Selenium Testing Tools Cookbook

Second Edition

Over 90 recipes to help you build and run automated tests for your web applications with Selenium WebDriver

Unmesh Gundecha

BIRMINGHAM - MUMBAI

Selenium Testing Tools Cookbook
Second Edition

First published: October 2015

Production reference: 1261015

Published by Packt Publishing Ltd.
Livery Place
35 Livery Street
Birmingham B3 2PB, UK.

ISBN 978-1-78439-251-2

www.packtpub.com

Credits

Author

Unmesh Gundecha

Reviewers

Alexander Afanasyev

Anuj Chaudhary

Oliver Gondža

Vatsala Dorairajan

Acquisition Editor

Tushar Gupta

Content Development Editor

Kirti Patil

Technical Editor

Rupali R. Shrawane

Copy Editor

Vatsal Surti

Project Coordinator

Nidhi Joshi

Proofreader

Safis Editing

Indexer

Tejal Daruwale Soni

Graphics

Jason Monteiro

Production Coordinator

Manu Joseph

Cover Work

Manu Joseph

About the Author

Unmesh Gundecha has a master's degree in software engineering and over 13 years of experience in software development and testing. He has architected functional test automation projects using industry-standard, in-house, and custom test automation frameworks, along with leading commercial and open source test automation tools. Presently, he is working as a test architect for a multinational company in Pune, India. Unmesh has also authored a book called *Learning Selenium Testing Tools with Python*, *Packt Publishing*.

About the Reviewers

Alexander Afanasyev is currently a Python developer and architect and a QA automation lead at Avenues International Inc. This is a data and analytics company that provides consulting solutions. He has completed his master's of science degree in electronics engineering. He has several years of experience in development and testing at various companies across different sectors, both in Russia and the United States. Alexander has always had a passion for testing, code quality, and web technologies. In his free time, he is likely to be found contributing to StackOverflow or GitHub, reading, or playing the guitar.

I would like to thank Daniel Lyakovetsky for "opening doors," for guidance, and for the confidence that he has shown in me. A huge thank you to my wonderful wife, Anna, and my little daughter, Kate, who have all been a constant source of support.

Anuj Chaudhary is a software engineer who enjoys working on software testing and automation. He has vast experience in different testing methodologies such as manual, automated, performance, and security testing. He has worked as an individual contributor and a technical lead on various software projects dealing with all stages of the application development life cycle.

Anuj has been awarded a Microsoft MVP two times in a row. He posts blogs at `www.anujchaudhary.com`. He has also reviewed the following books on Selenium:

- Selenium WebDriver Practical Guide (`http://www.packtpub.com/selenium-webdriver-practical-guide/book`)
- Selenium Design Patterns and Best Practices (`https://www.packtpub.com/web-development/selenium-design-patterns-and-best-practices`)
- Mastering Selenium WebDriver (`https://www.packtpub.com/web-development/mastering-selenium-webdriver`)

I would like to thank my wife Renu and son Arjun for always supporting me and letting me spend extra time on reviewing this book.

Oliver Gondža is a Java enthusiast, extreme programmer, OSS contributor, and Red Hatter.

Vatsala Dorairajan is a budding software technologist. She has mostly worked with "ideasmiths," transforming on-paper/in-concept ideas into working prototypes, which in turn have evolved into products. Her technical experience so far has been in Java, Flex, Python, PHP, and Ruby on Rails. She currently works with Jombay, an award-winning talent measurement and analytics company that helps companies hire, promote, and retain the right talent.

Vatsala has also reviewed the book *Selenium Testing Tools Starter, Packt Publishing*.

www.PacktPub.com

Support files, eBooks, discount offers, and more

For support files and downloads related to your book, please visit www.PacktPub.com.

Did you know that Packt offers eBook versions of every book published, with PDF and ePub files available? You can upgrade to the eBook version at www.PacktPub.com and as a print book customer, you are entitled to a discount on the eBook copy. Get in touch with us at service@packtpub.com for more details.

At www.PacktPub.com, you can also read a collection of free technical articles, sign up for a range of free newsletters and receive exclusive discounts and offers on Packt books and eBooks.

https://www2.packtpub.com/books/subscription/packtlib

Do you need instant solutions to your IT questions? PacktLib is Packt's online digital book library. Here, you can search, access, and read Packt's entire library of books.

Why Subscribe?

- Fully searchable across every book published by Packt
- Copy and paste, print, and bookmark content
- On demand and accessible via a web browser

Free Access for Packt account holders

If you have an account with Packt at www.PacktPub.com, you can use this to access PacktLib today and view 9 entirely free books. Simply use your login credentials for immediate access.

Table of Contents

Preface   **v**

Chapter 1: Getting Started   **1**

Introduction   1

Configuring the Selenium WebDriver test development environment
for Java with Eclipse and Maven   2

Using Ant for the Selenium WebDriver test execution   12

Configuring Microsoft Visual Studio for Selenium WebDriver
test development   15

Configuring Selenium WebDriver for Python and Ruby   19

Setting up Internet Explorer Driver Server   22

Setting up ChromeDriver for Google Chrome   27

Setting up Microsoft WebDriver for Microsoft Edge   30

Chapter 2: Finding Elements   **33**

Introduction   33

Using browser tools for inspecting elements and page structure   34

Finding an element using the findElement method   41

Finding elements using the findElements method   46

Finding links   47

Finding elements by tag name   48

Finding elements using XPath   49

Finding elements using CSS selectors   58

Locating elements using text   63

Finding elements using advanced CSS selectors   65

Using jQuery selectors   67

Chapter 3: Working with Elements   71

Introduction   71
Automating textboxes, text areas, and buttons   72
Checking an element's text   74
Checking an element's attribute and CSS values   76
Automating dropdowns and lists   77
Checking options in the Select element   81
Checking selected options in dropdowns and lists   83
Automating radio buttons and radio groups   86
Automating checkboxes   89
Working with WebTables   90

Chapter 4: Working with Selenium API   93

Introduction   93
Checking an element's presence   94
Checking an element's state   95
Using Advanced User Interactions API for mouse and keyboard events   96
Performing double-click on an element   98
Performing drag-and-drop operations   100
Working with context menus   101
Executing the JavaScript code   103
Capturing screenshots with Selenium WebDriver   105
Maximizing the browser window   107
Handling session cookies   108
Working with browser navigation   110
Working with WebDriver events   112

Chapter 5: Synchronizing Tests   117

Introduction   117
Synchronizing a test with an implicit wait   117
Synchronizing a test with an explicit wait   119
Synchronizing a test with custom-expected conditions   121
Synchronizing a test with FluentWait   123

Chapter 6: Working with Alerts, Frames, and Windows   127

Introduction   127
Handling a simple JavaScript alert box   128
Handling a confirm and prompt alert box   131
Identifying and handling frames   134
Working with IFRAME   139
Identifying and handling a child window   141
Identifying and handling a window by its title   144
Identifying and handling a pop-up window by its content   146

Chapter 7: Data-Driven Testing — 149

Introduction — 149
Creating a data-driven test using JUnit — 151
Creating a data-driven test using TestNG — 155
Reading test data from a CSV file using JUnit — 158
Reading test data from an Excel file using JUnit and Apache POI — 161
Creating a data-driven test in NUnit — 165
Creating a data-driven test in MSTEST — 169
Creating a data-driven test in Ruby using Roo — 173
Creating a data-driven test in Python using DDT — 178

Chapter 8: Using the Page Object Model — 181

Introduction — 181
Using the PageFactory class for exposing the elements on a page — 182
Using the PageFactory class for exposing an operation on a page — 187
Using the LoadableComponent class — 190
Implementing nested Page Object instances — 193
Implementing the Page Object model in .NET — 199
Implementing the Page Object model in Python — 203
Implementing the Page Object model in Ruby using the page-object gem — 206

Chapter 9: Extending Selenium — 209

Introduction — 209
Creating an extension class for web tables — 210
Creating an extension for the jQueryUI tab widget — 214
Implementing an extension for the WebElement object to set the element attribute values — 219
Implementing an extension for the WebElement object to highlight elements — 220
Creating an object map for Selenium tests — 222
Capturing screenshots of elements in the Selenium WebDriver — 228
Comparing images in Selenium — 230
Measuring performance with the Navigation Timing API — 235

Chapter 10: Testing HTML5 Web Applications — 239

Introduction — 239
Automating the HTML5 video player — 240
Automating interaction on the HTML5 canvas element — 243
Web storage – testing local storage — 245
Web storage – testing session storage — 247
Cleaning local and session storage — 250

Chapter 11: Behavior-Driven Development   251
Introduction   251
Using Cucumber-JVM and Selenium WebDriver in Java for BDD   252
Using SpecFlow.NET and Selenium WebDriver in .NET for BDD   261
Using Capybara, Cucumber, and Selenium WebDriver in Ruby   271
Using Behave and Selenium WebDriver in Python   274

Chapter 12: Integration with Other Tools   279
Introduction   279
Configuring Jenkins for continuous integration   280
Using Jenkins and Maven for Selenium WebDriver test execution
in continuous integration   282
Using Ant for Selenium WebDriver test execution   287
Using Jenkins and Ant for Selenium WebDriver test execution
in continuous integration   290
Automating a non-web UI in Selenium WebDriver with AutoIt   294
Automating a non-web UI in Selenium WebDriver with Sikuli   301

Chapter 13: Cross-Browser Testing   305
Introduction   305
Setting up Selenium Grid Server for parallel execution   307
Adding nodes to Selenium Grid for cross-browser testing   309
Creating and executing the Selenium script in parallel with TestNG   312
Creating and executing the Selenium script in parallel with Python   319
Using Cloud tools for cross-browser testing running tests in the Cloud 322
Running tests in headless mode with PhantomJS   325

Chapter 14: Testing Applications on Mobile Browsers   329
Introduction   329
Setting up Appium for testing mobile applications   330
Testing mobile web applications on iOS using Appium   332
Testing mobile web applications on Android using Appium   336

Index   343

Preface

Selenium is a set of tools used to automate browsers. It is largely used to test applications, but its usages are not limited to testing. It can also be used to perform screen scraping and automate repetitive tasks in a browser window. Selenium supports automation on all the major browsers, including Firefox, Internet Explorer, Google Chrome, Safari, and Opera. Selenium WebDriver is now a part of W3C standards and is supported by major browser vendors.

This book will help you learn advanced techniques to test web applications using the Selenium WebDriver API and related tools. In this book, you will learn how to test web applications effectively and efficiently with Selenium WebDriver on desktops, mobile web browsers, and in a distributed environment.

Along with the core features of Selenium WebDriver, this book also covers design patterns such as data-driven testing, page objects, and object maps, to design a highly maintainable and reliable test automation framework. You will also learn how to integrate Selenium WebDriver with ATDD/BDD, build and continuous integration tools, and perform mobile web testing with Appium.

This book also covers techniques to extend Selenium for your specific needs. There are more than 80 recipes that you can use to build or extend your existing test automation framework.

What this book covers

Chapter 1, Getting Started, demonstrates how to set up Selenium WebDriver with Eclipse, Maven, or ANT for test development on a Java platform. Then it shows how to set up Visual Studio, Ruby, and Python for test development. This chapter also shows how to set up various browsers for testing.

Chapter 2, Finding Elements, introduces you to the locator techniques supported by Selenium WebDriver to find elements on pages in your web applications. Selenium WebDriver provides a number of techniques to find elements on web pages with multiple locator strategies such as XPath, CSS, and DOM. We can also implement custom locator strategies to locate elements. This chapter will also help you get started with the Selenium WebDriver locator API.

Chapter 3, Working with Elements, demonstrates how to use the Selenium WebDriver API to automate interaction with various types of UI elements used in web applications, including textboxes, buttons, dropdowns, radio buttons, checkboxes, and tables.

Chapter 4, Working with Selenium API, demonstrates how to use the Selenium WebDriver API to build tests. We will explore the API and investigate advanced user interactions to perform complex mouse and keyboard operations and work with various types of UI elements used in web applications.

Chapter 5, Synchronizing Tests, demonstrates how to use the Selenium WebDriver API to handle synchronization with implicit and explicit waits to implement robust and reliable tests.

Chapter 6, Working with Alerts, Frames and Windows, demonstrates how to handle multiple windows, pop-ups, and alerts that are displayed during test execution.

Chapter 7, Data-Driven Testing, introduces the data-driven testing approach—a widely used methodology in test automation. Selenium WebDriver does not have built-in features to support data-driven testing. However, we can extend the Selenium WebDriver API to support data-driven testing. This chapter covers recipes to support data-driven testing using JUnit, TestNG, and Apache POI to read data from spreadsheets.

Chapter 8, Using the Page Object Model, introduces the Page Object model pattern, which is widely used for structuring Selenium WebDriver tests. This chapter provides examples and tips on how to build testing frameworks using the Page Object model pattern.

Chapter 9, Extending Selenium, demonstrates how to extend the Selenium WebDriver API and add features to build a scalable test automation framework. This chapter covers some of the important recipes in extending Selenium WebDriver for various practical scenarios such as to support custom UI controls, capture images of elements, and perform image-based verifications.

Chapter 10, Testing HTML5 Web Applications, introduces you to using Selenium WebDriver to test web applications using the HTML5 standard. This chapter explains how to test video and canvas elements and the web storage API of HTML5.

Chapter 11, Behavior-Driven Development, introduces behavior-driven development with Selenium WebDriver, using tools such as Cucumber-JVM, SpecFlow.NET for .NET, Behave for Python, and Capybara for Ruby.

Chapter 12, Integration with Other Tools, demonstrates how to set up Selenium WebDriver with Jenkins to run tests in Continuous Integration using Maven and ANR. This chapter also covers recipes to use tools such as AutoIt and Sikuli to test non-web UI.

Chapter 13, Cross-Browser Testing, demonstrates how to set up a distributed test environment with Selenium Grid for cross-browser testing. We will add nodes with various browser and operating system combinations. We will run tests in parallel using TestNG, which helps to reduce the time of test execution and increases test coverage. This chapter also covers how to use cloud-based services, such as Sauce Labs and BrowserStack, for cross browser testing.

Chapter 14, Testing Applications on Mobile Browsers, introduces you to testing mobile web applications with the Apple iOS and Android platforms using Appium. This chapter covers recipes to configure and use Selenium WebDriver to test a mobile web application on iPhone and Android-based devices/simulators.

What you need for this book

You will need the following software to follow the recipes in this book:

- Browsers: Mozilla Firefox, Google Chrome, or Microsoft Internet Explorer
- Selenium browser drivers: Chrome Driver and InternetExplorerDriver
- Selenium tools: The Selenium WebDriver client driver (based on your preference of programming language) and Selenium Standalone Server
- IDE: Eclipse, IntelliJ IDEA, and Microsoft Visual Studio (for .NET)
- BDD framework tools: Cucumber-JVM, SpecFlow.NET (for .NET), and Capybara (for Ruby)
- Build and integration tools: Maven, ANT, and Jenkins
- Other GUI automations tools: AutoIt and Sikuli
- Mobile tools: Apple Xcode (for iOS mobile browser testing), Android SDK, Android Server APK, and Appium
- Language runtimes: JDK 1.7 or JDK 1.8 (for Java), Ruby 1.9+ (for Ruby), and Python 2.7+ (for Python)

Who this book is for

This book is for software quality assurance/testing professionals, test managers, and software developers with prior experience in using Selenium and Java to test web-based applications.

Sections

In this book, you will find several headings that appear frequently (Getting ready, How to do it, How it works, There's more, and See also).

To give clear instructions on how to complete a recipe, we use these sections as follows:

Getting ready

This section tells you what to expect in the recipe and describes how to set up any software or any preliminary settings required for the recipe.

How to do it...

This section contains the steps required to follow the recipe.

How it works...

This section usually consists of a detailed explanation of what happened in the previous section.

There's more...

This section consists of additional information about the recipe in order to make the reader more knowledgeable about the recipe.

See also

This section provides helpful links to other useful information for the recipe.

Conventions

In this book, you will find a number of text styles that distinguish between different kinds of information. Here are some examples of these styles and an explanation of their meaning:

Code words in text, database table names, folder names, filenames, file extensions, pathnames, dummy URLs, user input, and Twitter handles are shown as follows: "This will open the pom.xml file in the editor area."

A block of code is written as follows:

```
<project xmlns="http://maven.apache.org/POM/4.0.0"
xmlns:xsi="http://www.w3.org/2001/XMLSchema-instance"
xsi:schemaLocation="http://maven.apache.org/POM/4.0.0
http://maven.apache.org/xsd/maven-4.0.0.xsd">
  <modelVersion>4.0.0</modelVersion>
```

When we wish to draw your attention to a particular part of a code block, the relevant lines or items are set in bold:

```
<artifactId>SeleniumCookbook</artifactId>
<version>0.0.1-SNAPSHOT</version>
<dependencies>
  <dependency>
    <groupId>org.seleniumhq.selenium</groupId>
```

Any command-line input or output is written as follows:

```
gem install selenium-webdriver
```

New terms and **important words** are shown in bold. Words that you see on the screen, for example, in menus or dialog boxes, appear in the text like this: "Select the **Create a simple project (skip archetype selection)** checkbox."

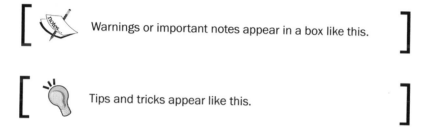

Warnings or important notes appear in a box like this.

Tips and tricks appear like this.

Reader feedback

Feedback from our readers is always welcome. Let us know what you think about this book—what you liked or disliked. Reader feedback is important for us as it helps us develop titles that you will really get the most out of.

To send us general feedback, simply e-mail feedback@packtpub.com, and mention the book's title in the subject of your message.

If there is a topic that you have expertise in and you are interested in either writing or contributing to a book, see our author guide at www.packtpub.com/authors.

Customer support

Now that you are the proud owner of a Packt book, we have a number of things to help you to get the most from your purchase.

Downloading the example code

You can download the example code files from your account at `http://www.packtpub.com` for all the Packt Publishing books you have purchased. If you purchased this book elsewhere, you can visit `http://www.packtpub.com/support` and register to have the files e-mailed directly to you.

Downloading the color images of this book

We also provide you with a PDF file that has color images of the screenshots/diagrams used in this book. The color images will help you better understand the changes in the output. You can download this file from `http://www.packtpub.com/sites/default/files/downloads/SeleniumTestingToolsCookbookSecondEdition_ColorImages.pdf`.

Errata

Although we have taken every care to ensure the accuracy of our content, mistakes do happen. If you find a mistake in one of our books—maybe a mistake in the text or the code—we would be grateful if you could report this to us. By doing so, you can save other readers from frustration and help us improve subsequent versions of this book. If you find any errata, please report them by visiting `http://www.packtpub.com/submit-errata`, selecting your book, clicking on the **Errata Submission Form** link, and entering the details of your errata. Once your errata are verified, your submission will be accepted and the errata will be uploaded to our website or added to any list of existing errata under the Errata section of that title.

To view the previously submitted errata, go to `https://www.packtpub.com/books/content/support` and enter the name of the book in the search field. The required information will appear under the **Errata** section.

Piracy

Piracy of copyrighted material on the Internet is an ongoing problem across all media. At Packt, we take the protection of our copyright and licenses very seriously. If you come across any illegal copies of our works in any form on the Internet, please provide us with the location address or website name immediately so that we can pursue a remedy.

Please contact us at `copyright@packtpub.com` with a link to the suspected pirated material.

We appreciate your help in protecting our authors and our ability to bring you valuable content.

Questions

If you have a problem with any aspect of this book, you can contact us at `questions@packtpub.com`, and we will do our best to address the problem.

1

Getting Started

In this chapter, we will see how to set up the **Selenium WebDriver** test development environment. We will also see some basic settings to help get started with Selenium WebDriver. You will learn the following:

- ▶ Configuring the Selenium WebDriver test development environment for Java with Eclipse and Maven
- ▶ Using Ant for Selenium WebDriver test execution
- ▶ Configuring Microsoft Visual Studio for Selenium WebDriver test development
- ▶ Configuring Selenium WebDriver for Python and Ruby
- ▶ Setting up Internet Explorer Driver Server
- ▶ Setting up ChromeDriver for Google Chrome
- ▶ Setting up Microsoft WebDriver for Microsoft Edge

Introduction

Selenium WebDriver has been widely used for automating web browsers in combination with various tools due to its neat and clean object-oriented design. We can integrate Selenium WebDriver with other tools to develop automated tests.

The initial sections of this chapter explore Selenium WebDriver's integration with development and build tools such as **Eclipse**, **Maven**, and **Microsoft Visual Studio**. These tools provide an easy way to develop test automation frameworks and extend the capabilities of Selenium WebDriver API. The following recipes will explain how to set up and configure these tools with Selenium.

Lastly, we will explore how to set up various browser drivers and initial settings for WebDriver.

Configuring the Selenium WebDriver test development environment for Java with Eclipse and Maven

Selenium WebDriver is a simple API that can help with browser automation. However, much more is needed when using it for testing and building a test framework. You will need an Integrated Development Environment (IDE) or a code editor to create a new Java project and add Selenium WebDriver and other dependencies in order to build a testing framework.

In the Java world, Eclipse is a widely used IDE, as well as **IntelliJ IDEA** and **NetBeans**. Eclipse provides a feature-rich environment for Selenium WebDriver test development.

Along with Eclipse, Apache Maven provides support for managing the entire life cycle of a test project. Maven is used to define project structure, dependencies, build, and test management.

You can use Eclipse and Maven to build your Selenium WebDriver test framework from a single window. Another important benefit of using Maven is that you can get all the Selenium library files and their dependencies by configuring the pom.xml file. Maven automatically downloads the necessary files from the repository while building the project.

This recipe will explain how to configure Eclipse and Maven for the Selenium WebDriver test development. Most of the code in this book has been developed in Eclipse and Maven.

Getting ready

You will need Eclipse and Maven to set up the test development environment. Download and set up Maven from http://maven.apache.org/download.html. Follow the instructions on the Maven download page (see the Installation Instructions section on the page).

Download and set up Eclipse IDE for Java Developers from https://eclipse.org/downloads/.

 The examples for this book are built in Eclipse version 4.4.2 (codenamed **Luna**) for Java Developers. This comes with the Maven plugin bundled with other packages.

How to do it...

Let's configure Eclipse with Maven to develop Selenium WebDriver tests using the following steps:

1. Launch the Eclipse IDE.

2. Create a new project by selecting **File** | **New** | **Other** from the Eclipse **Main** Menu.

3. On the **New** dialog, select **Maven** | **Maven Project**, as shown in the following screenshot, and click **Next**:

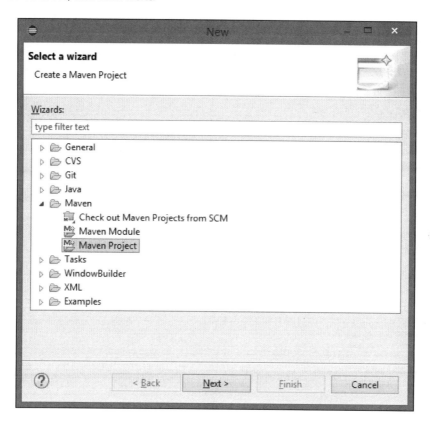

4. Next, the **New Maven Project** dialog will be displayed. Select the **Create a simple project (skip archetype selection)** checkbox and click on the **Next** button, as shown in the following screenshot:

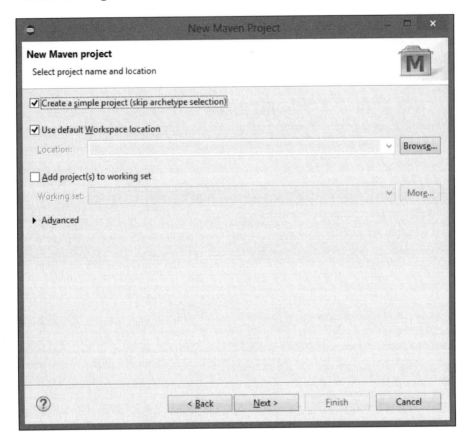

5. On the **New Maven Project** dialog box, enter `com.secookbook.examples` in the **Group Id:** textbox and `SeleniumCookbook` in the **Artifact Id:** `textbox`. You can also add a name and description optionally. Click on the **Finish** button, as shown in the following screenshot:

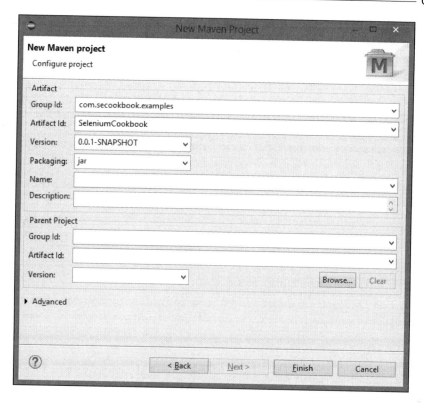

6. Eclipse will create the **SeleniumCookbook** project with a structure (in **Package Explorer**) similar to the one shown in the following screenshot:

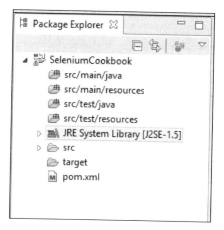

7. Select **pom.xml** from **Package Explorer**. This will open the `pom.xml` file in the editor area with the **Overview** tab open. Select the **pom.xml** tab next to the **Overview** tab, as shown in the following screenshot:

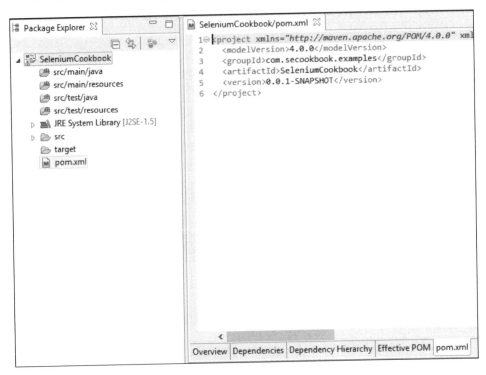

8. Add the WebDriver and JUnit dependencies highlighted in the following code snippet to `pom.xml` in the `<project>` node:

```
<project xmlns="http://maven.apache.org/POM/4.0.0"
xmlns:xsi="http://www.w3.org/2001/XMLSchema-instance"
xsi:schemaLocation="http://maven.apache.org/POM/4.0.0
http://maven.apache.org/xsd/maven-4.0.0.xsd">
   <modelVersion>4.0.0</modelVersion>
   <groupId>com.secookbook.examples</groupId>
   <artifactId>SeleniumCookbook</artifactId>
   <version>0.0.1-SNAPSHOT</version>
   <dependencies>
     <dependency>
       <groupId>org.seleniumhq.selenium</groupId>
       <artifactId>selenium-java</artifactId>
```

```
            <version>2.47.1</version>
    <scope>test</scope>
        </dependency>
        <dependency>
            <groupId>junit</groupId>
            <artifactId>junit</artifactId>
            <version>4.12</version>
    <scope>test</scope>
        </dependency>
        </dependencies>
    </project>
```

You can get the latest dependency information for Selenium WebDriver and JUnit from `http://seleniumhq.org/download/maven.html` and `http://maven.apache.org/plugins/maven-surefire-plugin/examples/junit.html` respectively.

 TestNG is another widely used unit-testing framework in Java World. If you want to add TestNG support to the project instead of JUnit, you can get its Maven entry at `http://testng.org/doc/maven.html`.

9. Select **src/test/java** in **Package Explorer** and right-click to show the menu. Select **New | Class**, as shown in the following screenshot:

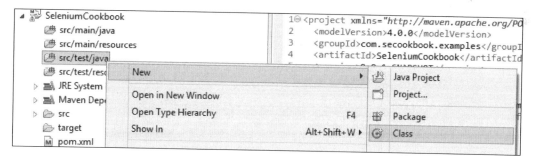

 Downloading the example code
You can download the example code files from your account at `http://www.packtpub.com` for all the Packt Publishing books you have purchased. If you purchased this book elsewhere, you can visit `http://www.packtpub.com/support` and register to have the files e-mailed directly to you.

10. Enter `com.seleniumcookbook.examples.chapter01` in the **Package:** textbox and `GoogleSearchTest` in the **Name:** textbox and click on the **Finish** button, as shown in the following screenshot:

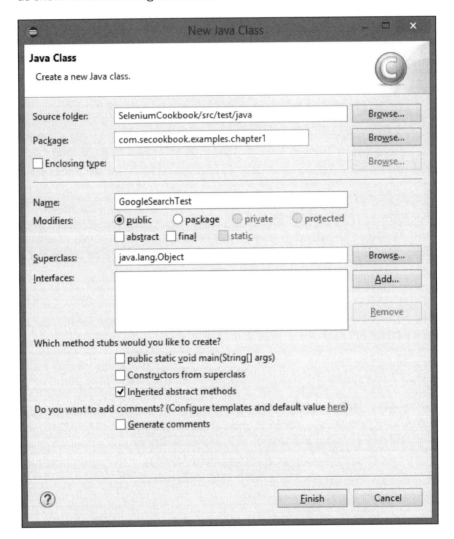

This will create the `GoogleSearchTest.java` class in the `com.secookbook.examples.chapter01` package.

11. Add the following code in the `GoogleSearchTest` class:

```
package com.secookbook.examples.chapter01;

import org.openqa.selenium.firefox.FirefoxDriver;
```

```java
import org.openqa.selenium.WebDriver;
import org.openqa.selenium.WebElement;
import org.openqa.selenium.By;
import org.openqa.selenium.support.ui.ExpectedCondition;
import org.openqa.selenium.support.ui.WebDriverWait;
import org.junit.*;

import static org.junit.Assert.*;

public class GoogleSearchTest {

  private WebDriver driver;

  @Before
  public void setUp() {
    // Launch a new Firefox instance
    driver = new FirefoxDriver();
    // Maximize the browser window
    driver.manage().window().maximize();
    // Navigate to Google
    driver.get("http://www.google.com");
  }

  @Test
  public void testGoogleSearch() {
    // Find the text input element by its name
    WebElement element = driver.findElement(By.name("q"));
    // Clear the existing text value
    element.clear();

    // Enter something to search for
    element.sendKeys("Selenium testing tools cookbook");

    // Now submit the form
    element.submit();

    // Google's search is rendered dynamically with JavaScript.
    // wait for the page to load, timeout after 10 seconds
    new WebDriverWait(driver, 10).until(new
ExpectedCondition<Boolean>() {
        public Boolean apply(WebDriver d) {
          return d.getTitle().toLowerCase()
            .startsWith("selenium testing tools cookbook");
        }
```

```
    });

        assertEquals("Selenium testing tools cookbook - Google
    Search",
            driver.getTitle());
    }

    @After
    public void tearDown() throws Exception {
      // Close the browser
      driver.quit();
    }
}
```

Downloading the example code:

You can download the example code files for all the Packt books you have purchased from your account at `http://www.packtpub.com`. If you have purchased this book elsewhere, you can visit `http://www.packtpub.com/support` and register to have the files e-mailed directly to you.

The example code is also hosted at `https://github.com/upgundecha/secookbook`.

12. To run the tests in the Maven life cycle, select the **SeleniumCookbook** project in **Package Explorer**. Right-click on the project name and select **Run As | Maven test**. Maven will execute all the tests from the project.

How it works...

Eclipse provides the ability to create Selenium WebDriver test projects easily with its Maven plugin, taking away the pain of project configurations, directory structure, dependency management, and so on. It also provides a powerful code editor to write the test code.

When you set up a project using Maven in Eclipse, it creates the `pom.xml` file, which defines the configuration of the project and its structure. This file also contains the dependencies needed for building, testing, and running the code. For example, the following code shows the dependency information about Selenium WebDriver that we added in `pom.xml`:

```
<dependency>
    <groupId>org.seleniumhq.selenium</groupId>
    <artifactId>selenium-java</artifactId>
    <version>2.47.1</version>
</dependency>
```

Most open source projects publish this information on their websites. In this case, you can check `http://seleniumhq.org/download/maven.html`; you can also get this information from Maven Central at `http://search.maven.org/#browse`. Maven will automatically download libraries and support files mentioned for all the dependencies and add to the project without you needing to find, download, and install these files to the project. This saves a lot of our time and effort while managing the dependency-related tasks.

Maven also generates a standard directory structure for your code, for easier management and maintenance. In the previous example, it created the `src/test/java` folder for the test code and the `src/test/resources` folder to maintain resources needed for testing, such as test data files, utilities, and so on.

Maven provides life cycle steps such as building the test code and running the test. If you are working with the Java development team, then you might find the application code and test code together in Maven. Here, Maven supports building the application code, then firing the tests, and releasing the software to production.

There's more...

Maven can also be used to execute the test from the command line. To run tests from the command line, navigate to the `SeleniumCookbook` project folder through the command line and type the following command:

```
mvn clean test
```

This command will traverse through all the subdirectories and run the clean command to delete/remove earlier build files. It will then build the project and run the tests. You will see the results at the end of execution on command line, as shown in the following screenshot:

Using Ant for the Selenium WebDriver test execution

Apache Ant is a popular build tool available for Java developers. It is similar to Apache Maven, but does not support project management and dependency management features like Maven. It's a pure build tool.

You can run Selenium WebDriver tests using Ant via command line or through **continuous integration** (**CI**) tools such as **Jenkins**.

In this recipe, we will add Ant support to the `SeleniumCookbook` project created in the *Configuring Selenium WebDriver test development environment for Java with Eclipse and Maven* recipe.

Getting ready

You can also download and configure Ant from `http://ant.apache.org/bindownload.cgi` for other OS platforms.

Windows users can download and install WinAnt on Windows. WinAnt comes with an installer that will configure Ant through the installer. The WinAnt installer is available at `http://code.google.com/p/winant/`.

This recipe uses WinAnt on the Windows OS.

You will also need Selenium WebDriver and JUnit JAR files. You can download Selenium JAR file from `http://selenium-release.storage.googleapis.com/` and JUnit JAR file from `https://github.com/junit-team/junit/wiki/Download-and-Install`.

How to do it...

Let's set up the `SeleniumCookbook` created in the previous recipe project for Ant with the following steps:

1. Create a `lib` folder and copy the JAR files for the dependencies used for this project, that is, Selenium WebDriver and JUnit, to the `lib` folder, as shown in screenshot below:

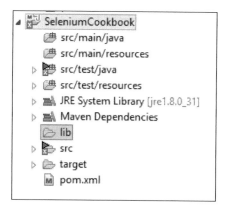

2. Create the `build.xml` file in the project folder with the following XML:

```xml
<?xml version="1.0" encoding="UTF-8"?>
<project name="test" default="exec" basedir=".">

    <property name="src" value="./src" />
    <property name="lib" value="./lib" />
    <property name="bin" value="./bin" />
    <property name="report" value="./report" />
    <path id="test.classpath">
        <pathelement location="${bin}" />
        <fileset dir="${lib}">
            <include name="**/*.jar" />
        </fileset>
    </path>

    <target name="init">
        <delete dir="${bin}" />
        <mkdir dir="${bin}" />
    </target>

    <target name="compile" depends="init">
        <javac source="1.8" srcdir="${src}" fork="true"
            destdir="${bin}" >
            <classpath>
                <pathelement path="${bin}" />
                <fileset dir="${lib}">
                  <include name="**/*.jar" />
                </fileset>
            </classpath>
```

```
            </javac>
        </target>

        <target name="exec" depends="compile">
            <delete dir="${report}" />
            <mkdir dir="${report}" />
                <mkdir dir="${report}/xml" />
            <junit printsummary="yes" haltonfailure="no">
                <classpath>
                    <pathelement location="${bin}" />
                    <fileset dir="${lib}">
                        <include name="**/*.jar" />
                    </fileset>
                </classpath>

                <test name="com.secookbook.examples.chapter1.
GoogleSearchTest"
                    haltonfailure="no" todir="${report}/xml"
                    outfile="TEST-result">
                    <formatter type="xml" />
                </test>
            </junit>
            <junitreport todir="${report}">
                <fileset dir="${report}/xml">
                    <include name="TEST*.xml" />
                </fileset>
                <report format="frames"
                    todir="${report}/html" />
            </junitreport>
        </target>
    </project>
```

3. Navigate to the project directory through the command line and type the
    following command:

    `ant`

    This will trigger the build process. You will see the test running. At the end, Ant will
    create a `report` folder in the project folder. Navigate to the `html` subfolder in the
    `report` folder and open the `index.html` file to view the results.

How it works...

Ant needs a `build.xml` file with all the configurations and steps required to build the project. We can add steps for report generation, sending e-mail notification, and so on to `build.xml`. Ant provides a very dynamic framework for defining steps in the build process.

Ant also needs the necessary library/JAR files to be copied in the `lib` folder, which are needed for building the project.

Ant scans for the complete set of tests in the project and executes these tests in a way similar to Maven.

Configuring Microsoft Visual Studio for Selenium WebDriver test development

Selenium WebDriver provides .NET bindings to develop Selenium tests with the .NET platform. To use the Selenium WebDriver API along with .NET, you need to refer the Selenium WebDriver libraries to the project. Microsoft Visual Studio being the major IDE used in the .NET world, setting up the Selenium WebDriver support has become easier with **NuGet Package Manager** (`http://nuget.org/`).

This recipe explains the process of setting up Selenium WebDriver in Microsoft Visual Studio 2013 using NuGet.

Getting ready

NuGet comes bundled with Microsoft Visual Studio 2012 onwards. However, for Microsoft Visual Studio 2010, you will need to download and install NuGet from `http://nuget.codeplex.com`.

How to do it...

Let's configure Microsoft Visual Studio 2013 to develop Selenium WebDriver tests using the following steps:

1. Launch the Microsoft Visual Studio.
2. Create a new project by selecting **File | New | Project** from the main menu.

3. In the **New Project** dialog box, select **Visual C# | Test | Unit Test Project**. Name the project as **SeleniumCookbook** and click on the **OK** button, as shown in the following screenshot:

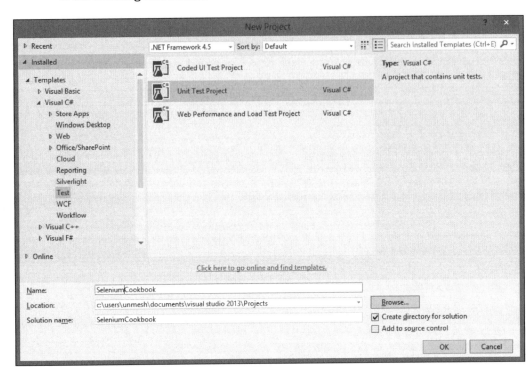

4. Next, add Selenium WebDriver packages using NuGet. Right-click on the **SeleniumCookbook** solution in **Solution Explorer** and select **Manage NuGet Packages...**, as shown in the following screenshot:

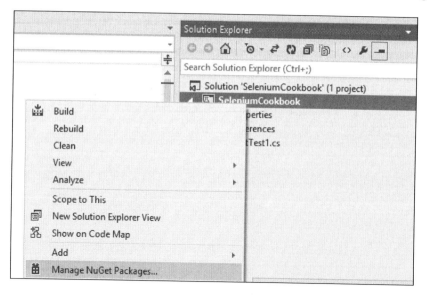

5. On the **SeleniumCookbook - Manage NuGet Packages** dialog box, select **Online** and search for the `WebDriver` package. The search will result in the suggestions shown in the following screenshot:

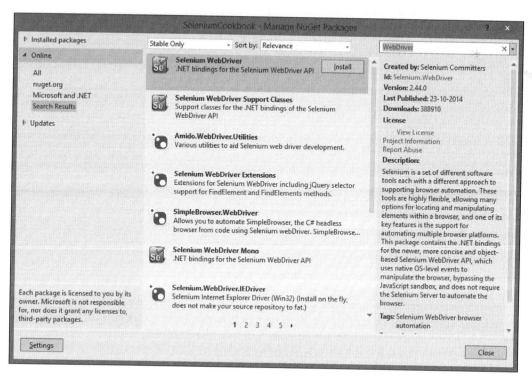

6. Select **Selenium WebDriver** from the list and click on the **Install** button. Repeat this step for **Selenium WebDriver Support Classes**. Successful installation will show a green tick mark for both the packages, as shown in the following screenshot:

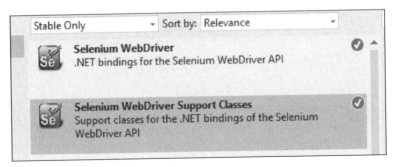

7. Close the **SeleniumCookbook - Manage NuGet Packages** dialog box.

8. Expand the **References** tree for the **SeleniumCookbook** solution in **Solution Explorer**. References for WebDriver are added to the project as shown in the following screenshot:

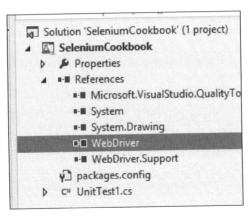

9. The `SeleniumCookbook` project is ready for test development. You can go on adding new tests as needed.

How it works...

NuGet Package Manager adds the external dependencies to Microsoft Visual Studio projects. It lists all available packages and automatically downloads and configures packages to the project. It also installs dependencies for the selected packages automatically. This saves a lot of effort in configuring the projects initially.

Configuring Selenium WebDriver for Python and Ruby

Along with Java and C#, Selenium WebDriver can also be used with various other programming languages. Among these, **Python** and **Ruby** are popular choices to create Selenium WebDriver tests. In this recipe, you will see how to install Selenium WebDriver client libraries in Python and Ruby.

Getting ready

You will need Python or Ruby installed before installing the Selenium WebDriver client library.

Installing Python

You can download and install the latest Python version from `https://www.python.org/`. In this recipe, Python 3.4 is used.

Installing Ruby

Similarly, you can download and install the latest Ruby version from `https://www.ruby-lang.org/en/installation/`. In this recipe, Ruby 2.1.3 is used.

How to do it...

Installation and setting up Selenium WebDriver with Python or Ruby is simple using following steps.

Installing Selenium WebDriver with Python

You can install Selenium WebDriver with Python using the `pip` tool with the following command line:

```
pip install selenium
```

This will get the latest version of Selenium WebDriver Python client library installed. That's it.

Let's create a simple test in Python using this installation. Create a `google_search.py` file in your favorite editor or IDE and copy the following code:

```
import unittest
from selenium.webdriver.support import expected_conditions
from selenium import webdriver
from selenium.webdriver.support.ui import WebDriverWait


class GoogleSearch(unittest.TestCase):
```

```python
    def setUp(self):
        self.driver = webdriver.Firefox()
        self.driver.implicitly_wait(30)
        self.base_url = "https://www.google.com/"

    def test_google_search(self):
        driver = self.driver
        driver.get(self.base_url)

        element = driver.find_element_by_idname("q")
        element.clear()
        element.send_keys("Selenium testing tools
cookbook")
        element.submit()

        WebDriverWait(driver, 30)\
            .until(expected_conditions.title_contains("Selenium
testing tools cookbook"))
        self.assertEqual(driver.title, "Selenium testing
tools cookbook - Google Search")

    def tearDown(self):
        self.driver.quit()

if __name__ == "__main__":
    unittest.main(verbosity=2, warnings="ignore")
```

You can run this test using the following command line:

```
python google_search.py
```

The Python interpreter will execute the test and you will see a Firefox window being opened and performing the search operation on Google.com. At the end of the execution you will see the results, as shown in the following screenshot:

Installing Selenium WebDriver with Ruby

You can install Selenium WebDriver with Ruby using the gem tool with following command line:

```
gem install selenium-webdriver
```

This will get the latest version of Selenium WebDriver Ruby client library installed. That's it.

Let's create a simple test in Ruby using this installation. Create a google_search.rb file in your favorite editor or IDE and copy the following code:

```ruby
require "selenium-webdriver"
gem "test-unit"
require "test/unit"

class GoogleSearch < Test::Unit::TestCase
  def setup
    @driver = Selenium::WebDriver.for :firefox
    @base_url = "https://www.google.com/"
    @driver.manage.timeouts.implicit_wait = 30
  end

  def test_google_search
    @driver.get(@base_url)

    element = @driver.find_element(:name, "q")
    element.clear
    element.send_keys "Selenium testing tools cookbook"
    element.submit()

    wait = Selenium::WebDriver::Wait.new(:timeout => 10)
    wait.until { @driver.title.include? "Selenium testing tools
cookbook" }

    assert_equal "Selenium testing tools cookbook - Google
Search", @driver.title
  end

  def teardown
    @driver.quit
  end
end
```

You can run this test using the following command line:

```
ruby google_search.rb
```

Ruby interpreter will execute the test and you will see a Firefox window being opened and performing the search operation on Google.com. At the end of the execution you will see the results, as shown in the following screenshot:

```
C:\Windows\system32\cmd.exe                                      _  □  ×

C:\Users\UNMESH>google_search.rb
Run options:

# Running tests:

Finished tests in 35.377895s, 0.0283 tests/s, 0.0283 assertions/s.
1 tests, 1 assertions, 0 failures, 0 errors, 0 skips

ruby -v: ruby 2.1.3p242 (2014-09-19 revision 47630) [x64-mingw32]
```

How it works...

Selenium WebDriver is supported on various programming languages. For each supported language, a client library or language binding is published by the Selenium developers. These client libraries have Selenium WebDriver classes and functions that are needed to create automation scripts.

These libraries can be installed using package installers available with the respective languages. In this case, we used pip for Python, which connected to the **PyPI** (**Python Package Index**) source using the Internet, downloaded the latest Selenium WebDriver Python client library and installed with the Python directory. Similarly, Selenium WebDriver Ruby Gem is installed using the gem utility.

Setting up Internet Explorer Driver Server

We saw how to automate the Firefox browser in previous recipes. Using Firefox was straightforward. In order to execute test scripts on the Internet Explorer browser, we need to use InternetExplorerDriver and a standalone Internet Explorer Driver Server executable.

Let's setup InternetExplorerDriver and create tests for testing the search feature on Internet Explorer.

Getting ready

You need to download **Internet Explorer Driver Server** from http://docs.seleniumhq.org/download/. It is available in both 32bit and 64bit versions.

After downloading the IEDriver server, unzip and copy the file to the same directory in which the scripts are stored.

How to do it...

Let's create a test that uses Internet Explorer Driver Server with the following steps:

1. In Eclipse, create a new folder named `drivers` in the **src/test/resources** folder of the **SeleniumCookbook** project. Copy the `IEDriverServer.exe` file to this folder, as shown in the following screenshot:

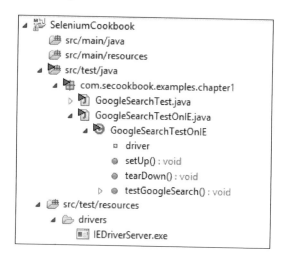

2. Add a new test and name it as `GoogleSearchTestOnIE`, and add the following code:

```
package com.secookbook.examples.chapter01;

import org.openqa.selenium.ie.InternetExplorerDriver;
import org.openqa.selenium.WebDriver;
import org.openqa.selenium.WebElement;
import org.openqa.selenium.By;
import org.openqa.selenium.remote.DesiredCapabilities;
import org.openqa.selenium.support.ui.ExpectedCondition;
import org.openqa.selenium.support.ui.WebDriverWait;
import org.junit.*;

import static org.junit.Assert.*;

public class GoogleSearchTestOnIE {

    private WebDriver driver;

    @Before
    public void setUp() {
```

```
System.setProperty("webdriver.ie.driver",
    "src/test/resources/drivers/IEDriverServer.exe");

DesiredCapabilities caps =
DesiredCapabilities.internetExplorer();

caps.setCapability(
    InternetExplorerDriver.INTRODUCE_FLAKINESS_BY_IGNORING_
SECU
RITY_DOMAINS,
    true);

// Launch Internet Explorer
driver = new InternetExplorerDriver(caps);
// Maximize the browser window
driver.manage().window().maximize();
// Navigate to Google
driver.get("http://www.google.com");
}

@Test
public void testGoogleSearch() {
    // Find the text input element by its name
    WebElement element = driver.findElement(By.name("q"));

    // Enter something to search for
    element.sendKeys("Selenium testing tools cookbook");

    // Now submit the form. WebDriver will find
    // the form for us from the element
    element.submit();

    // Google's search is rendered dynamically with
JavaScript.
    // Wait for the page to load, timeout after 10 seconds
    new WebDriverWait(driver, 10).until(new
ExpectedCondition<Boolean>() {
        public Boolean apply(WebDriver d) {
          return d.getTitle().toLowerCase()
              .startsWith("selenium testing tools cookbook");
        }
    });
```

```
        assertEquals("Selenium testing tools cookbook - Google
Search",
            driver.getTitle());
    }

    @After
    public void tearDown() throws Exception {
        // Close the browser
        driver.quit();
    }
}
```

Execute this test and you will see the Internet Explorer window being launched and all the steps executed.

How it works...

Internet Explorer Driver Server is a stand-alone server executable that implements WebDriver's JSON-wire protocol, which works as a glue between the test script and Internet Explorer, as shown in following diagram:

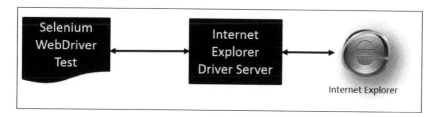

The tests should specify the path of the `IEDriverServer` executable before creating the instance of Internet Explorer. This is done by setting the `webdriver.ie.driver` property as shown in following code:

```
System.setProperty("webdriver.ie.driver",
    "src/test/resources/drivers/IEDriverServer.exe");
```

 We can also specify a path externally through the `Dwebdriver.ie.driver` option using Maven command line options. In this case, we don't need to set this property in test.

Internet Explorer Driver Server supports automating major IE versions on **Windows XP**, **Vista**, **Windows 7**, and **Windows 8** operating systems.

For more information on `InternetExplorerDriver`, please visit `https://code.google.com/p/selenium/wiki/InternetExplorerDriver`.

We need to create an instance of the `InternetExplorerDriver` class, which will connect to the Internet Explorer Driver Server to launch the Internet Explorer, shown as follows. It will then run the Selenium commands, which we will call by using various `WebDriver` and `WebElement` methods from the test script:

```
DesiredCapabilities caps = new
DesiredCapabilities().internetExplorer();

caps.setCapability(
InternetExplorerDriver.INTRODUCE_FLAKINESS_BY_IGNORING_SECU
RITY_DOMAINS,
true);

// Launch Internet Explorer
driver = new InternetExplorerDriver(caps);
```

We used the `DesiredCapabilities` class to set the `INTRODUCE_FLAKINESS_BY_IGNORING_SECURITY_DOMAINS` capability, which defines to ignore the browser protected mode settings during the start by IEDriverServer.

There's more...

Selenium provides the ability to run tests on remote machines by using the `RemoteWebDriver` class. We can configure any browser that Selenium supports for executing tests on a remote machine. To run tests on a remote machine, we need to run the Selenium Server and the Internet Explorer Driver Server on a remote machine and use `RemoteWebDriverClass`, as shown in the following code sample:

```
DesiredCapabilities caps = new
DesiredCapabilities().internetExplorer();

caps.setCapability(
InternetExplorerDriver.INTRODUCE_FLAKINESS_BY_IGNORING_SECU
RITY_DOMAINS,
true);

// Connect with Remote Selenium Server with specified URL
and capabilities
driver = new RemoteWebDriver(new
URL("http://192.168.1.3:4444/hub/wd"), caps);
```

We can connect any browser to a remote server using the preceding method.

Setting up ChromeDriver for Google Chrome

Similar to Internet Explorer, in order to execute test scripts on the Google Chrome browser, we need to use ChromeDriver and a standalone ChromeDriver executable.

ChromeDriver is maintained by the Google Chromium team. You can find more information at `https://sites.google.com/a/chromium.org/chromedriver/`.

Let's setup `ChromeDriver` and create a test for testing the search feature on Google Chrome.

Getting ready

You need to download ChromeDriver from `https://sites.google.com/a/chromium.org/chromedriver/downloads`.

How to do it...

1. After downloading the `ChromeDriver` server, unzip and copy the file to the driver's directory in the `src/test/resources` folder, as shown in the following screenshot:

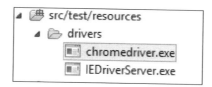

 On Linux and Mac operating systems, the `chromdriver` file needs to be made executable using the `chmod +x` command filename or the `chmod 775filename` command.

2. Add a new test and name it as `GoogleSearchTestOnChrome.java`, and add the following code:

```java
package com.secookbook.examples.chapter01;

import org.openqa.selenium.chrome.ChromeDriver;
import org.openqa.selenium.WebDriver;
import org.openqa.selenium.WebElement;
import org.openqa.selenium.By;
import org.openqa.selenium.support.ui.ExpectedCondition;
import org.openqa.selenium.support.ui.WebDriverWait;
import org.junit.*;
```

```
import static org.junit.Assert.*;

public class GoogleSearchTestOnChrome {

  private WebDriver driver;

  @Before
  public void setUp() {
    System.setProperty("webdriver.chrome.driver",
        "./src/test/resources/drivers/chromedriver.exe");

    // Launch Chrome
    driver = new ChromeDriver();
    // Maximize the browser window
    driver.manage().window().maximize();
    // Navigate to Google
    driver.get("http://www.google.com");
  }

  @Test
  public void testGoogleSearch() {
    // Find the text input element by its name
    WebElement element = driver.findElement(By.name("q"));

    // Enter something to search for
    element.sendKeys("Selenium testing tools cookbook");

    // Now submit the form. WebDriver will find
    // the form for us from the element
    element.submit();

    // Google's search is rendered dynamically with
JavaScript.
    // Wait for the page to load, timeout after 10 seconds
    new WebDriverWait(driver, 10).until(new
ExpectedCondition<Boolean>() {
        public Boolean apply(WebDriver d) {
          return d.getTitle().toLowerCase()
              .startsWith("selenium testing tools cookbook");
        }
      });

    assertEquals("Selenium testing tools cookbook - Google
Search",
```

```
        driver.getTitle());
  }

  @After
  public void tearDown() throws Exception {
    // Close the browser
    driver.quit();
  }
}
```

Execute this test and you will see a Chrome window being launched and all the steps executed.

How it works...

ChromeDriver is a standalone server executable that implements WebDriver's JSON-wire protocol and works as a glue between the test script and Google Chrome, as shown in the following diagram:

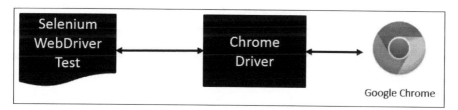

 For more information on ChromeDriver please visit `https://code.google.com/p/selenium/wiki/ChromeDriver`.

The tests should specify the path of the ChromeDriver executable before creating the instance of Chrome. This is done by setting the `webdriver.chrome.driver` property as shown in the following code:

```
System.setProperty("webdriver.chrome.driver","src/test/reso
urces/drivers/chromedriver.exe");
    "src/test/resources/drivers/chromedriver.exe");
```

We can also specify a path externally through the `-Dwebdriver.chrome.driver` option using Maven command line options. In this case, we don't need to set up this property in test; we need to create an instance of `ChromeDriver` class that will connect to the ChromeDriver Server, as shown in the following code. It will then run the Selenium commands that we will call by using various `WebDriver` and `WebElement` methods from the test script:

```
driver = new ChromeDriver();
```

Setting up Microsoft WebDriver for Microsoft Edge

Microsoft Edge is a new web browser launched with Microsoft Windows 10. Microsoft Edge implements the W3C WebDriver standard and provides in-built support for Selenium WebDriver.

Similar to Internet Explorer, in order to execute test scripts on the Microsoft Edge browser, we need to use `EdgeDriver` class and a standalone Microsoft WebDriver Server executable.

Microsoft WebDriver Server is maintained by the Microsoft Edge development team. You can find more information at `https://msdn.microsoft.com/en-us/library/mt188085(v=vs.85).aspx`.

Let's set up Microsoft WebDriver Server and create a test for testing the search feature on Microsoft Edge.

Getting ready

You need to download and install Microsoft WebDriver Server on Windows 10 from `https://www.microsoft.com/en-us/download/details.aspx?id=48212`.

How to do it...

Add a new test and name it as `GoogleSearchTestOnEdge.java` and add the following code:

```java
package com.secookbook.examples.chapter01;

import static org.junit.Assert.*;

import org.junit.After;
import org.junit.Before;
import org.junit.Test;
import org.openqa.selenium.By;
import org.openqa.selenium.WebDriver;
import org.openqa.selenium.WebElement;
import org.openqa.selenium.edge.EdgeDriver;
import org.openqa.selenium.edge.EdgeOptions;
import org.openqa.selenium.support.ui.ExpectedCondition;
import org.openqa.selenium.support.ui.WebDriverWait;

public class GoogleSearchTestOnEdge {

    private WebDriver driver;
```

```java
@Before
public void setUp() {
    System.setProperty("webdriver.edge.driver",
        "C:\\Program Files (x86)\\Microsoft Web
Driver\\MicrosoftWebDriver.exe");

    EdgeOptions options = new EdgeOptions();
    options.setPageLoadStrategy("eager");

    // Launch a new Edge instance
    driver = new EdgeDriver(options);

    // Navigate to Google
    driver.get("http://www.google.com");
}

@Test
public void testGoogleSearch() {
    // Find the text input element by its name
    WebElement element = driver.findElement(By.name("q"));

    // Clear the existing text value
    element.clear();

    // Enter something to search for
    element.sendKeys("Selenium testing tools cookbook");

    WebElement button = driver.findElement(By.name("btnG"));
    button.click();

    // Google's search is rendered dynamically with JavaScript.
    // Wait for the page to load, timeout after 10 seconds
    new WebDriverWait(driver, 10).until(new
ExpectedCondition<Boolean>() {
        public Boolean apply(WebDriver d) {
            return d.getTitle().toLowerCase()
                .startsWith("selenium testing tools cookbook");
        }
    });

    assertEquals("Selenium testing tools cookbook - Google
Search",
        driver.getTitle());
}
```

```
@After
public void tearDown() throws Exception {
  // Close the browser
  driver.quit();
}
}
```

Execute this test and you will see a Microsoft Edge window being launched and all the steps executed.

How it works...

Microsoft WebDriver Server is a standalone server executable that implements WebDriver's JSON-wire protocol, that works as a glue between the test script and the Microsoft Edge browser, as shown in the following diagram:

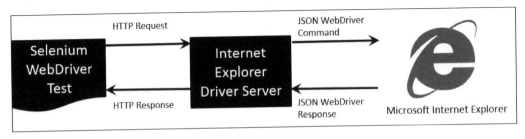

The tests should specify the path of Microsoft WebDriver Server executable before creating the instance of Microsoft Edge. This is done by setting the `webdriver.edge.driver` property as shown in the following code:

```
System.setProperty("webdriver.edge.driver",
        "C:\\Program Files (x86)\\Microsoft Web
Driver\\MicrosoftWebDriver.exe");
```

> We can also specify a path externally through the `-Dwebdriver.edge.driver` option using the Maven command line options. In this case, we don't need to set up this property in test.

2

Finding Elements

In this chapter, we will see how to use Selenium WebDriver API to find elements on a Web page and interact with these elements. We will explore various locator strategies supported by Selenium WebDriver. You will learn about:

- ▶ Using browser tools for inspecting elements and page DOM
- ▶ Finding an element using the findElement method
- ▶ Finding elements using the findElements method
- ▶ Finding links
- ▶ Finding elements by tag name
- ▶ Finding elements using CSS selectors
- ▶ Finding elements using XPath
- ▶ Finding elements using tag text contents
- ▶ Finding elements using advanced CSS selectors
- ▶ Using jQuery selectors

Introduction

Web applications, and the web pages within these applications, are commonly written in a mix of **Hyper Text Markup Language** (**HTML**), **Cascading Style Sheets** (**CSS**), and JavaScript code. Based on user actions like navigating to a website **Uniform Resource Locator** (**URL**) or clicking the submit button, a browser sends a request to a web server. Web server processes this request and sends back a response with HTML and related resources, such as JavaScript, CSS, Images, and so on, back to the Browser. The information received from a server is used by the browser to render a web page with various visual elements, such as textboxes, buttons, labels, tables, forms, checkboxes, radio boxes, lists, images, and so on, on the page. While doing so, the browser hides the HTML code and related resources from the user. The user is presented with a graphical user interface in the browser window.

When we want to automate browser interaction using Selenium, we need to tell Selenium how to find a particular element or set of elements on a web page programmatically and simulate user actions on these elements. Selenium provides various selector or locator methods to find elements based on the attribute/value criteria or selector value that we supply in the script.

Using browser tools for inspecting elements and page structure

Before we start exploring how to find elements on a page, we need to analyze the page to understand the **Document Object Model** (**DOM**) tree, what properties or attributes are defined for the elements displayed on the page, how JavaScript or AJAX calls are made from the application, and so on.

Browsers use the HTML code written for the page to render visual elements in the browser window. It uses other resources, including JavaScript, CSS, images, and so on, to decide the look, feel, and behavior of these elements.

Here is an example of a BMI Calculator application page and the HTML code written to render this page in a browser, as displayed in the following screenshot:

BMI Calculator

Enter Your Height and Weight (in Metric) to Calculate Your BMI

Height in Centimeters: *

Weight in Kilograms: *

Calculate

Your BMI is:

Category:

You can view the code written for a page by right-clicking in the browser window and selecting the **View Page Source** option from the pop-up menu. This will display the HTML code of the page in a separate window, as shown in the following screenshot:

```
108  <header id="header" class="info">
109  <h2>BMI Calculator</h2>
110  <div>Enter Your Height and Weight (in Metric) to Calculate Your BMI</div>
111  </header>
112
113  <ul>
114
115  <li id="foli1" class="notranslate        ">
116  <label class="desc" id="title1" for="heightCMS">
117  Height in Centimeters:
118  <span id="req_1" class="req">*</span>
119  </label>
120  <div>
121  <input name="heightCMS" id="heightCMS" type="number" class="field text medium" value="" maxlength="255" tabindex="1"
     onkeyup=""/>
122  </div>
123  </li><li id="foli2" class="notranslate       ">
124  <label class="desc" id="title2" for="weightKg">
125  Weight in Kilograms:
126  <span id="req_2" class="req">*</span>
127  </label>
128  <div>
129  <input name="weightKg" id="weightKg" type="number" class="field text medium" value="" maxlength="255" tabindex="2"
     onkeyup=""/>
130  </div>
131  </li>
132
133    <li class="buttons ">
134          <div>
```

We need tools that can display this information in a structured and easy to understand format. In this recipe, we will briefly explore some of these tools before we dive into locators and finding elements.

How to do it...

In the following sections, we will explore some of the tools that are available inbuilt in browsers or as Plugins to analyze elements and page DOM trees, JavaScript calls, CSS Style attributes, and so on.

Inspecting pages and elements with Mozilla Firefox using the Firebug add-on

The newer versions of **Mozilla Firefox** provide in-built ways to analyze the page and elements; however, we will use the Firebug add-on, which has more powerful features.

You need to install the Firebug add-on in Firefox from `https://addons.mozilla.org/en-us/firefox/addon/firebug/`.

To inspect an element from the page, move the mouse over the desired element and right-click to open the pop-up menu. Select the **Inspect Element with Firebug** option, as shown in the following screenshot:

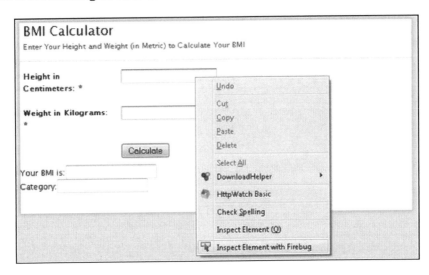

This will display Firebug with HTML code in a tree format, as shown in the following screenshot:

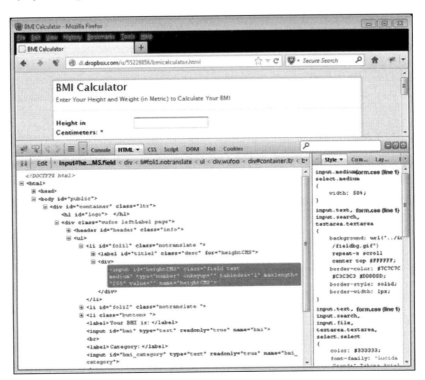

Using Firebug, we can also validate the XPath or CSS Selectors using the search box shown in the Firebug section. Just enter the XPath or CSS Selector and Firebug will highlight element(s) that match the expression, as shown in the following screenshot:

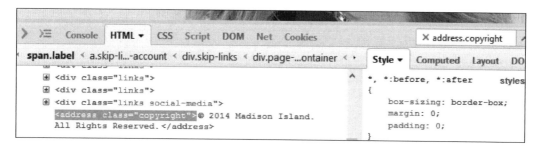

Firebug provides various other debugging features. It also generates XPath and CSS selectors for elements. For this, select the desired element in the tree, right-click, and select the **Copy XPath** or **Copy CSS Path** option from the pop-up menu, as shown in the following screenshot:

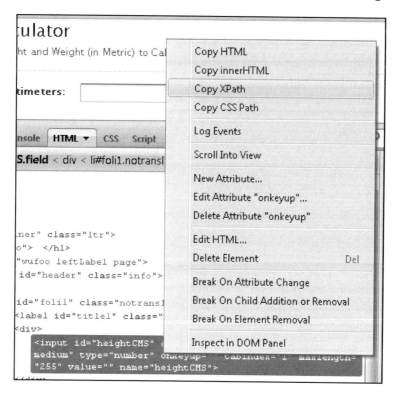

This will paste the Firebug-suggested XPath or CSS selector value to the clipboard.

Inspecting pages and elements with Google Chrome

Google Chrome provides an in-built feature to analyze pages and elements. This is very similar to Firebug but much more powerful. You can move the mouse over a desired element on the page and right-click to open the pop-up menu, then select the **Inspect element** option. This will open **Developer tools** in the browser, which displays information similar to that of Firebug, as shown in the following screenshot:

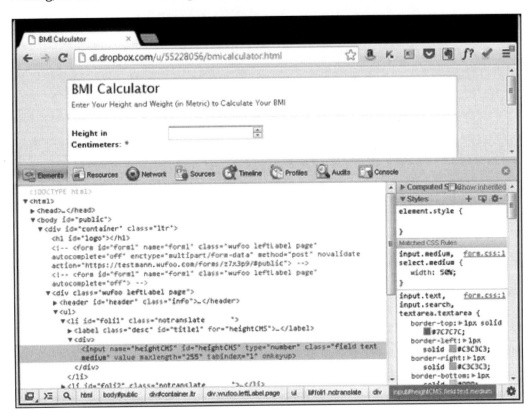

Similar to Firebug in Firefox, we can also test XPath and CSS Selectors in Google Chrome **Developer tools**. Press *Ctrl + F* (on Mac, use *Command + F*) in the **Elements** tab. This will display a search box. Just enter the XPath or CSS Selector, and matching elements will be highlighted in the tree, as shown in the following screenshot:

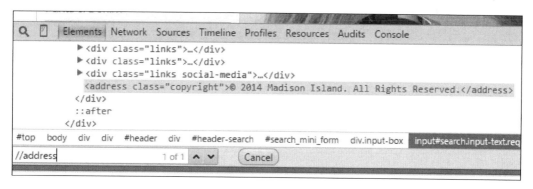

Chrome Developer Tools also provide a feature where you can get XPath for an element by right-clicking on the desired element in the tree and selecting the **Copy XPath** option from the pop-up menu.

Inspecting pages and elements with Microsoft Internet Explorer

Similar to Google Chrome, Microsoft Internet Explorer also provides an in-built feature to analyze pages and elements.

To open the Developer Tools, press the *F12* key. The Developer tools section will be displayed, as shown in the following screenshot:

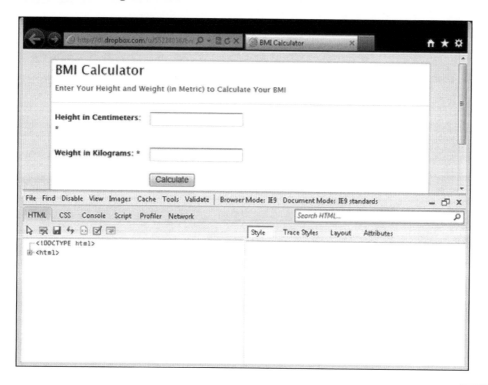

To inspect an element, click on the pointer () icon and hover over the desired element on the page. Developer tools will highlight the element with a blue outline and display the HTML code in a tree, as shown in the following screenshot:

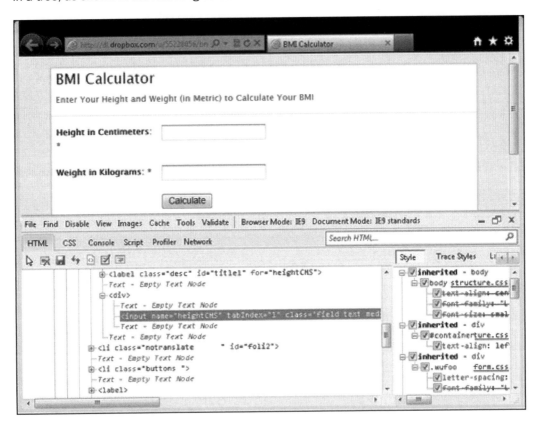

How it works...

Browser Developer tools come in really handy during the test script development. These tools will help you in finding the locator details for the elements with which you need to interact as part of the test. These tools parse the code for a page and display the information in a hierarchal tree. These tools also provide information on how styles have been applied, page resources, page DOM, JavaScript code, and so on.

Some of these tools also provide the ability to run JavaScript code for debugging and testing.

In the following recipes, we will explore various types of locators that are supported by Selenium WebDriver. These tools will help you in finding and deciding various locator strategies or methods provided by Selenium WebDriver API.

Finding an element using the findElement method

Finding elements in Selenium WebDriver is done by using the `findElement()` and `findElements()` methods provided by the `WebDriver` and `WebElement` interface.

The `findElement()` method returns an instance of a `WebElement` that is found in the page DOM based on specified locators, also called search criteria. If it does not find an element using the specified search criteria, it will throw the `NoSuchElementFound` exception.

The `findElements()` method returns a list of `WebElements` matching the search criteria. If no elements are found, it returns an empty list.

Find methods take a locator or a query object as an instance of a `By` class as an argument. Selenium WebDriver provides a `By` class to support various locator strategies. The following table lists various locator strategies supported by Selenium WebDriver:

Strategy	Syntax	Description
By ID	Java: `driver.findElement(By.id(<element ID>))` C#: `driver.FindElement(By.Id(<elementID>))` Python: `driver.find_element_by_id(<elementID>)` Ruby: `driver.find_element(:id,<elementID>)`	This will find element(s) using the ID attribute
By Name	Java: `driver.findElement(By.name(<element name>))` C#: `driver.FindElement(By.Name(<element name>))` Python: `driver.find_element_by_name(<element name>)` Ruby: `driver.find_element(:name,<element name>)`	This will find element(s) using the Name attribute

Strategy	Syntax	Description
By Class name	Java: `driver.findElement(By.className(<element class>))` C#: `driver.FindElement(By.ClassName(<element class>))` Python: `driver.find_element_by_class_name(<element class>)` Ruby: `driver.find_element(:class,<element class>)`	This will find element(s) using the Class attribute value
By Tag name	Java: `driver.findElement(By.tagName(<htmltagname>))` C#: `driver.FindElement(By.TagName(<htmltagname>))` Python: `driver.find_element_by_tag_name(<htmltagname >)` Ruby: `driver.find_element(:tag_name,< htmltagname >)`	This will find element(s) using its HTML tag
By Link text	Java: `driver.findElement(By.linkText(<linktext>))` C#: `driver.FindElement(By.LinkText(<linktext >))` Python: `driver.find_element_by_link_text(<linktext >)` Ruby: `driver.find_element(:link_text,<linktext >)`	This will find link(s) using its text
By Partial Link text	Java: `driver.findElement(By.partialLinkText(<linktext>))` C#: `driver.FindElement(By.PartialLinkText(<linktext >))` Python: `driver.find_element_by_partial_link_text(<linktext >)` Ruby: `driver.find_element(:partial_link_text,< linktext >)`	This will find link(s) using the link's partial text

Strategy	Syntax	Description
By CSS	Java: `driver.findElement(By.cssSelector(<css selector>))` C#: `driver.FindElement(By.CssSelector(<css selector >))` Python: `driver. find_elements_by_css_selector (<css selector>)` Ruby: `driver.find_element(:css,< css selector >)`	This will find element(s) using the CSS selector
By XPath	Java: `driver.findElement(By.xpath(<xpath query expression>))` C#: `driver.FindElement(By.XPath(<xpath query expression>))` Python: `driver. find_elements_by_xpath (<xpath query expression>)` Ruby: `driver.find_element(:xpath,<xpath query expression>)`	This will find element(s) using the XPath expression

In this recipe, we will use the `findElement()` method to locate elements.

How to do it...

Finding elements using the `id`, `name`, or `class` attributes is the preferred way to find elements. Let's try using these methods to locate elements as described in the following sections.

Finding elements by the ID attribute

We can find elements using the value of the `id` attribute. While searching through the DOM, browsers use `id` as the preferred way to identify the elements, and this provides the fastest locator strategy.

Let's now look at how to use `id` attributes to find elements on a login form, as shown in the following code:

```
<form name="loginForm">
    <label for="username">UserName: </label> <input type="text"
        id="username" /><br/>
    <label for="password">Password: </label> <input
        type="password" id="password" /><br/>
    <input name="login" type="submit" value="Login" />
</form>
```

To locate the **User Name** and **Password** fields, we can use the `id` attribute in the following way:

```
WebElement username = driver.findElement(By.id("username"));
WebElement password = driver.findElement(By.id("password"));
```

Finding elements by the Name attribute

We might find situations where we cannot use the `id` attribute due to the following reasons:

- Not all elements on a page have the `id` attribute specified
- The `id` attributes are not specified for key elements on a page
- The `id` attribute values are dynamically generated

In this example, the login form elements use the `name` attribute instead of the `id` attribute:

```
<form name="loginForm">
    <label for="username">UserName: </label> <input type="text"
        name="username" /><br/>
    <label for="password">Password: </label> <input
        type="password" name="password" /><br/>
    <input name="login" type="submit" value="Login" />
</form>
```

We can use the `name` attribute to find elements in the following way:

```
WebElement username = driver.findElement(By.name("username"));
WebElement password = driver.findElement(By.name("password"));
```

There could be multiple elements with similar `name` attributes. In such a case, the first element on the page with the specified value will be returned, which may not be the element we are looking for. This may cause the test to fail.

 When building an application, you should recommend that the developers add the `id` attribute for key elements as well as other unique attributes to enable the easy search of elements. This also brings greater testability.

Finding elements by the Class attribute

Apart from using the `id` and `name` attributes, we can also use the `class` attribute to find elements. The `class` attribute is commonly used to apply CSS to an element.

In this example, the login form elements use the `class` attribute instead of the `id` attribute:

```
<form name="loginForm">
    <label for="username">UserName: </label> <input type="text"
        class="username" /></br>
```

```
<label for="password">Password: </label> <input
    type="password" class="password" /></br>
<input name="login" type="submit" value="Login" />
</form>
```

We can use the `class` attribute to find elements in the following way:

```
WebElement username =
    driver.findElement(By.className("username"));
WebElement password =
    driver.findElement(By.className("password"));
```

Sometimes multiple CSS classes are given for an element. For example:

```
<input type="text"
    class="username textfield" />
```

In this case, use one of the class name with the `className()` method.

How it works...

Selenium WebDriver provides the `findElement()` method to locate the elements that are required in a test script from the page under test.

When finding an element, this method will look through the DOM for matching elements with the specified locator strategy and will return the first matching element to the test.

There's more...

The `WebElement` interface also supports find methods that find child elements. For example, if there are some duplicate elements on a page but they are located in the separate `<div>` elements, we can first locate the parent `<div>` element and then locate the child element within the context of the `<div>` element in the following way:

```
WebElement div = driver.findElement(By.id("div1"));
WebElement topLink = div.findElement(By.linkText("top"));
```

You can also a use a shortcut method in the following way:

```
WebElement topLink = driver.findElement
    (By.id("div1")).findElement(By.linkText("top"));
```

NoSuchElementFoundException

The `findElement()` methods will throw the `NoSuchElementFoundException` exception when they fail to find the desired element using the specified locator strategy. The `findElements()` method returns an empty list when it does not find elements matching the locator.

See also

▸   The *Finding elements using findElements method* recipe

Finding elements using the findElements method

Selenium WebDriver provides the `findElements()` method, using which we can find more than one element matching the specified search criteria. This method is useful when we want to work with a group of similar elements. For example, we can get all the links displayed on a page, or get all rows from a table, and so on.

In this recipe, we will get all the links and print their targets by using the `findElements()` method.

How to do it...

Let's create a test that will get all the links from a page, verify the count of links, and print a target for each link, as follows:

```
@Test
public void testFindElements() {
    //Get all the links displayed on Page
    List<WebElement> links = driver.findElements(By.tagName("a"));

    //Verify there are four links displayed on the page
    assertEquals(4, links.size());

    //Iterate though the list of links and print
    //target for each link
    for(WebElement link : links) {
        System.out.println(link.getAttribute("href"));
    }
}
```

How it works...

The `findElements()` method returns all the elements matching the search criteria as a list of `WebElements`.

```
List<WebElement> links = driver.findElements(By.tagName("a"));
```

The `size()` method of the `List` will tell us how many elements are there in the list:

```
assertEquals(4, links.size());
```

We can iterate by using this list in the following way, getting a link and printing its target value:

```
for(WebElement link : links) {
    System.out.println(link.getAttribute("href"));
}
```

See also

▶ The *Finding an element using the findElement method* recipe

Finding links

Selenium WebDriver provides two special methods to find links on a page. Links can be searched either by their text or by partial text.

Finding links with partial text comes in handy when links have dynamic text. In this recipe, we will see how to use these methods to find links.

How to do it...

Let's create a simple test to see how finding links works in Selenium WebDriver with the following options.

Finding a link by its text

Selenium WebDriver's `By` class provides the `linkText()` method to locate links using text displayed for the link. In the following example, we will locate the Gmail link displayed on the Google Home page:

```
WebElement gmailLink = driver.findElement(By.linkText("GMail"));
assertEquals("http://mail.google.com/",
    gmailLink.getAttribute("href"));
```

Finding a link by partial text

Selenium WebDriver's `By` class also provides a method to locate links using partial text. This method is useful where developers create links with dynamic text. In this example, a link is provided to open the inbox. This link also displays the number of new e-mails, which may change dynamically. Here, we can use the `partialLinkText()` method to locate the link using a fixed or known portion of the link text, which in this case would be `Index`. The following code shows an example:

```
WebElement inboxLink =
    driver.findElement(By.partialLinkText("Inbox"));
System.out.println(inboxLink.getText());
```

How it works...

The `linkText` and `partialLinkText` locator methods query the driver for all the links that meet the specified text and return the matching link(s).

There's more...

You can also locate links using the `id`, `name`, or `class` attributes, if developers have provided these attributes.

 Locating elements based on text can cause issues while testing applications in multiple locales. Using parameterized text locator values could work in such scenarios.

See also

- ▶ The *Finding an element using the findElement method* recipe
- ▶ The *Finding elements using findElements method* recipe

Finding elements by tag name

Selenium WebDriver's `By` class provides a `tagName()` method to find elements by their HTML tag name. This is similar to the `getElementsByTagName()` DOM method in JavaScript.

This is used when you want to locate elements using their tag name, for example, locating all `<tr>` tags in a table.

In this recipe, we will briefly see how to use the `tagName()` locator method.

How to do it...

Let's assume you have a single button element on a page. You can locate this button by using its tag in the following way:

```
WebElement loginButton = driver.findElement(By.tagName("button"));
loginButton.click();
```

Take another example where we want to count how many rows are displayed in <table>. We can do this in the following way:

```
WebElement table = driver.findElement(By.id("summaryTable"));
List<WebElement> rows = table.findElements(By.tagName("tr"));
assertEquals(10, rows.size());
```

How it works...

The `tagName()` locator method queries the DOM and returns a list of matching elements for the specified tag name. This method may not be reliable while locating individual elements and the page might have multiple instances of these elements.

See also

▶   The *Finding elements using findElements method* recipe

Finding elements using XPath

XPath (the XML path language) is a query language used to select nodes from an XML document. All the major browsers implement DOM Level 3 XPath (using `http://www.w3.org/TR/DOM-Level-3-XPath/`) specification, which provides access to a DOM tree.

The XPath language is based on a tree representation of the XML document and provides the ability to navigate around the tree and to select nodes using a variety of criteria.

Selenium WebDriver supports XPath to locate elements using XPath expressions, also known as XPath query.

One of the important differences between XPath and CSS is that, with XPath, we can search elements backwards or forwards in the DOM hierarchy, while CSS works only in a forward direction. This means that using XPath we can locate a parent element using a child element and vice versa.

In this recipe, we will explore some basic XPath queries to locate elements, and then examine some advanced XPath queries.

XML documents are treated as trees of nodes. The topmost element of the tree is called the root element. When an HTML document is loaded in DOM, it provides a similar tree of nodes. Here's an example of an HTML page:

```
<html>
  <head>
    <title>My Book List</title>
  </head>
<body>
  <h1>My Book List</h1>
  <div>
  <table class="main-list">
   <tr>
    <td>Title</td>
    <td>Author</td>
    <td>Publication Year</td>
    <td>Price</td>
    <td>Book Page</td>
   </tr>
   <tr id="book_1">
    <td>XML Developer's Guide</td>
    <td>Gambardella, Matthew</td>
    <td>Publication Year</td>
    <td class="price">44.95</td>
    <td><div class="desc">An in-depth look at creating applications
      with XML.</div></td>
    <td><a href="/book_1.html">
      <img src="/img/book1_png/" alt="XML Developers Guide">
      </a></td>
   </tr>
  </table>
 </div>
</body>
</html>
```

Let's understand some basic XPath terminology before we move on to using XPath, with the following listed terms. We will use the previous HTML document as an example:

Term	Description
Nodes	DOM represents an HTML document as trees of nodes. Here are examples of nodes from the previous HTML document: ▸ `html`: This is the root element node ▸ `title`: This is the element node ▸ `id="b00k_1"`: This represents the attributes and values The topmost element of the tree is called the root node or element.

Atomic Values	Atomic values are nodes with no children or parents. For example:
	
	`Gambardella, Matthew`
	
	`XML Developer's Guide`
	
	`44.95`

Parents	Each element and attribute has one parent. For example, the `body` element is the parent of `div`. Similarly, `div` is the parent of the `table` element.
Children	Element nodes may have zero, one, or more children. For example, there are two `tr` elements, which are children of the `table` element.
Siblings	Nodes that have the same parent. For example, h1 and `div` are all siblings and their parent is the `body` element.
Ancestors	A node's parent, parent's parent, and so on. For example, ancestors of the `table` element are `div`, `body` and `html`.
Descendants	A node's children, children's children, and so on. For example, the descendants of the `table` element are `tr`, `td` and `div`.

Selecting nodes

XPath uses path expressions to select nodes from the tree. The node is selected by following a path or steps. The most useful path expressions are listed as follows:

Expression	Description
nodename	This will select all nodes with the name "nodename". For example, table will select all the table elements.
/ (slash)	This will select element(s) relative to the root element. For example: ▸ /html: This will select the root HTML element. A slash (/) is used in the beginning and it defines an absolute path. ▸ html/body/table: will select all table elements that are children of HTML. The slash (/) is used at the start of a code element, and it defines an absolute path. It defines ancestor and descendant relationships if used in the middle; for example, //div/table returns the div containing a table object.
// (double slash)	This will select node(s) in the document from the current node that match the selection irrespective of its position. For example: ▸ //table will select all the table elements no matter where they are in the document ▸ //tr//td will select all the td elements ▸ //a//img will select all the img elements that are children of the "a" (anchor) element Double slash (//) defines a descendant relationship if used in the middle; for example, /html//title returns the title element that is descendant of the html element.
. (dot)	This represents the current node.
.. (double dot)	This will select the parent of the current node. For example, //table/.. will return the div element.
@	This represents an attribute. For example: ▸ //@id: This will select all the elements where the id attribute are defined no matter where they are in the document ▸ //img/@alt: This will select all the img elements where the @alt attribute is defined

How to do it...

Let's explore some basic XPath expressions that can be used in Selenium WebDriver. Selenium WebDriver provides the `xpath()` method to locate elements using XPaths.

Finding elements with an absolute path

XPath absolute paths refer to the very specific location of the element, considering its complete hierarchy in the DOM. Here is an example where the **Username Input** field is located using the absolute path. When providing an absolute path, a space is given between the elements:

```
WebElement userName =
    driver.findElement(By.xpath("/html/body/div/div/form/input"));
```

However, this strategy has limitations as it depends on the structure or hierarchy of the elements on a page. If this changes, the locator will fail to get the element.

Finding elements with a relative path

With a relative path, we can locate an element directly irrespective of its location in the DOM. For example, we can locate the **Username Input** field in the following way, assuming it is the first `<input>` element in the DOM:

```
WebElement userName = driver.findElement(By.xpath("//input"));
```

Finding elements using predicates

A predicate is embedded in square brackets and is used to find out specific node(s) or a node that contains a specific value.

In the previous example, the XPath query will return the first `<input>` element that it finds in the DOM. There could be multiple elements matching the specified XPath query. If the element is not the first element, we can also locate the element by using its index in the DOM. For example, in our login form, we can locate the **Password** field, which is the second `<input>` element on the page, in the following way:

```
WebElement userName = driver.findElement(By.xpath("//input[2]"));
```

Finding elements using attributes values with XPath

We can find elements using their attribute values in XPath. In the following example, the **Username** field is identified using the ID attribute:

```
WebElement userName =
    driver.findElement(By.xpath("//input[@id='username']"));
```

Here is another example where the image is located using the `alt` attribute:

```
WebElement previousButton =
    driver.findElement(By.xpath("//img[@alt='Previous']"));
```

You might come across situations where one attribute may not be sufficient to locate an element and you need combined additional attributes for a precise match. In the following example, multiple attributes are used to locate the `<input>` element for the **Login** button:

```
WebElement previousButton =
    driver.findElement(By.xpath
    ("//input[@type='submit'][@value='Login']"));
```

The same result can be achieved by using XPath `and` operator:

```
WebElement previousButton = driver.findElement
    (By.xpath("//input[@type='submit' and @value='Login']"));
```

In the following example, either of the attributes is used to locate the elements using XPath `or` operator:

```
WebElement previousButton = driver.findElement
    (By.xpath("//input[@type='submit'or @value='Login']"));
```

Finding elements using attributes with XPath

This strategy is a bit different from the earlier strategy where we want to find elements based only on the specific attribute defined for them but not attribute values. For example, we want to lookup all the `<img>` elements that have the `alt` attribute specified:

```
List<WebElement> imagesWithAlt = driver.findElements
    (By.xpath ("//img[@alt]"));
```

Here's another example where all the `<img>` elements will be searched and where the `alt` attribute is not defined. We will use the `not` function to check the negative condition:

```
List<WebElement> imagesWithAlt = driver.findElements
    (By.xpath ("//img[not(@alt)]"));
```

Performing partial match on attribute values XPath also provides a way to find elements matching partial attribute values using XPath functions. This is very useful to test applications where attribute values are dynamically assigned and change every time a page is requested. For example, ASP.NET applications exhibit this kind of behavior where IDs are generated dynamically.

The following table explains the use of these XPath functions:

Syntax	Example	Description
starts-with()	input[starts-with(@id,'ctrl')]	Starting with: For example, if the ID of an element is ctrl_12, this will find and return elements with ctrl at the beginning of the ID.
ends-with()	input[ends-with(@id,'_userName')]	Ending with: For example, if the ID of an element is a_1_userName, this will find and return elements with _userName at the end of the ID.
contains()	Input[contains(@id,'userName')]	Containing: For example, if the ID for an element is panel_login_userName_textfield, this will use the userName part in the middle to match and locate the element.

Matching any attribute using a value

XPath matches the attribute for all the elements for a specified value and returns the element. For example, in the following XPath query, 'userName' is specified. XPath will check all the elements and their attributes to see if they have this value and return the matching element.

```
WebElement userName =
    driver.findElement(By.xpath("//input[@*='username']"));
```

Here are more examples of using XPath predicates to find elements using their position and contents:

Expression	Description
/table/tr[1]	This will select the first tr (row) element that is the child of the table element.
/table/tr[last()]	This will select the last tr (row) element that is the child of the table element.
/table/tr[last()-1]	This will select the second last tr (row) element that is the child of the table element.
/table/tr[position()>4]	This will select the three tr (rows) elements that are child of the table element.
//tr[td>40]	This will select all the tr (rows) elements that have one of their children td with value greater than 40.

Selecting unknown nodes

Apart from selecting the specific nodes, XPath also provides wildcards to select a group of elements:

Wildcard	Description	Example
*	Matches any element node.	▸ `/table/*`: This will select all child elements of a table element ▸ `//*`: This will select all elements in the document ▸ `//*[@class='price']`: This will select any element in the document which has an attribute named `class` with a specified value, that is `price`
@	Matches any attribute node.	▸ `//td[@*]`: This will select all the `td` elements that have any attribute
`node()`	Matches any node of any kind.	▸ `//table/node()`: This will select all the child elements of `table`

Selecting several paths

Using the union | operator in XPath expressions, we can select several paths together, as shown in the following table:

Path Expression	Action
`//div|/p |` `//div/span`	This will select all the p (paragraph) and span elements of the div element.
`//p	//span`	This will select all the p (paragraph) and span elements in the document.

Locating elements with XPath axes

XPath axes help to find elements based on the element's relationship with other elements in a document. The following screenshot shows some examples for some common XPath axes used to find elements from a `<table>` element. This can be applied to any other element structure from your application.

Product	Price	Qty
Product 1	$100	12
Product 2	$150	5

The following image shows a graphical representation of the HTML elements:

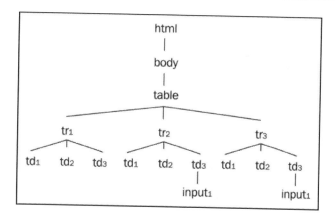

Axis	Description	Example	Result
ancestor	Selects all ancestors (parent, grandparent, and so on) of the current node.	`//td[text()='Product 1']/ancestor::table`	This will get the table element.
descendant	Selects all descendants (children, grandchildren, and so on) of the current node.	`/table/ descendant::td/input`	This will get the input element from the third column of the second row from the table.
following	Selects everything in the document after the closing tag of the current node.	`//td[text()='Product 1']/following::tr`	This will get the second row from the table.
following-sibling	Selects all siblings after the current node.	`//td[text()='Product 1']/following-sibling::td`	This will get the second column from the second row immediately after the column that has `Product 1` as the text value.

preceding	Selects all nodes that appear before the current node in the document, except ancestors, attribute nodes, and namespace nodes.	`//td[text()='$150']/preceding::tr`	This will get the header row.
preceding-sibling	Selects all siblings before the current node.	`//td[text()='$150']/preceding-sibling::td`	This will get the first column of third row from the table.

You can find more about XPath axes at `http://www.w3schools.com/xpath/xpath_axes.asp`.

How it works...

XPath is a powerful language to query and process DOM trees in browsers. XPath is used to navigate through elements and attributes in a DOM tree. XPath provides various rules, functions, operators, and syntax to find the elements.

The majority of browsers support XPath, and Selenium WebDriver provides the ability to find elements using the XPath language.

Using the `xpath()` method of the `By` class, we can locate elements using XPath syntax.

Finding elements using CSS selectors

The Cascading Style Sheets (CSS) is a style sheet language used to describe the presentation semantics (the looks and formatting) of a document written in a markup language such as HTML or XML.

Major browsers implement CSS parsing engines to format or style the pages using CSS syntax. CSS was introduced to keep the presentation information separate from the markup or content. For more information on CSS and CSS selectors, visit `http://en.wikipedia.org/wiki/Cascading_Style_Sheets`.

In CSS, the pattern-matching rules determine which style should be applied to elements in the DOM. These patterns, called **selectors**, may range from simple element names to rich contextual patterns. If all conditions in the pattern are true for a certain element, the selector matches the element, and the browser applies the defined style in CSS syntax.

In this recipe, we will explore some basic CSS selectors and then, later on, we will dive into advanced CSS selectors.

How to do it...

Let's explore some basic CSS selectors that can be used in Selenium WebDriver. Selenium WebDriver's `By` class provides the `cssSelector()` method to find elements using CSS selectors.

Finding elements with an absolute path

CSS absolute paths refer to the very specific location of the element considering its complete hierarchy in the DOM. Here is an example where the **Username Input** field is located using the absolute path. When providing an absolute path, a space is given between the elements, as shown in the following code example:

```
WebElement userName = driver.findElement(By.cssSelector("html body
    div div form input"));
```

You can also use the previous selector in the following way by describing the direct parent-to-child relationships with the > separator:

```
WebElement userName = driver.findElement(By.cssSelector("html >
    body > div > div > form > input"));
```

However, this strategy has limitations as it depends on the structure or hierarchy of the elements on a page. If this changes, the locator will fail to find the element.

Finding elements with a relative path

With a relative path, we can find an element directly, irrespective of its location in the DOM. For example, we can find the **Username Input** field in the following way, assuming it is the first `<input>` element in the DOM:

```
WebElement userName = driver.findElement(By.cssSelector("input"));
```

The following CSS selectors use Class and ID attributes to find elements using relative paths. This is the same as the `className()` and `id()` locator methods. However, there is another strategy where we can use any other attribute of the element that is not covered in the `By` class.

Finding elements using the Class selector

While finding elements using the CSS selector, we can use the `Class` attribute to locate an element. This can be done by specifying the type of HTML tag, then adding a dot followed by the value of the `class` attribute in the following way:

```
WebElement loginButton =
    driver.findElement(By.cssSelector("input.login"));
```

This will find the **Login** button's `<input>` tag whose `Class` attribute is `login`.

Sometimes, multiple CSS classes are given for an element. For example:

```
<input type="text"
    class="username textfield" />
```

In this case, we can use multiple class names, as shown in the following example:

```
WebElement loginButton =
    driver.findElement(By.cssSelector("input.login.textfield"));
```

There is also a shortcut where you can put a "." (period) and class attribute value and ignore the HTML tag. However, this will return all the elements with the class as `login` and the test may not return the correct element, as shown in the following code example:

```
WebElement loginButton =
driver.findElement(By.cssSelector(".login"));
```

This method is similar to the `className()` locator method.

Finding elements using the ID selector

We can find an element using the ID attribute. This can be done by specifying the type of HTML tag, then entering a # (hash) followed by the value of the `Class` attribute, as shown in the following code:

```
WebElement userName =
    driver.findElement(By.cssSelector("input#username"));
```

This will return the username `<input>` element using its `id` attribute.

There is also a shortcut where you can enter # and a class attribute value and ignore the HTML tag. However, this will return all the elements with the `id` set as `username` and the test may not return the correct element. This has to be used very carefully:

```
WebElement userName =
    driver.findElement(By.cssSelector("#username"));
```

This method is similar to the `id` locator strategy.

Finding elements using the attributes selector

Apart from the `class` and `id` attributes, CSS selectors also enable the finding of elements using other attributes of the element. In the following example, the `Name` attribute is used to locate an `<input>` element:

```
WebElement userName =
    driver.findElement(By.cssSelector("input[name=username]"));
```

Using the `name` attribute to locate an element is similar to the `name()` locator method of the `By` class.

Let's use some other attributes to find an element. In the following example, the `<img>` element is located by using its `alt` attribute:

```
WebElement previousButton =
    driver.findElement(By.cssSelector("img[alt='Previous']"));
```

You might come across situations where one attribute may not be sufficient to find an element and you need to combine additional attributes for a precise match. In the following example, multiple attributes are used to locate the **Login** button's `<input>` element:

```
WebElement previousButton =
driver.findElement(By.cssSelector("input[type='submit']
[value='Login']"));
```

Finding elements using the attributes name selector

This strategy is a bit different from the earlier strategy where we want to find elements based on only the specific attribute defined for them but not attribute values. For example, we want to look up all the `<img>` elements that have the `alt` attribute specified:

```
List<WebElement> imagesWithAlt =
    driver.findElements(By.cssSelector("img[alt]"));
```

A Boolean `not()` pseudo-class can also be used to find elements not matching the specified criteria. For example, to find all the `<img>` elements that do not have the `alt` attribute, the following method can be used:

```
List<WebElement> imagesWithoutAlt =
    driver.findElements(By.cssSelector("img:not([alt])"));
```

Selecting several paths

Using the `or` selector "`,`" in CSS selectors, we can select a single or several elements matching the given criteria, as shown in the following code:

```
List<WebElement> elements =
    driver.findElements(By.cssSelector("div, p"));
```

This will select all the `<div>` and all the `<p>` elements:

```
List<WebElement> elements =
    driver.findElements(By.cssSelector("div.first, div.last"));
```

This will select `<div>` with class first and last.

Performing a partial match on attribute values

CSS selector provides a way to find elements matching partial attribute values. This is very useful for testing applications where attribute values are dynamically assigned and change every time a page is requested. For example, ASP.NET applications exhibit this kind of behavior, where IDs are generated dynamically. The following table explains the use of CSS partial match syntax:

Syntax	Example	Description
^=	`input [id^='ctrl']`	Starting with: For example, if the ID of an element is `ctrl_12`, this will find and return elements with `ctrl` at the beginning of the ID.
$=	`input [id$='_userName']`	Ending with: For example, if the ID for an element is `a_1_userName`, this will find and return elements with `_userName` at the end of the ID.
*=	`Input [id*='userName']`	Containing: For example, if the ID of an element is `panel_login_userName_textfield`, this will use the `userName` part in the middle to match and find the element.

How it works...

CSS selector is a pattern and the part of a CSS rule that matches a set of elements in an HTML or XML document.

The majority of browsers support CSS parsing for applying styles to these elements. Selenium WebDriver uses a CSS parsing engine to locate the elements on a page. CSS selectors provide various methods, rules, and patterns to locate the element on a page.

Using CSS selector, the test can find elements in multiple ways using Class, ID, attribute values, and text contents, as described in this recipe.

See also

► The *Finding elements using advanced CSS selectors* recipe

Locating elements using text

When testing web applications, you will also encounter situations where developers don't assign any attributes to the elements and it becomes difficult to locate elements.

Using the CSS selectors or XPath, we can find elements based on their text contents. In this recipe, we will explore methods to find elements using text values.

How to do it...

To find elements using their text contents, CSS selectors and XPath provide methods to find text within the elements. If an element contains specific text, this will return the element in the test.

Using XPath's text function

XPath provides the `text()` function, which can be used to see if an element contains the specified text in the following way:

```
WebElement cell = driver.findElement
    (By.xpath("//td[contains(text(),'Item 1')]"));
```

We can also use a single period/dot, ".", instead of the `text()` function in following way:

```
WebElement cell = driver.findElement
    (By.xpath("//td[contains(.,'Item 1')]"));
```

Here, we are using the `contains` function along with the `text()` function. The `text()` function returns the complete text from the element and the `contains()` function checks for the specific value that we have mentioned.

XPath also offers the `normalize-space(.)` function to match the element using the element's and its sub-element's text.

Finding elements using exact text value in XPath

With XPath, elements can be searched by exact text value in the following way:

```
WebElement cell = driver.findElement
    (By.xpath("//td[.='Item 1']"));
```

This will locate the `<td>` element matching the exact text.

Using the CSS selector contains() pseudo-class

The CSS selectors provide the `contains()` pseudo-class which can be used to see if an element contains the specified text. For example, a test wants to find the cell of a table using its contents in the following way:

```
WebElement cell =
    driver.findElement(By.cssSelector("td:contains('Item 1')"));
```

The `contains()` pseudo-class accepts the text to be searched as a parameter. It then checks all the `<td>` elements in DOM for the specified text.

 The `contains()` pseudo-class may not work with browsers that don't natively support CSS selectors. Also, it has been deprecated from the CSS3 specification.

As an alternative to the `contains()` pseudo-class, you can use the `innerText` attribute (does not work with Firefox) or `textContent` attribute (for Firefox) in the following ways:

```
WebElement cell =
    driver.findElement(By.cssSelector("td[innerText='Item 1']"));
```

Or:

```
WebElement cell = driver.findElement
    (By.cssSelector("td[textContent='Item 1']"));
```

You can also use **jQuery** selectors, which support the `contains()` pseudo-class.

How it works...

CSS selector and XPath provide methods with which to find elements based on their text contents. This approach comes in handy when *elements don't have enough attributes or when no other strategies work when attempting to find these elements*.

To find elements using their text, both CSS selector and XPath search through the DOM for elements that have the specified text value and return the matching element(s).

Finding elements using advanced CSS selectors

We saw some basic CSS selectors in earlier recipes. In this recipe, we will explore some advanced CSS selectors for finding elements.

How to do it...

In the *Finding elements using CSS selectors* recipe, we explored some basic CSS selectors. Let's explore advanced CSS selectors such as adjacent sibling combinators and pseudo-classes, as described in the following sections.

Finding child elements

The CSS selectors provide various ways to find child elements from parent elements.

For example, to find the **Username** field in the login form, we can use the following selector. Here, > is used denote the parent and child relationship:

```
WebElement userName =
        driver.findElement(By.cssSelector("form#loginForm > input"));
```

Similarly, the nth-child() method can be used in the following way:

```
WebElement userName = driver.findElement
        (By.cssSelector("form#loginForm :nth-child(2)"));
```

Here, the second element in <form> is the **Username** field. The following table shows some of the structural pseudo-classes used to find child elements:

Pseudo-class	Example	Description
:first-child	form#loginForm :first-child	This will find the first element under the form, that is, the label for username.
:last-child	form#loginForm :last-child	This will find the last element under the form, that is, the **Login** button.
:nth-child(2)	form#loginForm :nth-child(2)	This will find the second child element under the form, that is, the **Username** field.

Finding sibling elements

With the CSS selector, we can find sibling elements using the + operator. For example, on the sample page, the <p> element with the Description for Product 2 text is selected in the following way:

```
WebElement productDescription =
    driver.findElement(By.cssSelector("div#top5 > p + p"));
```

In this example, the first child of div#top5 will be <p> with Description for Product 1 and its immediate sibling will be Description for Product 2. Here are a few more adjacent sibling combinations for finding siblings:

p + p	div#top5 > p + p	Immediately following sibling. This will locate Description for Product 2.
p + * + p	div#top5 > p + * + p	Following sibling with one intermediary. This will locate Description for Product 3.

Using user action pseudo-classes

Using the user action :focus pseudo-class, we can find an element which currently has the input focus in the following way:

```
WebElement productDescription =
    driver.findElement(By.cssSelector("input:focus"));
```

This will locate any element that currently has the input focus. You can also find elements using the :hover and :active pseudo-classes.

Using UI state pseudo-classes

Using UI state pseudo-classes, we can find elements for various states, such as when control is enabled, disabled, and checked. The following table describes these in detail:

Pseudo-class	Example	Description
:enabled	input:enabled	This will find all the elements that are enabled for user input.
:disabled	input:enabled	This will find all the elements that are disabled for user input.
:checked	input:checked	This will find all the elements (checkboxes) that are checked.

How it works...

Apart from the basic CSS selectors, you can also use various advanced CSS selector methods such as pseudo-classes or adjacent sibling combinators to find the elements with Selenium WebDriver API.

Visit `http://www.w3schools.com/cssref/css_selectors.asp` for an exhaustive list of CSS selectors and their usage.

See also

▸ The *Finding elements using CSS selectors* recipe

Using jQuery selectors

jQuery selectors are important features of the jQuery library. jQuery selectors are based on CSS1-3 selectors along with some additional selectors. These selectors use the familiar CSS Selector syntax to allow developers to quickly and easily identify page elements to operate using the jQuery library methods. Similar to CSS selectors, these selectors allow us to find and manipulate HTML elements as a single element or list of elements.

jQuery selectors can be used where CSS selectors are not supported natively by the browsers.

In this recipe, we will explore in brief how to use jQuery selectors with Selenium WebDriver.

How to do it...

Let's create a test that checks that specified checkboxes are selected when a page is displayed, as follows:

```
@Test
  public void testDefaultSelectedCheckbox() {

    // Expected list of selected Checkbox
    List<String> checked = Arrays
        .asList("user128_admin", "user220_browser");

    // Create an instance of JavaScript Executor from driver
    JavascriptExecutor js = (JavascriptExecutor) driver;

    // Locate all the Checkbox which are checked by calling jQuery
find()
    // method.
```

```
// find() method returns elements in array
@SuppressWarnings("unchecked")
List<WebElement> elements = (List<WebElement>) js
    .executeScript("return jQuery.find(':checked')");

// Verify two Checkbox are selected
assertEquals(elements.size(), 2);

// Verify correct Checkbox are selected
for (WebElement element : elements) {
  assertTrue(checked.contains(element.getAttribute("id")));
}
}
```

How it works...

Selenium WebDriver can be enhanced by jQuery selectors using the jQuery API. However, we need to make sure that the page has the jQuery API loaded before using these selectors. The jQuery API provides the `find()` function through which we can search for elements. We need to use the `JavaScriptExecutor` class to use jQuery's `find()` method. In this example, we will find all the selected checkboxes on a page by calling the `find()` method:

```
//Locate all the Checkbox which are checked by calling jQuery
    find() method.
//find() method returns elements in array
List<WebElement> elements = (List<WebElement>)
    js.executeScript("return jQuery.find(':checked')");
```

The `find()` method returns a single `WebElement` or a list of `WebElements` matching the selector criteria. For more details and a list of available jQuery selectors, please visit `http://api.jquery.com/category/selectors/`.

You can also use the CSS Selectors described in this chapter with the jQuery `find()` method.

There's more...

To use jQuery selectors, the page under test should have the jQuery library loaded. If your application does not use jQuery, you can load jQuery on the page by attaching the jQuery library at runtime with the following methods:

```
private void injectjQueryIfNeeded() {
    if (!jQueryLoaded())
        injectjQuery();
}
```

```
public Boolean jQueryLoaded() {
    Boolean loaded;
    try {
        loaded = (Boolean) driver.executeScript("return
            jQuery()!=null");
    } catch (WebDriverException e) {
        loaded = false;
    }
    return loaded;
}

public void injectjQuery() {
    driver.executeScript(" var headID =
        document.getElementsByTagName(\"head\")[0];"
    + "var newScript = document.createElement('script');"
    + "newScript.type = 'text/javascript';"
    + "newScript.src = 'http://ajax.googleapis.com/
        ajax/libs/jquery/1.7.2/jquery.min.js';"
    + "headID.appendChild(newScript);");
}
```

The `injectjQueryIfNeeded()` method will internally call the `jQueryLoaded()` method to see if the jQuery object is available on the page. If the page does not have the jQuery object defined, the `injectjQueryIfNeeded()` method will call the `injectjQuery()` method to attach the jQuery library to the page header at runtime. This is done by adding a `<script>` element, which refers to the Google **Content Delivery Network** (**CDN**) for the jQuery library file, to the page. You may change the version used in this example to the latest version of the jQuery library.

3
Working with Elements

In this chapter, we will explore the various methods of Selenium WebDriver that interact with HTML elements displayed on the page. We will cover the following recipes:

- ▶ Automating textboxes, text areas, and buttons
- ▶ Checking an element's text
- ▶ Checking an element's attribute and CSS values
- ▶ Automating dropdowns and lists
- ▶ Checking options in dropdowns and lists
- ▶ Checking selected options in dropdowns and lists
- ▶ Automating radio buttons and radio groups
- ▶ Automating checkboxes
- ▶ Working with WebTables

Introduction

Selenium WebDriver provides a very comprehensive API for working with different types of web elements performing User Interactions, executing JavaScript code, and supports various types of controls such as list, dropdown, radio buttons, and checkboxes.

In this chapter, we will explore how these features can be used to build simple to complex test steps. This chapter will also help you overcome some common issues faced while developing automated scripts with Selenium WebDriver. The chapter examples are created with Selenium WebDriver Java bindings. The sample code for this chapter contains some of these recipes implemented with C#, Ruby, and Python.

Automating textboxes, text areas, and buttons

The textbox and button elements are the most common elements used in any web application. Selenium WebDriver's **WebElement** interface provides methods to simulate keyboard entry into textboxes or text areas and perform clicks on a button control.

In this recipe, we will explore these methods to automate textbox, text-area, and button elements.

How to do it...

Here we will explore the `clear()`, `sendKeys()`, `submit()` and `click()` methods of the `WebElement` interface.

Clearing text from textbox and text-area elements

To clear the existing text value from textbox and text-area elements, we can use the `clear()` method, as shown in following code example:

```
// Find the text input element by its name
WebElement element = driver.findElement(By.name("q"));

// Clear the existing text value using clear method
element.clear();
```

Entering text in textbox and text-area elements

To enter text value in a textbox or a text-area element, we can use the `sendKeys()` method, as shown in following code example:

```
// Enter something to search for
element.sendKeys("Selenium testing tools cookbook");
```

Submitting forms

Normally, HTML data entry forms are created using the `<form>` element. When user fills the data and saves form, it is submitted on the remote web server to process the data. Here's an example where a Google search form is submitted by calling the `submit()` method on the search textbox shown on the Google homepage:

```
// Find the text input element by its name
WebElement element = driver.findElement(By.name("q"));

// Clear the existing text value
```

```
element.clear();

// Enter something to search for
element.sendKeys("Selenium testing tools cookbook");

// Now submit the form. WebDriver will find
// the form for us from the element
element.submit();
```

Performing a click on a button element

To click on a button element, we can use the `click()` method of the `WebElement` interface:

```
// Find the button element by its name
WebElement element = driver.findElement(By.name("btnG"));

// Click on the button
element.click();
```

How it works...

The `clear()` method of the `WebElement` interface works only on a textbox `<input>` and text area, having no effect on other types of elements. It will clear any previous value from an element.

The `sendKeys()` method can be used on any element that accepts values by typing on the element. This method simulates typing into an element that sets the given string as the value of that element. The `sendKeys()` method accepts `java.lang.CharSequence` or string value.

We can also simulate pressing non-text keys using the `sendKeys()` method by using the `Keys` enum. For example, after entering a value in the textbox, we can press the TAB key as shown in following code example:

```
element.sendKeys("123" + Keys.TAB);
```

For a complete list of keys visit `http://selenium.googlecode.com/git/docs/api/java/org/openqa/selenium/Keys.html`.

The `submit()` method is applicable on the `<form>` element or any element that is under the `<form>` element. Developers can create buttons or links for form submission. When a user clicks on the submission element, the `onsubmit` event is fired. In Selenium WebDriver, any element that is part of the form, or an element within a `<form>`, can call this event using the `submit()` method of the `WebElement` interface.

The `click()` method will click on an element. If clicking on an element causes the current page displayed in a browser to change, then the script will wait until the new page is loaded. However, if it causes a new page to be loaded via an event, or by sending a native event, then the method will not wait for it to be loaded. In such cases, we will have to verify that a new page has been loaded.

There are some preconditions for an element to be clicked using the `click()` method. The element must be visible and it must have a height and width greater then 0. Clicking on an invisible element will result in a `ElementNotVisibleException` exception.

See also

► The *Checking an element's text* recipe

► The *Checking an element's attribute and CSS values* recipe

Checking an element's text

While testing a web application, we need to verify that elements are displaying the correct values or text on the page. Selenium WebDriver's `WebElement` interface provides methods to retrieve and verify text from an element. Sometimes we need to retrieve text or values from an element into a variable at runtime and later use it at some other place in the test flow.

In this recipe, we will retrieve and verify text from an element using the `getText()` method of the `WebElement` interface.

How to do it...

Here, we will create a test that finds an element and then retrieves text from the element in a string variable. We will verify the contents of this string for correctness using the following code:

```
@Test
public void testElementText() {
  // Get the message Element
  WebElement message = driver.findElement(By.id("message"));

  // Get the message elements text
  String messageText = message.getText();

  // Verify message element's text displays "Click on me and my
  // color will change"
  assertEquals("Click on me and my color will change",
    messageText);

  // Get the area Element
```

```
WebElement area = driver.findElement(By.id("area"));

// Verify area element's text displays "Div's Text\nSpan's Text"
assertEquals("Div's Text\nSpan's Text", area.getText());
}
```

How it works...

The getText() method of the WebElement interface returns the visible innerText of the element, including sub-elements, without any leading or trailing whitespace.

If the element has child elements, the value of the innerText attribute of the child elements will also be returned along with the parent element. In the following example, we have a <span> element within a <div> element. While we are retrieving innerText from the <div> element it also appends innerText of the <span> element:

```
// Get the area Element
WebElement area = driver.findElement(By.id("area"));

// Verify element's text displays "Div's Text\nSpan's Text"
assertEquals("Div's Text\nSpan's Text",area.getText());
```

There's more...

The WebElement.getText() method does not work on hidden or invisible elements. Retrieval of text from such elements is possible through the getAttribute() method using the innerText or textContent attributes:

```
assertEquals("Div's Text\nSpan's
Text",area.getAttribute("innerText"));
```

The innerText attribute is not supported in Firefox and the textContent attribute is not supported in Internet Explorer.

See also

▶ The *Checking an element's attribute and CSS values* recipe

Checking an element's attribute and CSS values

Developers configure various attributes of elements displayed on the web page during design or at runtime to control the behavior or style of elements when they are displayed in the browser. For example, the `<input>` element can be set to read-only by setting the `readonly` attribute.

We can retrieve and check an element's attribute using the `getAttribute()` method of the `WebElement` interface.

Various styles are applied on elements displayed in a web application so that they look neat and become more usable. Developers add these styles using **Cascading Style Sheets** (**CSS**). This can be done using the `WebElement` class's `getCSSValue()` method, which returns the value of a specified style attribute.

In this recipe, we will use the `getCSSValue()` function to check the style attribute defined for an element.

In this recipe, we will check the attribute value of an element by using the `getAttribute()` method.

How to do it...

The following code can be used to create a test that locates an element and checks its attribute value:

```
@Test
public void testElementAttribute() {
    WebElement message = driver.findElement(By.id("message"));
    assertEquals("justify", message.getAttribute("align"));
}
```

Let's create a test that reads the CSS `width` attribute and verifies the value, using the following code:

```
@Test
public void testElementStyle() {
    WebElement message = driver.findElement(By.id("message"));
    String width = message.getCssValue("width");
    assertEquals("150px", width);
}
```

How it works...

By passing the name of the attribute to the `getAttribute()` method, it returns the value of the attribute back to the test. In this example, we are checking that the `align` attribute of the `<p>` element is set to justify:

```
assertEquals("justify", message.getAttribute("align"));
```

By passing the name of CSS attribute to the `getCSSValue()` method, it returns the value of the CSS attribute. In this example, we are checking that the width attribute of the `<div>` element is set to `150px`:

```
String width = message.getCssValue("width");
```

Automating dropdowns and lists

Selenium WebDriver supports testing dropdown and list elements using a special `Select` class.

The `Select` class provides various methods and properties to interact with dropdowns and lists created with the HTML `<select>` element.

In this recipe, we will automate dropdown and list control using the `Select` class.

How to do it...

Let's create a test for a dropdown control. This test will perform some basic checks and will then call various methods to select options in the dropdown:

```
@Test
public void testDropdown() {

    // Get the Dropdown as a Select using it's name attribute
    Select make = new Select(driver.findElement(By.name("make")));

    // Verify Dropdown does not support multiple selection
    assertFalse(make.isMultiple());
    // Verify Dropdown has four options for selection
    assertEquals(4, make.getOptions().size());

    // With Select class we can select an option in Dropdown using
    Visible text
    make.selectByVisibleText("Honda");
    assertEquals("Honda", make.getFirstSelectedOption().getText());
```

```
        // or we can select an option in Dropdown using value attribute
        make.selectByValue("audi");
        assertEquals("Audi", make.getFirstSelectedOption().getText());

        // or we can select an option in Dropdown using index
        make.selectByIndex(0);
        assertEquals("BMW", make.getFirstSelectedOption().getText());
    }
```

Create another test for a list control that has multi-selection enabled. The test will perform some basic checks and then call methods to select multiple options in a list. The test will check the selected options and then deselect the options by calling various deselection methods, namely, by visible text, by value, and by index respectively as shown in the following code example:

```
    @Test
    public void testMultipleSelectList() {
        // Get the List as a Select using it's name attribute
        Select color = new Select(driver.findElement(By.name("color")));

        // Verify List support multiple selection
        assertTrue(color.isMultiple());

        // Verify List has five options for selection
        assertEquals(5, color.getOptions().size());

        // Select multiple options in the list using visible text
        color.selectByVisibleText("Black");
        color.selectByVisibleText("Red");
        color.selectByVisibleText("Silver");

        // Deselect an option using value attribute of the option
        color.deselectByValue("rd");
        // Verify selected options count
        assertEquals(1, color.getAllSelectedOptions().size());

        // Deselect an option using index of the option
        color.deselectByIndex(0);
        // Verify selected options count
        assertEquals(0, color.getAllSelectedOptions().size());
    }
```

How it works...

We can find dropdown or list elements in a similar way to finding other elements on a page. However, we will use the `Select` class to interact with these elements. This is done in the following way:

```
Select color = new Select(driver.findElement(By.name("color")));
```

The HTML `<select>` element supports dropdowns or lists with multi-select options. We can check if the element supports multi-select by calling the `isMultiple()` method of the `Select` class, shown as follows. It returns `true` if the control supports multi-selection, and `false` if it does not:

```
assertFalse(make.isMultiple());
```

We can check the number of options available in the dropdown or list by calling the `getOptions()` method of the `Select` class and querying the size of the returned collection of `WebElements`:

```
assertEquals(4, make.getOptions().size());
```

The `Select` class provides three different ways to select and deselect the options from dropdowns and lists, as shown in the following sections.

Selection/deselection by visible text

We can select an option by its visible text. For example, here is the code snippet for the `<select>` element:

```
<select name="color" size="6" multiple="multiple"
  style="width:100px">
  <option value="bl">Black</option>
  <option value="wt">White</option>
  <option value="rd">Red</option>
  <option value="br">Brown</option>
  <option value="sl">Silver</option>
</select>
```

Each option in this `<select>` element has a value property as well as a text label specified between `<option>` and `</option>`. We can select an option using this text label by calling the `selectByVisibleText()` method of the `Select` class, as shown in the following code:

```
color.selectByVisibleText("Black");
```

Similarly, you can deselect an already selected option by calling the `deselectByVisibleText()` method, as shown in the following code:

```
color.deselectByVisibleText("Black");
```

Selection/deselection by value

We can also select an option using its value attribute. For example, the following option has the value attribute "bl" and text label "Black":

```
<option value="bl">Black</option>
```

To select this option by value we need to call the selectByValue() method of the Select class, as shown in the following line of code:

```
color.selectByValue("bl");
```

Similarly, you can deselect an already selected option by calling the deselectByValue() method, as shown in the following code:

```
color.deselectByValue("bl");
```

Selection/deselection by index

This is another way by which we can select an option, this time by using its index. When options are displayed on a page, they are indexed in the order in which they are defined on the page. We can call the selectByIndex() method of the Select class by specifying the index value, as shown in the following code:

```
color.selectByIndex("0");
```

Similarly, you can deselect an already selected option by calling the deselectByIndex() method. The following code shows the complete syntax:

```
color.deselectByIndex(0);
```

 This method may cause problems where options are dynamic and their index changes frequently.

There's more...

We can select/deselect multiple options from a dropdown or list by calling the select/deselect methods in a sequence. For example, in the color list that supports multiple selections, we can select options in the following way:

```
color.selectByVisibleText("Black");
color.selectByVisibleText("Red");
color.selectByVisibleText("Silver");
```

This will select Black, Red, and Silver options in the list.

See also

▸ The *Checking options in dropdowns and lists* recipe

▸ The *Checking selected options in dropdowns and lists* recipe

Checking options in the Select element

While testing the dropdowns and lists created with the `<select>` element, there will be a need to check to see that correct options are displayed for user selection. These options may be static or populated from a database via AJAX calls.

In this recipe, we will see how options can be checked against the expected values.

Getting ready

This recipe will need the test created from the earlier *Automating dropdowns and lists* recipe. We will add additional steps for checking the options.

How to do it...

Let's modify the `testDropdown()` test method for checking the options. Add the following highlighted code to the test:

```
@Test
public void testDropdown() {

    // Get the Dropdown as a Select using it's name attribute
    Select make = new Select(driver.findElement(By.name("make")));

    // Verify Dropdown does not support multiple selection
    assertFalse(make.isMultiple());
    // Verify Dropdown has four options for selection
    assertEquals(4, make.getOptions().size());

    // We will verify Dropdown has expected values as listed in a
array
    List<String> expectedOptions = Arrays.asList("BMW", "Mercedes",
"Audi",
        "Honda");
    List<String> actualOptions = new ArrayList<String>();

    // Retrieve the option values from Dropdown using getOptions()
method
```

```
    for (WebElement option : make.getOptions()) {
      actualOptions.add(option.getText());
    }


    // Verify expected options array and actual options array match
    assertArrayEquals(expectedOptions.toArray(), actualOptions.
  toArray());

    // With Select class we can select an option in Dropdown using
  Visible
    // Text
    make.selectByVisibleText("Honda");
    assertEquals("Honda", make.getFirstSelectedOption().getText());

    // or we can select an option in Dropdown using value attribute
    make.selectByValue("audi");
    assertEquals("Audi", make.getFirstSelectedOption().getText());

    // or we can select an option in Dropdown using index
    make.selectByIndex(0);
    assertEquals("BMW", make.getFirstSelectedOption().getText());

  }
```

How it works...

Checking options in a dropdown or list needs a slightly different approach, as there is no in-built method available in the `Select` class. In this approach, we create a list of expected values that we want to check in the dropdown or list, as shown in the following code:

```
List<String> expectedOptions = Arrays.asList("BMW",
  "Mercedes", "Audi","Honda");
```

The text labels for all the options will be retrieved in a similar list. For this, we will iterate through all the options using the `getOptions()` method of the `Select` class. The `getOptions()` method returns all the options as instances of the `WebElement` class in a list. Using the `getText()` method of the `WebElement` class, the text label of all the options will be added in the `actualOptions` array list:

```
List<String> act_options = new ArrayList<String>();

  //Retrieve the option values from Dropdown using getOptions()
  //method
  for(WebElement option : make.getOptions()) {
actualOptions.add(option.getText()); }
```

We will compare the `expectedOptions` list with `actualOptions` for any mismatch at the end:

```
assertArrayEquals(expectedOptions.toArray(),actualOptions.toArray());
```

There's more...

To check whether a specific option is available for selection, we can simply perform a check on the `actualOptions` array list in the following way:

```
assertTrue(actualOptions.contains("BMW"));
```

See also

- ▶ The *Automating dropdowns and lists* recipe
- ▶ The *Checking selected options in dropdowns and lists* recipe

Checking selected options in dropdowns and lists

In earlier recipes, we saw how to select options in the dropdown and list controls as well as how to check what options are available for selection. We also need to verify that the correct options are selected in these controls, either by default or by the user.

In this recipe, we will see how to check options that are selected in a dropdown or list.

Getting ready

This recipe will need the test created from the earlier *Automating dropdowns and lists* recipe. We will add additional steps for checking the options.

How to do it...

Let's modify the `testDropdown()` test method for checking the options. Add the following highlighted code to the test:

```
@Test
public void testDropdown()
{
    ...

    //With Select class we can select an option in Dropdown using
    //Visible Text
```

```
      make.selectByVisibleText("Honda");
      assertEquals("Honda", make.getFirstSelectedOption().getText());


      //or we can select an option in Dropdown using value attribute
      make.selectByValue("audi");
      assertEquals("Audi", make.getFirstSelectedOption().getText());


      //or we can select an option in Dropdown using index
      make.selectByIndex(0);
      assertEquals("BMW", make.getFirstSelectedOption().getText());
   }
```

Also, modify the testMultipleSelectList() test method for checking the options. Add the following highlighted code to the test:

```
@Test
public void testMultipleSelectList()
{
   ...


   //Select multiple options in the list using visible text
   color.selectByVisibleText("Black");
   color.selectByVisibleText("Red");
   color.selectByVisibleText("Silver");


   //We will verify list has multiple options selected as listed
   //in a array
   List<String> expectedSelection = Arrays.asList
      ("Black", "Red", "Silver");
   List<String> actualSelection = new ArrayList<String>();


   for(WebElement option : color.getAllSelectedOptions())
   {actualSelection.add(option.getText()); }


   //Verify expected array for selected options match with actual
   //options selected
   assertArrayEquals
      (expectedSelection.toArray(),actualSelection.toArray());


   //Verify there 3 options selected in the list
   assertEquals(3,color.getAllSelectedOptions().size());


   //Deselect an option using visible text
   color.deselectByVisibleText("Silver");
   //Verify selected options count
```

```
  assertEquals(2,color.getAllSelectedOptions().size());

  //Deselect an option using value attribute of the option
  color.deselectByValue("rd");
  //Verify selected options count
  assertEquals(1,color.getAllSelectedOptions().size());

  //Deselect an option using index of the option
  color.deselectByIndex(0);
  //Verify selected options count
  assertEquals(0,color.getAllSelectedOptions().size());
}
```

How it works...

When the user selects an option from a dropdown or list that supports only single option selection, the selected option can be queried through the `getFirstSelectedOption()` method of the `Select` class. It returns the option as an instance of `WebElement`. For example, in the `Make` dropdown, we selected the `Honda` option using the `selectByVisible()` method. To check this selection, we can use the `getFirstSelectedOption()` and the `getText()` methods in the following way:

```
//With Select class we can select an option in Dropdown using
Visible Text
  make.selectByVisibleText("Honda");
  assertEquals("Honda", make.getFirstSelectedOption().getText());
```

Checking selected options in a multi-select dropdown or list

To check selected options in a multi-select dropdown or list, we can use the `getAllSelectedOptions()` method of the `Select` class. It returns all the selected options as a list of `WebElement`. In this test, we created a list of expected selected items and then retrieved the selected options in a list by iterating `WebElement`, returned by `getAllSelectedOptions()`:

```
//We will verify list has multiple options selected as listed in a
//array
List<String> expectedSelection = Arrays.asList("Black",
  "Red", "Silver");
List<String> actualSelection = new ArrayList<String>();

for(WebElement option : color.getAllSelectedOptions()) {
  actualSelection.add(option.getText()); }
```

Using the `assertArrayEquals()` method of JUnit, we will compare both `expectedSelection` and `actualSelection` to check that correct options are selected in the list, as shown in the following code:

```
//Verify expected array for selected options match with actual
    //options selected
assertArrayEquals(expectedSelection.toArray(),
    actualSelection.toArray());
```

We can also check the number of options selected in a list by querying the size from the `getAllSelectedOptions()` method. For example, as shown in the following code, we selected three options in the list, so the `getAllSelectedOptions().size()` method should return 3:

```
assertEquals(3,color.getAllSelectedOptions().size());
```

There's more...

To check whether a specific option is selected, we can simply perform a check on the `actualSelection` array list in the following way:

```
assertTrue(actualSelection.contains("Red"));
```

See also

▶ The *Checking options in dropdowns and lists* recipe

▶ The *Checking selected options in dropdowns and lists* recipe

Automating radio buttons and radio groups

The Selenium WebDriver supports radio buttons and radio group elements using the `WebElement` interface. We can select and deselect the radio buttons using the `click()` method of the `WebElement` class, and check whether a radio button is selected or deselected using the `isSelected()` method.

In this recipe, we will see how to work with the radio button and radio group controls.

How to do it...

Let's create a test that will have radio buttons and the radio group controls. We will perform select and deselect operations, the following code shows an example:

```
@Test
public void testRadioButton() {
    // Get the Radio Button as WebElement using it's value attribute
```

```
WebElement petrol = driver.findElement(By
    .xpath("//input[@value='Petrol']"));

// Check if its already selected? otherwise select the Radio
Button
// by calling click() method
if (!petrol.isSelected()) {
  petrol.click();
}

// Verify Radio Button is selected
assertTrue(petrol.isSelected());

// We can also get all the Radio buttons from a Radio Group in a
list
// using findElements() method along with Radio Group identifier
List<WebElement> fuelType =
driver.findElements(By.name("fuel_type"));
  for (WebElement type : fuelType) {
    // Search for Diesel Radio Button in the Radio Group and
select it
    if (type.getAttribute("value").equals("Diesel")) {
      if (!type.isSelected()) {
        type.click();
      }
      assertTrue(type.isSelected());
      break;
    }
  }
}
```

How it works...

We can locate a radio button similar to any other element. In this example, **XPath** is used to locate the radio button using its `value` attribute:

```
//Get the Radiobutton as WebElement using it's value attribute
WebElement petrol = driver.findElement(By.xpath
  ("//input[@value='Petrol']"));
```

We can select or deselect a radio button by using the `click()` method. There are no separate methods to perform these operations. When we want to select a radio button, we need to be careful and see to it that it's not already selected, or else, calling the `click()` method will deselect the radio button. We can check if a radio button is already selected by calling the `isSelected()` method, which returns `true` if it's selected and `false` if it's not selected. In the following example, the `click()` method will be called only when the radio button is not selected:

```
//Check if its already selected? otherwise select the Radiobutton
//by calling click() method
if (!petrol.isSelected()) {
  petrol.click();
}
```

Working with radio groups

Instead of just locating a single radio button, we can also work with a group of radio buttons by locating all the radio buttons from a group shown as a list of `WebElement` using the `findElements()` method. In the following example, a radio button from `fuel_type` radio group is retrieved in a list of `WebElement`:

```
//We can also get all the Radiobuttons from a Radio Group in a
//list using findElements() method along with Radio Group
//identifier
List<WebElement> fuelType =
  driver.findElements(By.name("fuel_type"));
```

We can then iterate through this list to find a specific radio button and select or deselect a radio button as shown in the following example:

```
for (WebElement type : fuelType)
{
  //Search for Diesel Radiobutton in the Radio Group and select it
  if(type.getAttribute("value").equals("Diesel"))
  {
    if(!type.isSelected()) {
      type.click();
  }

    assertTrue(type.isSelected());
    break;
  }
}
```

Automating checkboxes

Selenium WebDriver supports the **checkbox** element using the `WebElement` interface. We can select or deselect a checkbox using the `click()` method and check whether a checkbox is selected or deselected using the `isSelected()` method.

In this recipe, we will see how to work with the checkbox element.

How to do it...

Here is the code for a test that has a checkbox and performs the select and deselect operations:

```java
@Test
public void testCheckBox() {
  //Get the Checkbox as WebElement using it's value attribute
  WebElement airbags = driver.findElement(By.xpath("//input[@
value='Airbags']"));

  //Check if its already selected? otherwise select the Checkbox
  //by calling click() method
  if (!airbags.isSelected()) {
    airbags.click();
  }

  //Verify Checkbox is Selected
  assertTrue(airbags.isSelected());

  //Check Checkbox if selected? If yes, deselect it
  //by calling click() method
  if (airbags.isSelected()) {
    airbags.click();
  }

  //Verify Checkbox is Deselected
  assertFalse(airbags.isSelected());
}
```

How it works...

We can locate a checkbox in a way similar to locating any other element on a page. In this example, XPath is used to locate the checkbox by its `value` attribute:

```
WebElement airbags = driver.findElement
    (By.xpath("//input[@value='Airbags']"));
```

We can select or deselect a checkbox by using the `click()` method. There are no separate methods to perform these operations. When we want to select a checkbox, we need to be careful that it's not already selected, otherwise calling the `click()` method will deselect the checkbox. We can check if a checkbox is already selected by calling the `isSelected()` method, which returns `true` if it's selected and `false` if it's not selected. Here, the `click()` method will be called only when the checkbox is not selected:

```
if (!airbags.isSelected()) {
    airbags.click();
}
```

Similarly, to deselect the checkbox, we need to see if it is already selected:

```
if (airbags.isSelected()) {
  airbags.click();
}
```

Working with WebTables

Similar to other element types that we have seen in earlier sections, an HTML **table** is represented as `WebElement`. However, there are no table-specific methods that are available with the `WebElement` interface.

While working with tables, we can find the rows and cells effectively by using a set of the `By` class methods. In this recipe, we will see how to get rows and columns in table.

How to do it...

Let's create a simple test that will print data from a table, as shown in the following code example:

```
@Test
public void testWebTable() {

    WebElement simpleTable = driver.findElement(By.id("items"));

    // Get all rows
```

```
    List<WebElement> rows =
  simpleTable.findElements(By.tagName("tr"));
    assertEquals(3, rows.size());

    // Print data from each row
    for (WebElement row : rows) {
      List<WebElement> cols = row.findElements(By.tagName("td"));
      for (WebElement col : cols) {
        System.out.print(col.getText() + "\t");
      }
      System.out.println();
    }
  }
```

How it works...

A table in HTML is a collection of the `<tr>` and `<td>` elements for rows and cells respectively. In the sample test, the table can be found as a `WebElement` using its ID attribute, as follows:

```
WebElement simpleTable = driver.findElement(By.id("items"));
```

To get all the rows from a table, the `findElements()` method is called on `simpleTable` and the `tagName` strategy is used to get all `<tr>` elements as shown in the following way:

```
List<WebElement> rows =
    simpleTable.findElements(By.tagName("tr"));
```

Each `<tr>` element then holds the `<td>` elements, which are the columns or cells of the table. The test iterates through the rows and columns to print the data in the following way:

```
//Print data from each row
for (WebElement row : rows) {
    List<WebElement> cols = row.findElements(By.tagName("td"));
    for (WebElement col : cols) {
        System.out.print(col.getText() + "\t");
    }
    System.out.println();
}
```

This method is useful when you have a test that needs to verify data in a table.

There's more...

We can also use CSS selectors or XPath to find table rows and cells using the index matching technique. In the following example, CSS selector is used to find the first cell of the second row in the table:

```
WebElement cell = driver.findElement
        (By.cssSelector("table#items tbody tr:nth-child(2) td"));
```

Similarly, using XPath, it can be done in the following way:

```
WebElement cell = driver.findElement
        (By.xpath("//table[@id='items']/tbody/tr[2]/td"));
```

4
Working with Selenium API

In this chapter, we will cover:

- ▸ Checking for an element's presence
- ▸ Checking for an element's state
- ▸ Using Advanced User Interactions API for mouse and keyboard events
- ▸ Performing double-click on an element
- ▸ Performing drag-and-drop operations
- ▸ Working with context menus
- ▸ Executing the JavaScript code
- ▸ Capturing screenshots with Selenium WebDriver
- ▸ Maximizing the browser window
- ▸ Handling session cookies
- ▸ Working with browser navigation
- ▸ Working with WebDriver events

Introduction

Selenium WebDriver implements a very comprehensive API to work with web elements, perform advanced user interactions such as complex mouse and keyboard events, execute JavaScript code, capture screenshots, and so on.

In this chapter, we will explore how these features can be used to build simple to complex test steps. This chapter will also help in overcoming some common issues when building tests with Selenium WebDriver.

Checking an element's presence

The Selenium WebDriver does not implement Selenium RC's isElementPresent() method to check if an element is present on a page. This method is useful for building a reliable test that checks an element's presence before performing any action on it.

In this recipe, we will write a method similar to the isElementPresent() method.

How to do it...

To implement the isElementPresent() method, follow these steps:

1. Create a method isElementPresent() and keep it accessible to your tests, shown as follows:

```java
private boolean isElementPresent(By by) {
  try {
    driver.findElement(by);
      return true;
    } catch (NoSuchElementException e) {
      return false;
  }
}
```

2. Now, implement a test that calls the isElementPresent() method. It will check if the desired element is present on a page. If found, it will click on the element; else it fails the test. This is done as follows:

```java
@Test
public void testIsElementPresent() {
    // Check if element with locator criteria exists on Page
    if (isElementPresent(By.name("airbags"))) {
      // Get the checkbox and select it
      WebElement airbag =
driver.findElement(By.name("airbags"));
        if (!airbag.isSelected()) {
          airbag.click();
        }
    } else {
      fail("Airbag Checkbox doesn't exists!!");
    }
}
```

How it works...

The `isElementPresent()` method takes a locator using an instance of `By`. It then calls the `findElement()` method. If the element is not found, a `NoSuchElementException` exception will be thrown. Using the try and catch block, the `isElementPresent()` method will return true if the element is found and no exception is thrown; otherwise, it will return false if `NoSuchElementException` is thrown by the `findElement()` method.

See also

▸   The *Checking an element's status* recipe

Checking an element's state

Many a time a test fails to click on an element or enter text in a field, as the element is disabled or exists in the DOM but is hidden on the page. This will result in an error being thrown and the test resulting in failure. To build reliable tests that can run unattended, a robust exception and error handling is needed in the test flow.

We can handle these problems by checking the state of elements. The `WebElement` interface provides the following methods to check the state of an element:

Method	Purpose
`isEnabled()`	This method checks if an element is enabled. It returns `true` if enabled, else `false` if disabled.
`isSelected()`	This method checks if an element is selected (radio button, checkbox, and so on). It returns `true` if selected, else `false` if deselected.
`isDisplayed()`	This method checks if an element is displayed.

In this recipe, we will use some of these methods to check the status and handle possible errors.

How to do it...

We will create a test where a checkbox for the LED headlamp option needs to be selected on a page. This checkbox will be enabled or disabled based on the previously selected option. Before selecting this checkbox, we will make sure that it's enabled for selection, as follows:

```
@Test
public void testElementIsEnabled() {
    // Get the Checkbox as WebElement using it's name attribute
    WebElement ledheadlamp = driver.findElement(By
        .name("ledheadlamp"));
```

```
    // Check if its enabled before selecting it
    if (ledheadlamp.isEnabled()) {
        // Check if its already selected? otherwise select the
Checkbox
        if (!ledheadlamp.isSelected()) {
          ledheadlamp.click();
        }
    } else {
        fail("LED Lamp Checkbox is disabled!!");
    }
}
```

How it works...

We are selecting a checkbox by checking the two states of an element—first, it is enabled, and second, it is not selected. We can use the isEnabled() function of the WebElement interface, which returns true if the element is enabled or false if it's disabled. The test will fail if the checkbox is disabled. If we do not check this condition, the test will possibly throw an exception saying the object is disabled, as follows:

```
    // Check if its enabled before selecting it
    if (ledheadlamp.isEnabled()) {
        // Check if its already selected? otherwise select the Checkbox
        if (!ledheadlamp.isSelected()) {
          ledheadlamp.click();
        }
    } else {
        fail("LED Lamp Checkbox is disabled!!");
    }
```

Using Advanced User Interactions API for mouse and keyboard events

The Selenium WebDriver's **Advanced User Interactions** API allows us to perform operations from keyboard events and simple mouse events to complex events such as dragging-and-dropping, holding a key and then performing mouse operations using the Actions class, and building a complex chain of events exactly like a user doing these manually.

The Actions class implements the builder pattern to create a composite action containing a group of other actions.

In this recipe, we will use the Actions class to build a chain of events to select rows in a table.

How to do it...

Let's create a test to select the multiple rows from different positions in a table using the *Ctrl* key (*Command* key on a Mac). We can select multiple rows by selecting the first row, then holding the *Ctrl* key (*Command* key on a Mac), and then selecting another row and releasing the *Ctrl* key (*Command* key on a Mac). This will select the desired rows from the table, as shown in the following code:

```
@Test
public void testRowSelectionUsingControlKey() {

    List<WebElement> tableRows = driver.findElements
        (By.xpath("//table[@class='iceDatTbl']/tbody/tr"));

    //Select second and fourth row from table using Control Key.
    //Row Index start at 0
    Actions builder = new Actions(driver);
    builder.click(tableRows.get(1))
            .keyDown(Keys.CONTROL)
            .click(tableRows.get(3))
            .keyUp(Keys.CONTROL)
            .build().perform();

    //Verify Selected Row table shows two rows selected
    List<WebElement> rows = driver.findElements
        (By.xpath("//div[@class='icePnlGrp
        exampleBox']/table[@class='iceDatTbl']/tbody/tr"));
    assertEquals(2, rows.size());
}
```

 On a Mac OS X machine, you need to use the Command key syntax instead of the Control key syntax. For example:

```
Actions builder = new Actions(driver);
builder.click(tableRows.get(1)).keyDown(Keys.COMMAND)
    click(tableRows.get(3)).keyUp(Keys.COMMAND).
perform();}
```

How it works...

We need to create an instance of the `Actions` class by passing the instance of the `driver` class to the constructor in the following way:

```
Actions builder = new Actions(driver);
```

We will build a chain of events that we need to perform to select the rows. This will require performing a `click()` operation on the first row, then holding the *Ctrl* key (*Command* key on Mac) using the `keyDown()` operation, clicking on the end row, and then releasing the *Ctrl* key (*Command* key on Mac) by calling `keyUp()`. The `Actions` class provides various methods to perform keyboard and mouse operations:

```
Actions builder = new Actions(driver);
builder.click(tableRows.get(1)).keyDown(Keys.CONTROL)
    .click(tableRows.get(3)).keyUp(Keys.CONTROL)
    .build().perform();
```

We can create a composite action that is ready to be performed by calling the `perform()` method of the `Actions` class.

The Keys class will represent all non-textual keys on the keyboard, for example, the *Ctrl* key, the *Shift* key, the function keys, and so on. In the previous example, we used `keyDown(Keys.CONTROL)` to press and hold the *Ctrl* key (*Command* key on a Mac) until the next operation was completed.

 Actions may not work properly for elements that are not visible or enabled. Before using these events, make sure that elements are visible and enabled.

See also

▶ The *Performing double-click on an element* recipe

Performing double-click on an element

There will be elements in a web application that need double-click events fired to perform some actions. For example, double-clicking on a row of a table will launch a new window. The Advanced User Interaction API provides a method to perform a double-click.

In this recipe, we will use the `Actions` class to perform double-click operations.

How to do it...

Let's create a test that locates an element for which a double-click event is implemented. When we double-click on this element, it changes its color:

```java
package com.secookbook.examples.chapter04;

import org.openqa.selenium.WebDriver;
import org.openqa.selenium.chrome.ChromeDriver;
import org.openqa.selenium.WebElement;
import org.openqa.selenium.By;
import org.openqa.selenium.interactions.Actions;
import static org.junit.Assert.*;
import org.junit.Test;

public class DoubleClickTest {
  @Test
  public void testDoubleClick() throws Exception {
    WebDriver driver = new ChromeDriver();
    driver.get("http://cookbook.seleniumacademy.com/DoubleClickDemo.html");

    try {
      WebElement message = driver.findElement(By.id("message"));

      // Verify color is Blue
      assertEquals("rgba(0, 0, 255, 1)",
          message.getCssValue("background-color"));

      Actions builder = new Actions(driver);
      builder.doubleClick(message).perform();

      // Verify Color is Yellow
      assertEquals("rgba(255, 255, 0, 1)",
          message.getCssValue("background-color"));
    } finally {
      driver.quit();
    }
  }
}
```

How it works...

To perform a double-click on an element, the `doubleClick()` method of the `Actions` class is called. To call this method, we need to create an instance of the `Actions` class, as shown in the following code:

```
Actions builder = new Actions(driver);
```

The `doubleClick()` method needs the element on which the double-click event will be fired. We can call the `doubleClick()` method by passing the element, as follows:

```
builder.doubleClick(message).perform();
```

See also

▶ The *Using Advanced User Interactions API for mouse and keyboard events* recipe

▶ The *Performing drag-and-drop operations* recipe

Performing drag-and-drop operations

Selenium WebDriver implements Selenium RC's `dragAndDrop` command using the `Actions` class. As seen in earlier recipes, the `Actions` class supports advanced user interactions such as firing various mouse and keyboard events. We can build simple or complex chains of events using this class.

In this recipe, we will use the `Actions` class to perform drag-and-drop operations.

How to do it...

Let's implement a test that will perform a drag-and-drop operation on a page using the `Actions` class:

```
@Test
public void testDragDrop() {
    driver.get("http://cookbook.seleniumacademy.com/DragDropDemo.html");

    WebElement source = driver.findElement(By.id("draggable"));
    WebElement target = driver.findElement(By.id("droppable"));

    Actions builder = new Actions(driver);
    builder.dragAndDrop(source, target) .perform();
    assertEquals("Dropped!", target.getText());
}
```

How it works...

To drag an element on to another element and drop it, we need to locate these elements and pass them to the `dragAndDrop()` method of the `Actions` class. To call this method, we need to create an instance of the `Actions` class in the following way:

```
Actions builder = new Actions(driver);
```

The `dragAndDrop()` method needs the source element and target element, where the source element will be dragged and dropped. We can call the `dragAndDrop()` method in the following way:

```
builder.dragAndDrop(source, target).perform();
```

> While writing this book, drag & drop for HTML5 was not supported by Selenium WebDriver. Please visit `https://code.google.com/p/selenium/issues/detail?id=3604` for more details. There is a workaround available to simulate the drag & drop feature on HTML5 web applications. Visit `https://gist.github.com/rcorreia/2362544` for more details.

See also

▸ The *Using Advanced User Interactions API for mouse and keyboard events* recipe

▸ The *Performing double-click on an element* recipe

Working with context menus

A context menu (also known as a shortcut, a popup, or a pop-up menu) is a menu displayed on a web page that appears when a user performs a right-click mouse operation. For example, here is a jQuery `contextMenu` plug-in from `http://bit.ly/1CAV05I`, which displays the editing menu when a user performs a right-click operation.

The Selenium WebDriver `Actions` class provides the `contextClick()` method to perform a right-click operation. In this recipe, we will explore how to automate interaction on a context menu.

How to do it...

Let's implement a test that will open a context menu and select one of the menu options using the `Actions` class:

```
@Test
public void testContextMenu() {
  WebElement clickMeElement =
      driver.findElement(By.cssSelector("div.context-menu-
one.box.menu-1"));
  WebElement editMenuItem =
      driver.findElement(By.cssSelector("li.context-menu-
item.icon-edit"));

  Actions builder = new Actions(driver);
  builder.contextClick(clickMeElement)
    .moveToElement(editMenuItem)
    .click()
    .perform();

  WebDriverWait wait = new WebDriverWait(driver, 10);

  Alert alert = wait.until(ExpectedConditions.alertIsPresent());
  assertEquals("clicked: edit", alert.getText());
  alert.dismiss();
}
```

How it works...

To open the context menu on right click, the `Actions` class provides the `contextClick()` method. This method will perform a right click on a specified element:

```
WebElement clickMeElement =
      driver.findElement(By.cssSelector("div.context-menu-
one.box.menu-1"));
  WebElement editMenuItem =
      driver.findElement(By.cssSelector("li.context-menu-
item.icon-edit"));

  Actions builder = new Actions(driver);
  builder.contextClick(clickMeElement)
    .moveToElement(editMenuItem)
    .click()

    .perform();
```

We can then move to the desired element, in this case a `<li>` element, which represents one of the menu items. To perform the menu action, the `click()` method is called. In this example, when the `click()` method is called, an alert is displayed and a test checks the message on the alert box.

There's more...

In the preceding example, the test finds the menu item and then performs the click operation. You might come across menus with shortcut keys. Using the `Actions` class, we can use a combination of mouse events and keyboard key press events to open the desired menu option. For example, the Edit menu has "e" as a shortcut key. We can open the context menu and then send the *Alt + E* key combination to open the menu option in following way:

```
@Test
public void testContextMenuWithKeys() {
    WebElement clickMeElement =
        driver.findElement(By.cssSelector("div.context-menu-
one.box.menu-1"));

    Actions builder = new Actions(driver);
    builder.contextClick(clickMeElement)
    .sendKeys(Keys.chord(Keys.ALT, "e"))
    .perform();

    WebDriverWait wait = new WebDriverWait(driver, 10);

    Alert alert = wait.until(ExpectedConditions.alertIsPresent());
    assertEquals("clicked: edit", alert.getText());
    alert.dismiss();
}
```

See also

▸ The *Using Advanced User Interactions API for mouse and keyboard events* recipe

Executing the JavaScript code

The Selenium WebDriver API provides the ability to execute JavaScript code with the browser window. This is a very useful feature when tests need to interact with the page using JavaScript. Using this API, client-side JavaScript code can also be tested using Selenium WebDriver. Selenium WebDriver provides a `JavascriptExecutor` interface that can be used to execute arbitrary JavaScript code within the context of the browser.

In this recipe, we will explore how to use `JavascriptExecutor` to execute JavaScript code. This book has various other recipes where `JavascriptExecutor` has been used to perform some advanced operations that are not yet supported by Selenium WebDriver.

How to do it...

Let's create a test that will call JavaScript code to return title and count of links (that is a count of `Anchor` tags) from a page. Returning a page title can also be done by calling the `driver.getTitle()` method. The following is an example code for this:

```
@Test
public void testJavaScriptCalls() throws Exception {
   WebDriver driver = new ChromeDriver();
   driver.get("http://www.google.com");
   try {
      JavascriptExecutor js = (JavascriptExecutor) driver;

      String title = (String) js.executeScript("return
document.title");
      assertEquals("Google", title);

      long links = (Long) js
           .executeScript("var links = document.
getElementsByTagName('A'); return links.length");
      assertEquals(42, links);
   } finally {
      driver.quit();
   }
}
```

How it works...

By casting the WebDriver instance to a `JavascriptExecutor` interface, we can execute the JavaScript code in Selenium WebDriver:

```
JavascriptExecutor js = (JavascriptExecutor) driver;
```

In the following example, a single line of JavaScript code is executed to return the title of the page displayed in the driver. The `JavascriptExecutor` interface provides the `executeScript()` method to which we need to pass the JavaScript code:

```
String title = (String) js.executeScript("return document.title");
```

When returning values from the JavaScript code, we need to use the `return` keyword. Based on the type of return value, we need to cast the `executeScript()` method. For decimal values, `Double` can be used; for non-decimal numeric values, `Long` can be used; and for Boolean values, `Boolean` can be used. If JavaScript code is returning an HTML element, then `WebElement` can be used. For text values, `String` can be used. If a list of objects is returned, then any of the values will work based on the type of objects. Otherwise, a null will be returned.

In the following example, we execute a multiline JavaScript code to retrieve the count of links on a page:

```
long links = (Long) js.executeScript("var links =
    document.getElementsByTagName('A'); return links.length");
```

There's more...

Arguments can also be a passed to the JavaScript code being executed by using the `executeScript()` method. In the following example, we want to set the value of an element. A special `arguments` array will be used inside the JavaScript code, as shown in the following code:

```
js.executeScript("document.getElementByID('name').value =
    arguments[0]","John");
```

Capturing screenshots with Selenium WebDriver

Selenium WebDriver provides the `TakesScreenshot` interface to capture a screenshot of a web page. This helps in test runs, showing exactly what happened when an exception or error has occurred during execution, and so on. We can also capture screenshots during verification of element state, values displayed in elements, or state after an action is completed.

Capturing screenshots also helps in the verification of layouts, field alignments, and so on, where we compare screenshots taken during test execution with baseline images.

In this recipe, we will use the `TakesScreenshot` interface to capture a screenshot of the web page under test.

How to do it...

Let's create a test that will open our test application and take a screenshot of the page in **PNG** (**Portable Network Graphics**) format, as shown in the following code example:

```
@Test
public void testTakesScreenshot() throws Exception {
    File scrFile = ((TakesScreenshot) driver)
        .getScreenshotAs(OutputType.FILE);
    FileUtils.copyFile(scrFile, new File("target/main_page.png"));
}
```

How it works...

The `TakesScreenshot` interface provides the `getScreenshotAs()` method to capture a screenshot of the page displayed in the `driver` instance. In the following example, we specified `OutputType.FILE` as an argument to the `getScreenshotAs()` method, so that it will return the captured screenshot in a file:

```
File scrFile =
    ((TakesScreenshot)driver).getScreenshotAs(OutputType.FILE);
```

We can save the file object returned by the `getScreenshotAs()` method using the `copyFile()` method of the `FileUtils` class from the `org.apache.commons.io.FileUtils` class.

 `TakesScreenshot` relies on the browser API to capture the screenshots. The `HtmlUnit` driver does not support the `TakesScreenshot` interface.

There's more...

The `OutputType` class provides multiple ways to output the screenshot data using the `getScreenshotAs()` method. In the previous example, we saw a screenshot captured in a file. Screenshots can also be captured in a Base64 string format or in raw bytes. In the following example, a screenshot is captured as Base64 string:

```
String base64 =
    ((TakesScreenshot)driver).getScreenshotAs(OutputType.BASE64);
```

Capturing screenshots with RemoteWebDriver/Selenium Grid

While running tests with `RemoteWebDriver` or Selenium Grid, it is not possible to take the screenshots, as the `TakesScreenshot` interface is not implemented in `RemoteWebDriver`.

However, we can use the `Augmenter` class, which adds the `TakesScreenshot` interface to the remote driver instance, as shown in the following code example:

```
driver = new Augmenter().augment(driver);
File scrFile =
  ((TakesScreenshot)driver).getScreenshotAs(OutputType.FILE);
FileUtils.copyFile(scrFile, new File("c:\\tmp\\screenshot.png"));
```

The `Augmenter` class enhances the `RemoteWebDriver` by adding various interfaces to it, including the `TakesScreenshot` interface:

```
driver = new Augmenter().augment(driver);
```

Later, we can use the `TakesScreenshot` interface from `RemoteWebDriver` to capture the screenshot.

See also

▸ The *Capturing screenshots of elements in the Selenium WebDriver* recipe in *Chapter 9, Extending Selenium*

▸ The *Comparing images in Selenium* recipe in *Chapter 9, Extending Selenium*

Maximizing the browser window

Selenium RC's `windowMaximize()` command was missing in Selenium WebDriver. However, starting from release 2.21, Selenium WebDriver supports maximizing the browser window.

In this short recipe, we will see how to maximize the browser window.

Getting ready

Create a new test that will get an instance of WebDriver, navigate to a site, and perform some basic actions and verifications.

How to do it...

To maximize a browser window, we need to call the `maximize()` method of the `Window` interface of the `driver` class. Add the second line of code from the following code; this is where you define an instance of `FirefoxDriver`:

```
driver = new FirefoxDriver();
driver.manage().window().maximize();
```

Handling session cookies

Websites use cookies to store user preferences, login information, and various other details of the client. The Selenium WebDriver API provides various methods to manage these cookies during testing. Using these methods, we can read cookie values, add cookies, and delete cookies during the test. This can be used to test how the application reacts when cookies are manipulated. The `WebDriver.Options` interface provides the following methods to manage cookies:

Method	Description
`addCookie(Cookie cookie)`	This method adds a cookie.
`getCookieNamed(String name)`	This method returns the cookie with a specified name.
`getCookies()`	This method returns all the cookies for current domain.
`deleteCookieNamed(String name)`	This method deletes the cookie with a specified name.
`deleteCookie(Cookie cookie)`	This method deletes a cookie.
`deleteAllCookies()`	This method deletes all the cookies for current domain.

In this recipe, we will see how to read a cookie and check it's value.

Getting ready

Create a new test that will get an instance of `WebDriver`, navigate to a site, and perform some basic actions and verifications.

How to do it...

Let's create a test that reads a cookie and checks its value, as shown in the following code example:

```
@Test
public void testCookies() {
    driver.get("http://demo.magentocommerce.com/");

    // Get the Your language dropdown as instance of Select class
    Select language = new Select(driver.findElement(By
        .id("select-language")));

    // Check default selected option is English
    assertEquals("English",
language.getFirstSelectedOption().getText());

    // Store cookies should be none
    Cookie storeCookie = driver.manage().getCookieNamed("store");
    assertEquals(null, storeCookie);

    // Select an option using select_by_visible text
    language.selectByVisibleText("French");

    // Store cookie should be populated with selected country
    storeCookie = driver.manage().getCookieNamed("store");
    assertEquals("french", storeCookie.getValue());
}
```

How it works...

The WebDriver.Options interface provides various methods to add, read, change, and delete cookies. In this example, when we change the language of the store, a cookie is used to store language preference. We can read this cookie and its value in following way:

```
Cookie storeCookie = driver.manage().getCookieNamed("store");
assertEquals("french", storeCookie.getValue());
```

We called the getCookieNamed() method by passing the name of the cookie. It returns an instance of the Cookie object. The Cookie object has various methods of reading value, domain, and so on.

Working with browser navigation

Browsers provide various navigation methods to access web pages from the browser history or by refreshing the current page with the back, forward, and refresh/reload buttons on the browser window's toolbar. The Selenium WebDriver API provides access to these buttons with various methods of `WebDriver.Navigation` interface. We can test the behavior of the application when these methods are used.

Method	Description
`back()`	This method moves back to the page in browser history.
`forward()`	This method moves forward to the page in browser history.
`refresh()`	This method reloads the current page.

`to(String url)`
 	
`to(java.net.URL url)`
	This method loads the specified URL in the current browser window.

In this recipe, we will see browser navigation methods.

Getting ready

Create a new test that will get an instance of `WebDriver`, navigate to a site, and perform some basic actions and verifications.

How to do it...

Let's create a test that calls various navigation methods and checks the behavior of the application in following code example:

```
@Test
public void testNavigation() {
    driver.get("http://www.google.com");

    // Get the search textbox
    WebElement searchField = driver.findElement(By.name("q"));
    searchField.clear();

    // Enter search keyword and submit
    searchField.sendKeys("selenium webdriver");
    searchField.submit();
```

```
WebElement resultLink = driver.findElement(By
    .linkText("Selenium WebDriver"));
resultLink.click();

new WebDriverWait(driver, 10).until(ExpectedConditions
    .titleIs("Selenium WebDriver"));

assertEquals("Selenium WebDriver", driver.getTitle());

driver.navigate().back();

new WebDriverWait(driver, 10).until(ExpectedConditions
    .titleIs("selenium webdriver - Google Search"));

assertEquals("selenium webdriver - Google Search", driver.
getTitle());

driver.navigate().forward();

new WebDriverWait(driver, 10).until(ExpectedConditions
    .titleIs("Selenium WebDriver"));

assertEquals("Selenium WebDriver", driver.getTitle());

driver.navigate().refresh();

new WebDriverWait(driver, 10).until(ExpectedConditions
    .titleIs("Selenium WebDriver"));

assertEquals("Selenium WebDriver", driver.getTitle());
}
```

How it works...

The WebDriver.Navigation interface provide back() and forward() to load pages from browser history. These methods represent the back and forward arrow buttons available in any web browser. We can also refresh or reload a page by calling the refresh() method.

Working with WebDriver events

The Selenium WebDriver provides the `EventFiringWebDriver` class, which listens to various events happening during the test execution. For example, events are raised when we navigate to a page, when a click is performed on an element, or value is changed. The following table lists all the events that we can track during the test execution:

Event	Description
beforeNavigateTo	This method is called before the `get(String url)` or the `navigate().to(String url)` method is called.
afterNavigateTo	This method is called after the `get(String url)` or the `navigate().to(String url)` method is called.
beforeNavigateBack	This method is called before the `navigate().back()` method.
afterNavigateBack	This method is called after the `navigate().back()` method.
beforeNavigateForward	This method is called before the `navigate().forward()` method.
afterNavigateForward	This method is called after the `navigate().forward()` method.
beforeFindBy	This method is called before the following methods: ▸ `WebDriver.findElement(...)` ▸ `WebDriver.findElements(...)` ▸ `WebElement.findElement(...)` ▸ `WebElement.findElements(...)`
afterFindBy	This method is called after the following methods: ▸ `WebDriver.findElement(...)` ▸ `WebDriver.findElements(...)` ▸ `WebElement.findElement(...)` ▸ `WebElement.findElements(...)`
beforeChangeValueOf	This method is called before the `WebElement.clear()` or the `WebElement.sendKeys(...)` method.
afterChangeValueOf	This method is called after the `WebElement.clear()` or the `WebElement.sendKeys(...)` method.
beforeClickOn	This method is called before the `WebElement.click()` method.
afterClickOn	This method is called after the `WebElement.click()` method.

Event	Description
`beforeScript`	This method is called before the `RemoteWebDriver.executeScript(java.lang.String, java.lang.Object[])` method.
`afterScript`	This method is called after the `RemoteWebDriver.executeScript(java.lang.String, java.lang.Object[])` method.
`onException`	This method is called whenever an exception would be thrown.

We can use these event handlers to process extra commands. For example, before entering a value into a textbox, we can clear the existing value or capture a screenshot even if an exception is raised by `WebDriver`. This is done with the following steps:

▶ Create your own user-defined event listener class. We can add the code that will be invoked when specific events are called to this class

▶ Create an `EventFiringWebDriver` instance using `WebDriver` instance

▶ And register the event listener class to the `EventFiringWebDriver` instance

The event listener class can be created in two ways:

▶ By implementing the `WebDriverEventListener` interface

▶ By extending the `AbstractWebDriverEventListener` class

In this recipe, we will see how to use `EventFiringWebDriver` to listen to the `WebDriver` events.

Getting ready

Create a new test that will get an instance of `WebDriver`, navigate to a site, and perform some basic actions and verifications.

How to do it...

First, we will define an event listener class by implementing the `WebDriverEventListener` interface in the following way:

```
package com.secookbook.examples.chapter04;

import org.openqa.selenium.*;
import org.openqa.selenium.support.events.WebDriverEventListener;

public class MyListener implements WebDriverEventListener {
```

```
   public void beforeChangeValueOf(WebElement element, WebDriver
driver) {
      element.clear();
   }


}
```

Next, we will create a test that uses EventFiringWebDriver:

```
package com.secookbook.examples.chapter04;

import org.openqa.selenium.By;
import org.openqa.selenium.WebDriver;
import org.openqa.selenium.firefox.FirefoxDriver;
import org.openqa.selenium.support.events.EventFiringWebDriver;
import org.junit.After;
import org.junit.Before;
import org.junit.Test;

public class EventFiringTest {
  private WebDriver driver;

  @Before
  public void setUp() throws Exception {
    driver = new FirefoxDriver();
  }

  @Test
  public void testEventFiringWebDriver() throws Exception {

    EventFiringWebDriver eventDriver =
    new EventFiringWebDriver(driver);
    MyListener myListener = new MyListener();
    eventDriver.register(myListener);

    eventDriver.get("http://bit.ly/1DbdhsW");
    eventDriver.findElement(By.id("q"))
      .sendKeys("Selenium Testing Tools Cookbook");
  }

  @After
  public void tearDown() throws Exception {
    driver.quit();
  }
}
```

There's more...

Let's add one more event handler to the event listener class to capture a screenshot when an exception is thrown:

```java
public void onException(Throwable exception, WebDriver driver) {
   try {
     if
(driver.getClass().getName().equals("org.openqa.selenium.remote.Re
moteWebDriver")) {
        driver = new Augmenter().augment(driver);
      }
     File scrFile = ((TakesScreenshot)
driver).getScreenshotAs(OutputType.FILE);
      FileUtils.copyFile(scrFile, new
File("target/screenshots/error.png"));
   } catch (Exception e) {
     e.printStackTrace();
   }
}
```

5

Synchronizing Tests

In this chapter, we will cover the following:

- ▸ Synchronizing a test with an implicit wait
- ▸ Synchronizing a test with an explicit wait
- ▸ Synchronizing a test with custom-expected conditions
- ▸ Synchronizing a test with FluentWait

Introduction

While building automated scripts for a complex web application using Selenium WebDriver, we need to ensure that the test flow is maintained for reliable test automation.

When tests are run, the application may not always respond with the same speed. For example, it might take a few seconds for a progress bar to reach 100 percent, a status message to appear, a button to become enabled, and a window or pop-up message to open.

You can handle these anticipated timing problems by synchronizing your test to ensure that Selenium WebDriver waits until your application is ready before performing the next step. There are several options that you can use to synchronize your test. In this chapter, we will see various features of Selenium WebDriver to implement synchronization in tests.

Synchronizing a test with an implicit wait

The Selenium WebDriver provides an implicit wait for synchronizing tests. When an implicit wait is implemented in tests, if WebDriver cannot find an element in the DOM, it will wait for a defined amount of time for the element to appear in the DOM. Once the specified wait time is over, it will try searching for the element once again. If the element is not found in specified time, it will throw the `NoSuchElement` exception.

In other terms, an implicit wait polls the DOM for a certain amount of time when trying to find an element or elements if they are not immediately available. The default setting is 0.

Once set, the implicit wait is set for the life of the WebDriver object's instance.

In this recipe, we will briefly explore the use of an implicit wait. However, it is recommended that you avoid or minimize the use of an implicit wait.

How to do it...

Let's create a test on a demo AJAX-enabled application as follows:

```
@Test
public void testWithImplicitWait() {
    WebDriver driver = new FirefoxDriver();
    // Launch the sample Ajax application
    driver.get("http://cookbook.seleniumacademy.com/AjaxDemo.html");

    // Set the implicit wait time out to 10 Seconds
    driver.manage().timeouts().implicitlyWait(10, TimeUnit.SECONDS);

    try {
        // Get link for Page 4 and click on it
        driver.findElement(By.linkText("Page 4")).click();

        // Get an element with id page4 and verify it's text
        WebElement message = driver.findElement(By.id("page4"));
        assertTrue(message.getText().contains("Nunc nibh tortor"));
    } finally {
        driver.quit();
    }
}
```

How it works...

The Selenium WebDriver provides the `Timeouts` interface to configure the implicit wait. The `Timeouts` interface provides an `implicitlyWait()` method , which accepts the time the driver should wait when searching for an element. In this example, `driver` will wait for an element to appear in DOM for 10 seconds after an initial try:

```
driver.manage().timeouts().implicitlyWait(10, TimeUnit.SECONDS);
```

Until the end of a test, or until an implicit wait is set back to 0, every time an element is searched for using the `findElement()` method, the test will wait for 10 seconds for an element to appear.

Using an implicit wait may slow down tests when an application responds normally, as it will wait for each element appearing in the DOM and increase the overall execution time. Minimize or avoid using an implicit wait. Use an explicit wait, which provides more control when compared with an implicit wait.

See also

▶ The *Synchronizing a test with an explicit wait* recipe

▶ The *Synchronizing a test with custom-expected conditions* recipe

▶ The *Synchronizing a test with FluentWait* recipe

Synchronizing a test with an explicit wait

The Selenium WebDriver provides an explicit wait for synchronizing tests, which provides a better way to wait over an implicit wait. Unlike an implicit wait, you can write and use pre-defined conditions or custom conditions for wait before proceeding further in the code.

The Selenium WebDriver provides the `WebDriverWait` and `ExpectedConditions` classes to implement an explicit wait.

The `ExpectedConditions` class provides a set of predefined conditions to wait for before proceeding further in the code. The following table shows some common conditions that we frequently come across when automating web browsers supported by the `ExpectedConditions` class:

Predefined condition	Selenium method
An element is visible and enabled	`elementToBeClickable(By locator)`
An element is selected	`elementToBeSelected(WebElement element)`
Presence of an element	`presenceOfElementLocated(By locator)`
Specific text present in an element	`textToBePresentInElement(By locator, java.lang.String text)`
Element value	`textToBePresentInElementValue(By locator, java.lang.String text)`
Title	`titleContains(java.lang.String title)`

For more conditions, visit `http://seleniumhq.github.io/selenium/docs/api/java/index.html`.

In this recipe, we will explore some of these conditions with the `WebDriverWait` class.

How to do it...

Let's implement a test that uses the `ExpectedConditions.titleContains()` method to implement an explicit wait, as follows:

```
@Test
public void testExplicitWaitTitleContains()
{
  //Go to the Google Home Page
  WebDriver driver = new FirefoxDriver();
  driver.get("http://www.google.com");

  //Enter a term to search and submit
  WebElement query = driver.findElement(By.name("q"));
  query.sendKeys("selenium");
  query.click();

  //Create Wait using WebDriverWait.
  //This will wait for 10 seconds for timeout before title is
updated with search term
  //If title is updated in specified time limit test will move to
the text step
  //instead of waiting for 10 seconds
  WebDriverWait wait = new WebDriverWait(driver, 10);
  wait.until(ExpectedConditions.titleContains("selenium"));

  //Verify Title
  assertTrue(driver.getTitle().toLowerCase().startsWith("selenium"));

  driver.quit();
}
```

How it works...

We can define an explicit wait for a set of common conditions using the `ExpectedConditions` class. First, we need to create an instance of the `WebDriverWait` class by passing the driver instance and timeout for a wait, as follows:

```
WebDriverWait wait = new WebDriverWait(driver, 10);
```

Next, the `ExpectedCondition` is passed to the `wait.until()` method, as follows:

```
wait.until(ExpectedConditions.titleContains("selenium"));
```

The `WebDriverWait` object will call the `ExpectedConditions` class object every 500 milliseconds until it returns successfully.

- ▸ The *Synchronizing a test with an implicit wait* recipe
- ▸ The *Synchronizing a test with custom-expected conditions* recipe
- ▸ The *Synchronizing a test with FluentWait* recipe

Synchronizing a test with custom-expected conditions

With the explicit wait mechanism, we can also build custom-expected conditions along with common conditions using the `ExpectedConditions` class. This comes in handy when a wait cannot be handled with a common condition supported by the `ExpectedConditions` class.

In this recipe, we will explore how to create a custom condition.

How to do it...

We will create a test that will create a wait until an element appears on the page using the `ExpectedCondition` class as follows:

```
@Test
public void testExplicitWait() {

    WebDriver driver = new FirefoxDriver();
    // Launch the sample Ajax application
    driver.get("http://cookbook.seleniumacademy.com/AjaxDemo.html");

    try {
        driver.findElement(By.linkText("Page 4")).click();
        WebElement message = new WebDriverWait(driver, 5)
            .until(new ExpectedCondition<WebElement>() {
                public WebElement apply(WebDriver d) {
                    return d.findElement(By.id("page4"));
                }
            });
        assertTrue(message.getText().contains("Nunc nibh tortor"));
    } finally {
        driver.quit();
    }
}
```

How it works...

The Selenium WebDriver provides the ability to implement the custom `ExpectedCondition` interface along with the `WebDriverWait` class to create a custom-wait condition, as needed by a test. In this example, we created a custom condition, which returns a `WebElement` object once the inner `findElement()` method locates the element within a specified timeout, as follows:

```
WebElement message = new WebDriverWait(driver, 5)
.until(new ExpectedCondition<WebElement>(){
    @Override
    public WebElement apply(WebDriver d) {
    return d.findElement(By.id("page4"));
}});
```

There's more...

A custom wait can be created in various ways. In the following section, we will explore some common examples to implement a custom wait.

Waiting for an element's attribute value update

Based on the events and actions performed, the value of an element's attribute might change at runtime. For example, a disabled textbox gets enabled based on the user's rights. A custom wait can be created on the attribute value of the element. In the following example, `ExpectedCondition` waits for a `Boolean` return value, based on the attribute value of an element:

```
new WebDriverWait(driver, 10).until(new
ExpectedCondition<Boolean>() {
    public Boolean apply(WebDriver d) {
        return
d.findElement(By.id("userName")).getAttribute("readonly").contains
("true");
}});
```

Waiting for an element's visibility

Developers can hide or display elements based on the sequence of actions, user rights, and so on. The specific element might exist in the DOM but are hidden from the user, and when the user performs a certain action, it appears on the page. A custom wait condition can be created based on the element's visibility, as follows:

```
new WebDriverWait(driver, 10).until(new
ExpectedCondition<Boolean>() {
```

```
public Boolean apply(WebDriver d) {
    return d.findElement(By.id("page4")).isDisplayed();
}});
```

Waiting for DOM events

The web application may be using a JavaScript framework such as jQuery for AJAX and content manipulation. For example, jQuery is used to load a big JSON file from the server asynchronously on the page. While jQuery is reading and processing this file, a test can check its status using the `active` attribute. A custom wait can be implemented by executing the JavaScript code and checking the return value, as follows:

```
new WebDriverWait(driver, 10).until(new
ExpectedCondition<Boolean>() {
    public Boolean apply(WebDriver d) {
        JavascriptExecutor js = (JavascriptExecutor) d;
        return (Boolean)js.executeScript("return jQuery.active ==
0");
}});
```

See also

▶ The *Synchronizing a test with an implicit wait* recipe

▶ The *Synchronizing a test with an explicit wait* recipe

▶ The *Synchronizing a test with FluentWait* recipe

Synchronizing a test with FluentWait

The `FluentWait` class is an implementation of Selenium WebDriver's `Wait` interface. Using the `FluentWait` class, we can define the maximum amount of time to wait for an element or condition as well as the frequency with which to check for the condition. We can also configure it to ignore specific types of exceptions such as the `NoSuchElement` exception while searching for an element.

Unlike implicit and explicit wait, `FluentWait` uses a maximum timeout value and polling frequency. For example, if we set the maximum timeout value as 20 seconds and polling frequency as 2 seconds, WebDriver will check for an element every 2 seconds until the maximum value. In addition to this, we can configure `FluentWait` to ignore specific types of exceptions while waiting for the condition.

The `FluentWait` class is helpful in automating AJAX applications or scenarios where element load time varies often.

In this recipe, we will explore some of these conditions with the `FluentWait` class.

How to do it...

Let's implement a test that uses the `FluentWait` class to find and wait for an element, as shown in following code example:

```java
@Test
public void testFluentWait() {
  WebDriver driver = new ChromeDriver();
  // Launch the sample Ajax application
  driver.get("http://cookbook.seleniumacademy.com/AjaxDemo.html");

  try {
    driver.findElement(By.linkText("Page 4")).click();

    Wait<WebDriver> wait = new FluentWait<WebDriver>(driver)
        .withTimeout(10, TimeUnit.SECONDS)
        .pollingEvery(2, TimeUnit.SECONDS)
        .ignoring(NoSuchElementException.class);

    WebElement message = wait
        .until(new Function<WebDriver, WebElement>() {
          public WebElement apply(WebDriver d) {
            return d.findElement(By.id("page4"));
          }
        });

    assertTrue(message.getText().contains("Nunc nibh tortor"));
  } finally {
    driver.quit();
  }
}
```

How it works...

We can define a fluent wait by using the `FluentWait` class. We can configure the maximum timeout for 10 seconds, polling frequency for every 2 seconds, and exceptions to be ignored by setting up methods of the `FluentWait` class, as shown in following code example:

```java
Wait<WebDriver> wait = new FluentWait<WebDriver>(driver)
    .withTimeout(10, TimeUnit.SECONDS)
    .pollingEvery(2, TimeUnit.SECONDS)
     .ignoring(NoSuchElementException.class);
```

When we use this instance further to find an element, WebDriver will wait for 10 seconds, polling for the given element every 2 seconds in the DOM:

```
WebElement message = wait
    .until(new Function<WebDriver, WebElement>(){
        public WebElement apply(WebDriver d) {
            return d.findElement(By.id("page4"));
        }});
```

In this example, we are finding an element with `FluentWait`, and returning the found element back to the test.

There's more...

Unlike the previous example where we returned the element, we can also wait for given conditions. The `FluentWait` class can be configured in multiple ways to handle wait conditions, as shown in the following code example:

```
@Test
public void testFluentWaitWithPredicate() {

    final WebDriver driver = new ChromeDriver();
    // Launch the sample Ajax application
    driver.get("http://cookbook.seleniumacademy.com/AjaxDemo.html");

    try {
        FluentWait<By> wait = new FluentWait<By>(By.linkText("Page 4"))
            .withTimeout(1000, TimeUnit.MILLISECONDS)
            .pollingEvery(200, TimeUnit.MILLISECONDS)
            .ignoring(NoSuchElementException.class);

        wait.until(new Predicate<By>() {
            public boolean apply(By by) {
                try {
                    return driver.findElement(by).isDisplayed();
                } catch (NoSuchElementException ex) {
                    return false;
                }
            }
        });
        driver.findElement(By.linkText("Page 4")).click();
    } finally {
        driver.quit();
    }
}
```

See also

- ▶ The *Synchronizing a test with an implicit wait* recipe
- ▶ The *Synchronizing a test with an explicit wait* recipe
- ▶ The *Synchronizing a test with custom-expected conditions* recipe

6

Working with Alerts, Frames, and Windows

In this chapter, we will cover the following:

- ▸ Handling a simple JavaScript alert box
- ▸ Handling a confirm and prompt alert box
- ▸ Identifying and handling frames
- ▸ Working with IFRAME
- ▸ Identifying and handling a child window
- ▸ Identifying and handling a window by its title
- ▸ Identifying and handling a pop-up window by its content

Introduction

To build a great user interface, developers use features similar to desktop applications in the form of pop-up windows and alerts. While testing complex workflows, tests need to flow from the browser window to a pop-up window in order to alert the user and perform operations as needed. This chapter will explain common issues that pertain to the handling of pop-up windows and alerts, and how best to use Selenium WebDriver API for this.

Handling a simple JavaScript alert box

Web developers use JavaScript alerts to inform users about validation errors, warnings, getting a response for an action, accepting an input value, and so on. Alert's are modal windows displayed by browsers where user has to take action before processing further. You can find more about JavaScript `alert()` method at `http://www.w3schools.com/jsref/met_win_alert.asp`.

JavaScript alerts are implemented differently by browsers compared to other dialog windows such as Print, Save, File Download, and so on.

Tests will need to verify that the user is shown correct alerts while testing. It is also required to handle alerts while performing an end-to-end workflow. The Selenium WebDriver provides an `Alert` interface for working with JavaScript alerts.

In this recipe, we will automate interaction with a simple alert box that is often used to notify the user with information such as errors, warnings, and success. When an alert box pops up, the user will have to click on the **OK** button to proceed, as shown in the following screenshot:

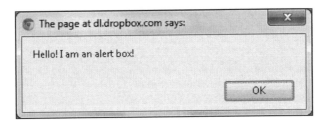

How to do it...

We will use a simple page on which a simple alert box is displayed to the user after a button is clicked. Let's create a test that checks that correct information is displayed in the alert box, as shown in the following code example:

```
package com.secookbook.examples.chapter06;

import org.openqa.selenium.WebDriver;
import org.openqa.selenium.firefox.FirefoxDriver;
import org.openqa.selenium.support.ui.ExpectedConditions;
import org.openqa.selenium.support.ui.WebDriverWait;
import org.openqa.selenium.By;
import org.openqa.selenium.Alert;
import org.junit.AfterClass;
import org.junit.BeforeClass;
import org.junit.Test;
```

```
import static org.junit.Assert.*;

public class AlertsTest {

    private static WebDriver driver;

    @BeforeClass
    public static void setUp() {
        driver = new FirefoxDriver();
        driver.get("http://cookbook.seleniumacademy.com/Alerts.html");
        driver.manage().window().maximize();
    }

    @Test
    public void testSimpleAlert() {
        // Click Simple button to show an Alert box
        driver.findElement(By.id("simple")).click();

        // Optionally we can also wait for an Alert box using the
WebDriverWait
        new WebDriverWait(driver, 10)
            .until(ExpectedConditions.alertIsPresent());

        // Get the Alert
        Alert alert = driver.switchTo().alert();

        // Get the text displayed on Alert
        String textOnAlert = alert.getText();

        // Check correct message is displayed to the user on Alert box
        assertEquals("Hello! I am an alert box!", textOnAlert);

        // Click OK button, by calling accept method
        alert.accept();
    }

    @AfterClass
    public static void tearDown() {
        driver.quit();
    }
}
```

How it works...

The Selenium WebDriver provides an `Alert` interface for handling alerts. It provides various methods for interacting with an alert box. The `driver.switchTo().alert()` method returns an instance of the `Alert` for the alert box displayed on the screen, as follows:

```
Alert alert = driver.switchTo().alert();
```

We might need to verify what message is displayed in an alert box. We can get the text from an alert box by calling the `getText()` method provided by `Alert`, as follows:

```
String textOnAlert = alert.getText();
```

An alert box is closed by clicking on the **OK** button; this is be done by calling the `accept()` method, as follows:

```
alert.accept();
```

> An alert box can also be accessed by directly calling desired methods. The following code shows an example:
> ```
> driver.switchTo().alert().accept();
> ```

There's more...

We can also create an explicit wait condition for an alert to be displayed on the page using the `WebDriverWait` class and the `alertIsPresent()` method of the `ExpectedConditions` class, as shown in the following code example:

```
new WebDriverWait(driver, 10)
    .until(ExpectedConditions.alertIsPresent());

// Get the Alert
Alert alert = driver.switchTo().alert();
```

This is useful when there is a delay after a user performs an action and an alert is displayed.

The NoAlertPresentException

The `driver.switchTo().alert()` method throws a `NoAlertPresentException` exception when it tries to access an alert box that doesn't exist.

See also

> ▶ The *Handling a Confirm and Prompt Alert Box* recipe

Handling a confirm and prompt alert box

A confirm box is often used to verify or accept something from the user. When a confirm alert is displayed, the user will have to click on either the **OK** or the **Cancel** button to proceed, as shown in the following screenshot:

If the user clicks on the **OK** button, the confirm box returns a `true` value response. If the user clicks on the **Cancel** button, then it returns `false`.

The prompt alert box

A prompt box is often used to accept a value from a user. When a prompt box pops up, the user will have to enter a value and click on either the **OK** or the **Cancel** button to proceed, as shown in the following screenshot:

If the user clicks on the **OK** button, the box returns the input value. If the user clicks on the **Cancel** button, the box returns `null`.

In this recipe, we will handle confirm and prompt boxes using the Selenium WebDriver's `Alert` interface.

How to do it...

Let's create a set of tests that can handle a confirm box displayed on a page, as follows:

1. In the `testConfirmAccept` test, we will accept the confirm box and verify a message on the page when the confirm box is accepted, that is, when the **OK** button is clicked, as shown in following code:

```
@Test
  public void testConfirmAccept() {
      // Click Confirm button to show Confirmation Alert box
      driver.findElement(By.id("confirm")).click();

      // Get the Alert
      Alert alert = driver.switchTo().alert();

      // Click OK button, by calling accept method
      alert.accept();

      // Check Page displays correct message
      WebElement message = driver.findElement(By.id("demo"));
      assertEquals("You Accepted Alert!", message.getText());
  }
```

2. In the `testConfirmDismiss` test as shown in the following code, we will dismiss the confirm box by calling the `dismiss()` method; this is the same as clicking the **Cancel** button:

```
@Test
  public void testConfirmDismiss() {
      // Click Confirm button to show Confirmation Alert box
      driver.findElement(By.id("confirm")).click();

      // Get the Alert
      Alert alert = driver.switchTo().alert();

      // Click Cancel button, by calling dismiss method
      alert.dismiss();

      // Check Page displays correct message
      WebElement message = driver.findElement(By.id("demo"));
      assertEquals("You Dismissed Alert!", message.getText());
  }
```

Handling a prompt box

Let's create a test that handles a prompt box. We will enter text into the prompt box's input field and later verify if the same value is displayed on the page, as shown in following code example:

```
@Test
  public void testPrompt() {
    // Click Confirm button to show Prompt Alert box
    driver.findElement(By.id("prompt")).click();

    // Get the Alert
    Alert alert = driver.switchTo().alert();

    // Enter some value on Prompt Alert box
    alert.sendKeys("Foo");

    // Click OK button, by calling accept method
    alert.accept();

    // Check Page displays message with value entered in Prompt
    WebElement message = driver.findElement(By.id("prompt_demo"));
    assertEquals("Hello Foo! How are you today?",
message.getText());
  }
```

How it works...

Handling a confirm box works in a similar way to handling a simple alert box. To cancel a confirm box, the `dismiss()` method of `Alert` is used, as follows:

```
alert.dismiss();
```

To handle a prompt box, the `Alert` interface provides an extra `sendKeys()` method to enter text in the prompt box's input field. We can enter the text and either accept or dismiss a prompt box using the `Alert` method, as follows:

```
alert.sendKeys("Foo");
alert.accept();
```

See also

▸ The *Handling a simple JavaScript alert box* recipe

Identifying and handling frames

HTML frames allow developers to present documents in multiple views, which may be in a separate child window or sub-window. Multiple views offer developers a way to keep certain information visible while other views are scrolled or replaced. For example, within the same window, one frame might display a static banner, the second a navigation menu, and the third the main document that can be scrolled through or replaced by navigating in the second frame.

A page with frames is created using the `<frameset>` tag or the `<iframe>` tag. All frame tags are nested with a `<frameset>` tag. In the following example, a page will display three frames, each loading different HTML pages:

```html
<html>
    <frameset cols="25%,*,25%" frameborder="NO" framespacing="0"
border="0">
        <frame id="left" src="frame_a.htm" />
        <frame src="frame_b.htm" />
        <frame name="right" src="frame_c.htm" />
    </frameset>
</html>
```

Frames can be identified by an ID or through the `name` attribute. In this recipe, we will identify and work with frames using the `driver.switchTo().frame()` method of the `WebDriver.TargetLocator` interface, which is used to locate a given frame or window using the `id`, `name`, instance of `WebElement`, and the index.

How to do it...

Let's create a test on a simple page that has three frames. We will use `id`, `name` and index to identify these frames and interact with contents of these frames, as shown in the following examples:

1. In the `testFrameWithIdOrName` test, we will use the `name` and `id` attributes to identify frames, as shown in the following code:

   ```java
   package com.secookbook.examples.chapter06;

   import org.openqa.selenium.WebDriver;
   import org.openqa.selenium.firefox.FirefoxDriver;
   import org.openqa.selenium.By;
   import org.openqa.selenium.WebElement;

   import org.junit.AfterClass;
   import org.junit.BeforeClass;
   import org.junit.Test;
   ```

```
import static org.junit.Assert.*;

public class FramesTest {

  public static WebDriver driver;

  @BeforeClass
  public static void setUp() {
    driver = new FirefoxDriver();
    driver.get("http://cookbook.seleniumacademy.com/Frames.html");
    driver.manage().window().maximize();
  }

  @Test
  public void testFrameWithIdOrName() {
    try {

      // Activate the frame on left side using it's id
attribute
      driver.switchTo().frame("left");

      // Get an element from the frame on left side and
verify it's
      // contents
      WebElement msg = driver.findElement(By.tagName("p"));
      assertEquals("This is Left Frame", msg.getText());
    } finally {
      // Activate the Page, this will move context from
frame back to the
      // Page
      driver.switchTo().defaultContent();
    }

    try {
      // Activate the frame on right side using it's name
attribute
      driver.switchTo().frame("right");

      // Get an element from the frame on right side and
verify it's
      // contents
      WebElement msg = driver.findElement(By.tagName("p"));
      assertEquals("This is Right Frame", msg.getText());
    } finally {
```

```
        // Activate the Page, this will move context from
frame back to the
        // Page
        driver.switchTo().defaultContent();
    }
  }

  @AfterClass
  public static void tearDown() {
    // Close the Parent Popup Window
    driver.close();
    driver.quit();
  }
}
```

2. In the second test, `testFrameByIndex`, we will use index for identifying the frame, as shown in the following code:

```
@Test
public void testFrameByIndex() {
  try {
    // Activate the frame in middle using it's index. Index starts
at 0
    driver.switchTo().frame(1);

    // Get an element from the frame in the middle and verify it's
    // contents
    WebElement msg = driver.findElement(By.tagName("p"));
    assertEquals("This Frame doesn't have id or name", msg.
getText());
  } finally {
    // Activate the Page, this will move context from frame back
to the
    // Page
    driver.switchTo().defaultContent();
  }
}
```

How it works...

The Selenium WebDriver's `WebDriver.TargetLocator` interface provides the `driver.switchTo().frame()` method to activate a frame on a page and perform operations. This method takes the `id` or `name` attribute value or instance of a `WebElement` (the `<frame>` element can be located using the `driver.findElement()` method).

In the following example, the id attribute is used to identify a frame:

```
//Activate the frame on left side using it's id attribute
driver.switchTo().frame("left");
```

When frames do not have the id or name attributes defined, index can be used to identify a frame. In the preceding example, the frame in the middle does not have the id or name attributes. The middle frame's index will be 1, as it has a frame on the left-hand side with the index as 0, and on the right-hand side with the index 2:

```
//Activate the frame in middle using it's index. Index starts at 0
driver.switchTo().frame(1);
```

Once a frame is activated, we can leave the driver instance to interact with the page loaded in the frame. To return to the main page, use the driver.switchTo().defaultContent() method.

Warning: While working with multiple frames, when an operation is completed on a frame and a test flow needs to move to another frame, calling the driver.switchTo().frame() method will not move the context to the desired frame. The test will first need to activate the main page by calling the driver.switchTo().defaultContent() method and then later activating the desired frame.

There's more...

While working with frames, you will find that the id or name attributes are not defined. Still, frames can be identified using their index. This may not be a reliable way when applications are dynamic and there is a need to ensure that the correct frame is activated.

Let's look at an example in which we will identify frames by the contents of the page loaded in these frames to make tests more reliable, as shown in following code example:

```
@Test
public void testFrameByContents() {
  // Get all frames on the Page, created with <frame> tag
  List<WebElement> frames =
driver.findElements(By.tagName("frame"));

  // In this example frame in the middle is activated by checking
the
  // contents
  // Activate frame and check if it has the desired content. If
found
  // perform the operations
```

```
        // if not, then switch back to the Page and continue checking
    next frame
       try {
          for (WebElement frame : frames) {
             // switchTo().frame() also accepts frame elements apart from
    id,
             // name or index
             driver.switchTo().frame(frame);
             String title = driver.getTitle();
             if (title.equals("Frame B")) {
                WebElement msg = driver.findElement(By.tagName("p"));
                assertEquals("This is Left Frame", msg.getText());
                break;
             } else
                driver.switchTo().defaultContent();
          }
       } finally {
          // Activate the Page, this will move context from frame back
    to the
          // Page
          driver.switchTo().defaultContent();
       }
    }
```

In Selenium WebDriver, we can get multiple elements matching the same criteria in a list. Here we will get all frame elements from the page using the `tagName()` method, as shown in following code example:

```
//Get all frames on the Page, created with <frame> tag
List<WebElement> frames = driver.findElements(By.tagName("frame"));
```

The test will iterate through each frame element, passing this element to the `driver.switchTo().frame()` method and checking its content. If the frame has matching content, then we can continue operations on the frame and later switch back to the main page, as shown in the following code example:

```
for (WebElement frame : frames) {
       // switchTo().frame() also accepts frame elements apart from
    id,
          // name or index
          driver.switchTo().frame(frame);
          String title = driver.getTitle();
          if (title.equals("Frame B")) {
             WebElement msg = driver.findElement(By.tagName("p"));
             assertEquals("This is Left Frame", msg.getText());
             break;
```

```
  } else
    driver.switchTo().defaultContent();
}
```

 You can create a utility method to switch between frames using their content.

See also

▸ The *Working with IFRAME* recipe

Working with IFRAME

Developers can also embed external documents or documents from another domain using the `<iframe>` tag, also known as inline frames. Various social media websites provide buttons that can be embedded in your web applications to link to these websites. For example, you can add a Twitter-follow button in your application, as follows:

```
<iframe allowtransparency="true" frameborder="0" scrolling="no"
src="http://platform.twitter.com/widgets/follow_button.html?screen
_name=upgundecha" style="width:300px; height:20px;"></iframe>
```

Identifying and working with the `<iframe>` tag is similar to a frame that is created with the `<frameset>` tag. In this recipe, we will identify the `<iframe>` tag that is nested in another frame.

How to do it...

We will create a test on a sample page which embeds the `<iframe>` tag within a frame. We will move to the parent frame first and then to the `<iframe>` tag. The test will click the element within the `<iframe>` tag and operate on a pop-up window currently displayed. Finally, it will switch back to the main document. This is implemented as shown in the following code example:

```
@Test
public void testIFrame() {
  // Store the handle of current driver window
  String currentWindow = driver.getWindowHandle();

  // The frame on the right side has a nested iframe containing
'Twitter
  // Follow' Button
```

```java
    // Activate the frame on right side using it's name attribute
    try {
      driver.switchTo().frame("right");

      // Get the iframe element
      WebElement twitterFrame =
    driver.findElement(By.tagName("iframe"));

      try {
        // Activate the iframe
        driver.switchTo().frame(twitterFrame);
        // Get and Click the follow button from iframe
        // a Popup Window will appear after click
        WebElement button = driver.findElement(By.id("follow-
  button"));
        button.click();

        try {
          // The Twitter Popup does not have name or title.
          // Script will get handles of all open windows and
          // desired window will be activated by checking it's Title

          for (String windowId : driver.getWindowHandles()) {
            driver.switchTo().window(windowId);
            if (driver.getTitle().equals(
                "Unmesh Gundecha (@upgundecha) on Twitter")) {
              assertTrue("Twitter Login Popup Window Found", true);
              driver.close();
              break;
            }
          }

        } finally {
          // Switch back to original driver window
          driver.switchTo().window(currentWindow);
        }
      } finally {
        // switch back to Page from the frame
        driver.switchTo().defaultContent();
      }

    } finally {
      // switch back to Page from the frame
      driver.switchTo().defaultContent();
    }
  }
```

How it works...

Working with IFRAME or inline frame is similar to working with a normal frame. In this example, the `<iframe>` element is located using the `findElement()` method by passing the tag:

```
WebElement twitterFrame =
driver.findElement(By.tagName("iframe"));
```

To activate the frame, the `driver.switchTo().frame()` method is called by passing it an instance of the `WebElement`, as follows:

```
driver.switchTo().frame(twitterFrame)
```

See also

▶ The *Identifying and handling frames* recipe

Identifying and handling a child window

In Selenium WebDriver, testing multiple windows involves identifying a window, switching the driver context to the window, then executing steps on the window, and finally, switching back to the browser.

The Selenium WebDriver allows us to identify a window by its `name` attribute or window handle, and switching between the window and the browser window is done using the `WebDriver.switchTo().window()` method of `WebDriver.TargetLocator`.

In this recipe, we will identify and handle a window by using its `name` attribute. Developers provide the `name` attribute for a window that is different from its title. In the following example, a user can open a window by clicking on the **Help** button. In this case, the developer has provided `HelpWindow` as its name:

```
<button id="helpbutton" on
Click='window.open("help.html","HelpWindow","width=500,height=500"
);'>Help</button>
```

How to do it...

Let's create a test that identifies a window using its `name` attribute, as shown in the following code example:

```
package com.secookbook.examples.chapter06;

import org.openqa.selenium.firefox.FirefoxDriver;
import org.openqa.selenium.WebDriver;
```

```java
import org.openqa.selenium.By;

import static org.junit.Assert.*;
import org.junit.AfterClass;
import org.junit.BeforeClass;
import org.junit.Test;

public class WindowTest {

  public static WebDriver driver;

  @BeforeClass
  public static void setUp() {
    driver = new FirefoxDriver();
    driver.get("http://cookbook.seleniumacademy.com/Config.html");
    driver.manage().window().maximize();
  }

  @Test
  public void testWindowUsingName() {
    // Store WindowHandle of parent browser window
    String parentWindowId = driver.getWindowHandle();

    // Clicking Help button will open Help Page in a new child window
    driver.findElement(By.id("helpbutton")).click();

    try {
      // Switch to the Help window using name
      driver.switchTo().window("HelpWindow");

      try {
        // Check the driver context is in Help window
        assertEquals("Help", driver.getTitle());
      } finally {
        // Close the Help window
        driver.close();
      }
    } finally {
      // Switch to the parent browser window
      driver.switchTo().window(parentWindowId);
    }
    // Check driver context is in parent browser window
    assertEquals("Build my Car - Configuration",
  driver.getTitle());
```

```
    }

    @AfterClass
    public static void tearDown() {
      driver.quit();
    }
  }
```

How it works...

The Selenium WebDriver provides a way to switch between the browser and windows and change the context of the driver. To move to a child window from the parent or the browser window, the `driver.switchTo().window()` method is used. This method accepts the `name` or `handle` attribute of the window. In the following example, the `name` attribute is used:

```
//Switch to the Help window
driver.switchTo().window("HelpWindow");
```

Now we can perform actions or verifications on the window through the driver instance as usual.

During a test, when you want to move to a window called from a parent window, save the parent window's `handle` attribute in a variable so that, when operations on the pop-up window are over and we want to switch back to the parent window, we can use the `handle` attribute, as follows:

```
//Save the WindowHandle of parent browser window
String parentWindowId = driver.getWindowHandle();
```

A test can switch back to the parent window using its `handle` attribute, as follows:

```
//Move back to the parent browser Window
driver.switchTo().window(parentWindowId);
```

 NoSuchWindowException: The `driver.switchTo().window()` method throws the `NoSuchWindowException` exception when it fails to identify the desired window.

There's more...

Windows can be closed by calling the `driver.close()` method. However, developers might implement the closing of a window by clicking on a button or a link. In this case, closing a window directly might lead to errors or exceptions.

See also

▸ The *Identifying and handling a window by its title* recipe

▸ The *Identifying and handling a window by its content* recipe

Identifying and handling a window by its title

Many a time, developers don't assign the `name` attribute to windows. In such cases, we can use its window `handle` attribute. However, the `handle` attributes keep changing and it becomes difficult to identify the window, especially when there is more than one window open. Using the `handle` and `title` attributes of the page displayed in a window, we can build a more reliable way to identify child windows.

In this recipe, we will use the `title` attribute to identify the window and then perform operations on it.

How to do it...

We will create a test that retrieves the handles of all the open windows in the current driver context. We will iterate through this list and check the title matching the criteria, as follows:

```java
@Test
public void testWindowUsingTitle() {
    // Store WindowHandle of parent browser window
    String parentWindowId = driver.getWindowHandle();

    // Clicking Visit Us Button will open Visit Us Page in a new child
    // window
    driver.findElement(By.id("visitbutton")).click();

    // Get Handles of all the open windows
    // iterate through list and check if tile of
    // each window matches with expected window title
    try {
        for (String windowId : driver.getWindowHandles()) {
            String title = driver.switchTo().window(windowId).getTitle();
            if (title.equals("Visit Us")) {
                assertEquals("Visit Us", driver.getTitle());
                // Close the Visit Us window
                driver.close();
```

```
        break;
    }
  }
} finally {
  // Switch to the parent browser window
  driver.switchTo().window(parentWindowId);
}

// Check driver context is in parent browser window
assertEquals("Build my Car - Configuration", driver.getTitle());
}
```

How it works...

The `driver.getWindowHandles()` method returns the handles of all the open windows in a list. We can then iterate through this list and find out the matching window by checking the title of each window using the `handle` attribute, as follows:

```
for (String windowId : driver.getWindowHandles()) {
    String title =
driver.switchTo().window(windowId).getTitle();
    if (title.equals("Visit Us")) {
      assertEquals("Visit Us", driver.getTitle());
      // Close the Visit Us window
      driver.close();
      break;
    }
  }
```

 You can create a reusable function for identifying pop-up windows using the `title` attribute.

See also

▶ The *Identifying and handling windows* recipe
▶ The *Identifying and handling a window by its content* recipe

Identifying and handling a pop-up window by its content

In certain situations, developers neither assign a name attribute nor provide a title to the page displayed in a window. This becomes more complex when a test needs to deal with multiple windows open at the same time and identify the desired window.

As a workaround to this problem, we can check the contents of each window returned by the driver.getWindowHandles() method to identify the desired window.

How to do it...

Let's create a test that retrieves the handles of all the open windows in the current driver context. It will then iterate through this list, switching to the window and then checking for the content, which will help in identifying the correct window, as shown in the following code example:

```java
@Test
public void testWindowUsingContents() {
    // Store WindowHandle of parent browser window
    String currentWindowId = driver.getWindowHandle();

    // Clicking Chat Button will open Chat Page in a new child
window
    driver.findElement(By.id("chatbutton")).click();

    // There is no name or title provided for Chat Page window
    // We will iterate through all the open windows
    // and check the contents to find out if it's Chat window
    try {
      for (String windowId : driver.getWindowHandles()) {
        driver.switchTo().window(windowId);

        // We will use the page source to check the contents
        String pageSource = driver.getPageSource();

        if (pageSource.contains("Configuration - Online Chat")) {

          // Check the page for an element displaying a expected
          // message
          assertTrue(driver.findElement(By.tagName("p")).getText()
              .equals("Wait while we connect you to Chat..."));
```

```
        // Find the Close Button on Chat Window and close the
window
            // by clicking Close Button
            driver.findElement(By.id("closebutton")).click();
            break;
        }
    }
} finally {
    // Switch back to the parent browser window
    driver.switchTo().window(currentWindowId);
}
// Check driver context is in parent browser window
assertEquals("Build my Car - Configuration", driver.getTitle());
}
```

How it works...

By calling the `driver.getWindowHandles()` method, the test will iterate through each open window, switching to the window and then checking if the desired content is present in the window with the help of the following code snippet:

```
for (String windowId : driver.getWindowHandles()) {
    driver.switchTo().window(windowId);

    // We will use the page source to check the contents
    String pageSource = driver.getPageSource();

    if (pageSource.contains("Configuration - Online Chat")) {

        // Check the page for an element displaying a expected
        // message
        assertTrue(driver.findElement(By.tagName("p")).getText()
            .equals("Wait while we connect you to Chat..."));

        // Find the Close Button on Chat Window and close the
window
        // by clicking Close Button
        driver.findElement(By.id("closebutton")).click();
        break;
    }
}
```

In this example, it checks for specific text appearing on a page by calling the `driver.getPageSource()` method.

If a window is found with the specific text, it will be closed by clicking on the **Close** button instead of calling the `driver.close()` method. You can implement this in your test when windows cannot be identified by using the `name` attribute or the title. This will help in building more reliable tests.

See also

- ▶ The *Identifying and handling windows* recipe
- ▶ The *Identifying and handling a window by its title* recipe

7

Data-Driven Testing

In this chapter, we will cover:

- ▸ Creating a data-driven test using JUnit
- ▸ Creating a data-driven test using TestNG
- ▸ Reading test data from a CSV file using JUnit
- ▸ Reading test data from an Excel file using JUnit and Apache POI
- ▸ Creating a data-driven test in NUnit
- ▸ Creating a data-driven test in MSTEST
- ▸ Creating a data-driven test in Ruby using Roo
- ▸ Creating a data-driven test in Python using DDT

Introduction

The data-driven testing approach is a widely used methodology in software test automation. We can use the same test script to check different test conditions by passing set of data to the test script.

We will use the BMI calculator application as an example to understand the data-driven testing approach.

When testing whether the BMI calculator application indicates BMI categories correctly, instead of having a separate test script for each category, we can have one script that will enter the height and weight by referring to a set of values and checking the expected values.

We can use the following combinations of test conditions to test the BMI calculator application:

Height (centimeters)	Weight (kilograms)	BMI	Category
160	45	17.6	Underweight
168	70	24.8	Normal
181	89	27.2	Overweight
178	100	31.6	Obesity

In the simplest form, the tester supplies inputs from a row in the table and expected outputs, which occur in the same row.

Data-driven approach – workflow

In the data-driven approach, we can maintain the test data in form tables in a variety of formats, such as CSV files, Excel spreadsheets, and databases.

We implement test scripts after reading input and output values from data files row by row, then passing the values to the main test code. Then, the test code navigates through the application, executing the steps needed for the test case using the variables loaded with data values.

Data-driven tests are great for applications involving calculations for testing ranges of values, boundary values, and corner cases.

Benefits of data-driven testing

The benefits of data-driven testing are as follows:

▶ With data-driven tests, we can get greater test coverage while minimizing the amount of test code we need to write and maintain

▶ Data-driven testing makes creating and running a lot of test conditions very easy

▶ Test data can be designed and created before the application is ready for testing

▶ Data tables can also be used in manual testing

Selenium WebDriver, being a pure browser automation API, does not provide built-in features to support data-driven testing. However, we can add support for data-driven testing using various options in Selenium WebDriver. In this chapter, we will create some basic data-driven tests in **JUnit** and **TestNG**. Later, we will build some advanced data-driven tests using different data sources in JUnit, and a data-driven test in Ruby using Roo and Python.

We will also create data driven tests for .NET bindings using **NUnit** and **MSTest**.

Creating a data-driven test using JUnit

JUnit is a popular testing framework used to create Selenium WebDriver tests in Java. We can create data-driven Selenium WebDriver tests using the JUnit 4 parameterization feature. This can be done by using the JUnit parameterized class runner.

In this recipe, we will create a simple JUnit test case to test our BMI calculator application. We will specify the test data within our JUnit test case class. We will use various JUnit annotations to create a data-driven test.

Getting ready

The following are the things we need to do:

- ▶ Set up a new project and add JUnit4 to the project's build path. You can set up the project in an IDE of your choice.

- ▶ Identify the set of values that need to be tested.

How to do it...

Let's create a data-driven test using JUnit by following these steps:

1. Create a new JUnit test class that uses a parameterized runner using `@RunWith(Parameterized.class)`:

```
package com.secookbook.examples.chapter07;

import org.openqa.selenium.firefox.FirefoxDriver;
import org.openqa.selenium.WebDriver;
import org.openqa.selenium.WebElement;
import org.openqa.selenium.By;
import org.junit.*;
import org.junit.runner.RunWith;
import org.junit.runners.Parameterized.Parameters;
import org.junit.runners.Parameterized;

import static org.junit.Assert.*;

import java.util.Arrays;
import java.util.List;

@RunWith(Parameterized.class)
public class SimpleDDT {
```

```
            private static WebDriver driver;


        }
```

2. Declare instance variables for the parameterized values in the `SimpleDDT` class:

```
private String height;
private String weight;
private String bmi;
private String bmiCategory;
```

3. Define a method that will return the collection of parameters to the `SimpleDDT` class by using the `@Parameters` annotation:

```
@Parameters
public static List<String[]> testData() {
    return Arrays.asList(new String[][] {
            { "160", "45", "17.6", "Underweight" },
            { "168", "70", "24.8", "Normal" },
            { "181", "89", "27.2", "Overweight" },
            { "178", "100", "31.6", "Obesity" } });
}
```

4. Add a constructor to the `SimpleDDT` class, which will be used by the test runner to pass the parameters to the `SimpleDDT` class instance:

```
public SimpleDDT(String height, String weight, String bmi,
String bmiCategory)
{
    this.height = height;
    this.weight = weight;
    this.bmi = bmi;
    this.bmiCategory = bmiCategory;
}
```

5. Finally, add the test case method `testBMICalculator()` that uses parameterized variables. Also, add the `setup()` and `teardown()` methods to the `SimpleDDT` class:

```
@Test
public void testBMICalculator() throws Exception {
    // Get the Height element and set the value using height
variable
    WebElement heightField =
driver.findElement(By.name("heightCMS"));
    heightField.clear();
    heightField.sendKeys(height);
```

```
    // Get the Weight element and set the value using weight
variable
    WebElement weightField =
driver.findElement(By.name("weightKg"));
    weightField.clear();
    weightField.sendKeys(weight);

    // Click on Calculate Button
    WebElement calculateButton =
driver.findElement(By.id("Calculate"));
    calculateButton.click();

    // Get the Bmi element and verify its value using bmi
variable
    WebElement bmiLabel = driver.findElement(By.name("bmi"));
    assertEquals(bmi, bmiLabel.getAttribute("value"));

    // Get the Bmi Category element and verify its value
using
    // bmiCategory variable
    WebElement bmiCategoryLabel = driver.findElement(By
        .name("bmi_category"));
    assertEquals(bmiCategory,
bmiCategoryLabel.getAttribute("value"));
    }
```

How it works...

When the test is executed for each row in the test data collection, the test runner will instantiate the test case class, passing the test data as parameters to the `SimpleDDT` class constructor. It will then execute all the tests in the `SimpleDDT` class.

Instance variables are declared to store the test data passed by the test runner, as shown in the following code snippet:

```
private String height;
private String weight;
private String bmi;
private String bmiCategory;
```

In the test case class constructor, these variables are assigned with values at runtime by the test runner from the test data collection, using the test method arguments as shown in following code:

```
public SimpleDDT(String height, String weight, String bmi, String
bmiCategory)
{
  this.height = height;
  this.weight = weight;
  this.bmi = bmi;
  this.bmiCategory = bmiCategory;
}
```

In the `testBMICalculator()` method, we passed these variables to Selenium `WebDriver` `API`. For example, to enter a value in the `height` field, we used the instance variable of the test case class as follows:

```
WebElement heightField = driver.findElement(By.name("heightCMS"));
heightField.sendKeys(this.height);
```

The expected result is also parameterized using the instance variable for BMI value, as shown in following code:

```
WebElement bmiLabel = driver.findElement(By.name("bmi"));
assertEquals(this.bmi, bmiLabel.getAttribute("value"));
```

JUnit will display results for each set of test data along with the time taken to execute it, as shown in the following screenshot:

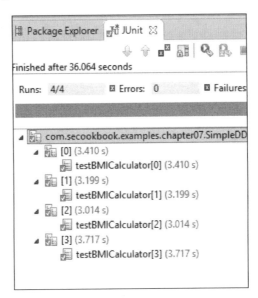

This is one of the simplest ways to parameterize a test; however, test data is hardcoded within the test case class, which could become difficult to maintain. It is always recommended that we store the test data in an external source such as a CSV, Excel, or database file for easier maintenance.

See also

▶ The _Reading test data from a CSV file using JUnit_ recipe

▶ The _Reading test data from an Excel file using JUnit and Apache POI_ recipe

Creating a data-driven test using TestNG

TestNG is another widely used testing framework with Selenium WebDriver. It is very similar to JUnit. TestNG has rich features for testing, such as parameterization, parallel test execution, and so on.

TestNG provides the `DataProvider` feature to create data-driven tests. In this recipe, we will use the `DataProvider` feature to create a simple test. Creating data-driven tests in TestNG is fairly easy when compared with JUnit.

Getting ready

The following are the steps we need to begin with:

▶ Add TestNG dependency to the Maven `pom.xml` file:

```
<dependency>
  <groupId>org.testng</groupId>
  <artifactId>testng</artifactId>
  <version>6.9.4</version>
  <scope>test</scope>
</dependency>
```

▶ Identify the set of values that we need to test.

How to do it...

Let's create a new test and parameterize a TestNG test using the following steps:

```
import org.openqa.selenium.WebDriver;
import org.openqa.selenium.firefox.FirefoxDriver;
import org.openqa.selenium.WebElement;
import org.openqa.selenium.By;
```

```java
import org.testng.annotations.*;
import static org.testng.Assert.*;

public class TestNGDDT {

  private WebDriver driver;

  @DataProvider
  public Object[][] testData() {
    return new Object[][] {
        new Object[] { "160", "45", "17.6", "Underweight"
},
        new Object[] { "168", "70", "24.8", "Normal" },
        new Object[] { "181", "89", "27.2", "Overweight" },
        new Object[] { "178", "100", "31.6", "Obesity" }, };
  }

  @BeforeTest
  public void setUp() {
    // Create a new instance of the Firefox driver
    driver = new FirefoxDriver();
    driver.get("http://cookbook.seleniumacademy.com/bmicalculat
or.html");

  }

  @Test(dataProvider = "testData")
  public void testBMICalculator(String height, String
weight, String bmi,
      String category) {
    WebElement heightField =
driver.findElement(By.name("heightCMS"));
    heightField.clear();
    heightField.sendKeys(height);

    WebElement weightField =
driver.findElement(By.name("weightKg"));
    weightField.clear();
    weightField.sendKeys(weight);

    WebElement calculateButton =
driver.findElement(By.id("Calculate"));
    calculateButton.click();

    WebElement bmiLabel = driver.findElement(By.name("bmi"));
    assertEquals(bmiLabel.getAttribute("value"), bmi);

    WebElement bmiCategoryLabel = driver.findElement(By
        .name("bmi_category"));
```

```
        assertEquals(bmiCategoryLabel.getAttribute("value"),
    category);
      }

    @AfterTest
    public void tearDown() {
      driver.quit();
    }
}
```

How it works...

Unlike the JUnit, where parameterization is done on a class level, TestNG supports parameterization at the test level.

> In TestNG, we do not need a constructor and instance variable for the test case class to pass the parameter values. TestNG does the mapping automatically.

When a method is annotated with @DataProvider, it becomes a data feeder method by passing the test data to the test case. In this example, the testData() method will become the data feeder method, and TestNG will pass the array of data rows to the test method one by one:

```
@DataProvider
public Object[][] testData() {
    return new Object[][] {
      new Object[] {"160","45","17.6","Underweight"},
      new Object[] {"168","70","24.8","Normal"},
      new Object[] {"181","89","27.2","Overweight"},
      new Object[] {"178","100","31.6","Obesity"},
    };
}
```

The test case method is linked to the data feeder method by passing the name of the dataProvider method to the @Test annotation:

```
@Test(dataProvider = "testData")
public void testBMICalculator(String height, String weight, String
bmi, String category)
```

TestNG will execute the test four times with different test combinations. TestNG also generates a well-formatted report at the end of the test execution.

There's more...

To run Selenium tests in parallel, the TestNG parameterization feature comes in very handy. TestNG supports running Selenium tests parallel in a multithreading safe environment.

See also

> ▸ The *Reading test data from a CSV file using JUnit* recipe
>
> ▸ The *Reading test data from an Excel file using JUnit and Apache POI* recipe

Reading test data from a CSV file using JUnit

We saw a simple data-driven test using JUnit and TestNG. The test data was hardcoded in the test script code. This could become difficult to maintain. It is recommended that we store the test data separately from the test scripts.

Often we use data from the production environment for testing. This data can be exported in CSV format. We will use OpenCSV library to read a CSV file. For more details on OpenCSV, headon to `http://opencsv.sourceforge.net/`.

In this recipe, we will read data from a CSV file and use this data to execute the test script.

Getting ready

To begin, follow these steps:

> ▸ Add OpenCSV dependency to the Maven `pom.xml` file:

```
<dependency>
    <groupId>com.opencsv</groupId>
    <artifactId>opencsv</artifactId>
    <version>3.4</version>
    <scope>test</scope>
</dependency>
```

> ▸ Prepare a CSV file with the required data.

How to do it...

Let's create a new JUnit test and CSV parametrization, as shown in the following example:

```java
package com.secookbook.examples.chapter07;

import org.openqa.selenium.firefox.FirefoxDriver;
import org.openqa.selenium.WebDriver;
import org.openqa.selenium.WebElement;
import org.openqa.selenium.By;
import org.junit.*;
import org.junit.runner.*;
import org.junit.runners.*;
import org.junit.runners.Parameterized.Parameters;

import com.opencsv.CSVReader;

import static org.junit.Assert.*;

import java.io.*;
import java.util.*;

@RunWith(Parameterized.class)
public class CsvTestData {

  private static WebDriver driver;

  private String height;
  private String weight;
  private String bmi;
  private String bmiCategory;

  @Parameters
  public static List<String[]> testData() throws
IOException {
     return getTestData("./src/test/resources/testdata/data.csv");
  }

  public CsvTestData(String height, String weight, String
bmi,
      String bmiCategory) {
    this.height = height;
    this.weight = weight;
    this.bmi = bmi;
```

```java
        this.bmiCategory = bmiCategory;
    }

    public static List<String[]> getTestData(String fileName)
        throws IOException {
      CSVReader reader = new CSVReader(new
FileReader(fileName));
      List<String[]> myEntries = reader.readAll();
      reader.close();
      return myEntries;
    }

    @BeforeClass
    public static void setUp() throws Exception {
      // Create a new instance of the Firefox driver
      driver = new FirefoxDriver();
      driver.get("http://cookbook.seleniumacademy.com/bmicalculat
or.html");
    }

    @Test
    public void testBMICalculator() throws Exception {
      WebElement heightField =
driver.findElement(By.name("heightCMS"));
      heightField.clear();
      heightField.sendKeys(height);

      WebElement weightField =
driver.findElement(By.name("weightKg"));
      weightField.clear();
      weightField.sendKeys(weight);

      WebElement calculateButton =
driver.findElement(By.id("Calculate"));
      calculateButton.click();

      WebElement bmiLabel =
driver.findElement(By.name("bmi"));
      assertEquals(bmi, bmiLabel.getAttribute("value"));

      WebElement bmiCategoryLabel = driver.findElement(By
          .name("bmi_category"));
      assertEquals(bmiCategory,
bmiCategoryLabel.getAttribute("value"));
    }
```

```
@AfterClass
public static void tearDown() throws Exception {
  // Close the browser
  driver.quit();
}
}
```

How it works...

When the test is executed, the `testData()` method will call the `getTestData()` helper method by passing the path of the CSV file. Inside the `getTestData()` method, the `BufferedReader` class from the `java.io` namespace is used to read the file line by line. Lines are then split into an array of strings using the comma delimiter. This array is then added to `Collection` or `ArrayList`, either of which is then returned to the `testData()` method.

For each row in the test data collection returned by the `testData()` method, the test runner will instantiate the test case class, passing the test data as parameters to the test class constructor, and it will then execute all the tests in the `test` class.

See also

- ▶ The *Creating a data-driven test using JUnit* recipe
- ▶ The *Reading test data from an Excel file using JUnit and Apache POI* recipe

Reading test data from an Excel file using JUnit and Apache POI

To maintain test cases and test data, Microsoft Excel is the favorite tool used by testers. Compared to the CSV file format, Excel gives numerous features and a structured way to store data. A tester can create and maintain tables of test data in an Excel spreadsheet easily.

In this recipe, we will use an Excel spreadsheet as your data source. We will use the Apache POI API, developed by the Apache Foundation, to manipulate the Excel spreadsheet. This recipe also implements some negative test handling.

Getting ready

To begin, follow these steps:

- ▶ Add OpenCSV dependency to the Maven `pom.xml` file:

```
<dependency>
  <groupId>com.opencsv</groupId>
```

```
        <artifactId>opencsv</artifactId>
        <version>3.4</version>
        <scope>test</scope>
    </dependency>
```

▸ Prepare an Excel spreadsheet with the required data

We will also need a `SpreadsheetData` helper class to read the Excel spreadsheets. This is available in the source code bundle for this book. This class supports both the old `.xls` and newer `.xlsx` formats.

How to do it...

Let's create a test that uses Excel spreadsheet test data for parameterization, as shown in the following code example:

```
package com.secookbook.examples.chapter07;

import org.openqa.selenium.WebDriver;
import org.openqa.selenium.chrome.ChromeDriver;
import org.openqa.selenium.WebElement;
import org.openqa.selenium.By;

import org.junit.*;
import org.junit.runner.RunWith;
import org.junit.runners.Parameterized.Parameters;
import org.junit.runners.Parameterized;
import static org.junit.Assert.*;

import java.io.FileInputStream;
import java.io.InputStream;
import java.util.Collection;

@RunWith(Parameterized.class)
public class ExcelTestData {

    private static WebDriver driver;

    private String height;
    private String weight;
    private String bmi;
    private String bmiCategory;
    private String error;
```

```
    @Parameters
    public static Collection testData() throws Exception {
        InputStream spreadsheet = new FileInputStream("./src/test/
resources/testdata/Data.xlsx");
        return new SpreadsheetData(spreadsheet).getData();
    }

    public ExcelTestData(String height, String weight, String bmi,
        String bmiCategory, String error) {
        this.height = height;
        this.weight = weight;
        this.bmi = bmi;
        this.bmiCategory = bmiCategory;
        this.error = error;
    }

    @BeforeClass
    public static void setUp() throws Exception {

        // Create a new instance of the Chrome driver
        driver = new ChromeDriver();
        driver.get("http://cookbook.seleniumacademy.com/bmicalculator.
html");
    }

    @Test
    public void testBMICalculator() throws Exception {
        WebElement heightField = driver.findElement(By.name("heightCMS"));
        heightField.clear();
        if (!height.equals("<Blank>")) {
            heightField.sendKeys(this.height);
        }

        WebElement weightField =
driver.findElement(By.name("weightKg"));
        weightField.clear();
        if (!weight.equals("<Blank>")) {
            weightField.sendKeys(this.weight);
        }

        WebElement calculateButton =
driver.findElement(By.id("Calculate"));
        calculateButton.click();
```

```
      if (error.equals("<Blank>")) {
        WebElement bmiField = driver.findElement(By.name("bmi"));
        assertEquals(this.bmi, bmiField.getAttribute("value"));

        WebElement bmiCategoryField = driver.findElement(By
            .name("bmi_category"));
        assertEquals(this.bmiCategory,
            bmiCategoryField.getAttribute("value"));
      } else {
        WebElement errorLabel =
  driver.findElement(By.id("error"));
        assertEquals(this.error, errorLabel.getText());
      }
    }
  }

  @AfterClass
  public static void tearDown() throws Exception {
    driver.quit();
  }
}
```

How it works...

When the test is executed, the `testData()` method will create an instance of the `SpreadsheetData` class. The `SpreadsheetData` class reads the contents of the Excel spreadsheet row by row in a collection and returns this collection back to the `testData()` method:

```
InputStream spreadsheet = new
FileInputStream("./src/test/resources/testdata/Data.xlsx");
return new SpreadsheetData(spreadsheet).getData();
```

For each row in the test data collection returned by the `testData()` method, the test runner will instantiate the test case class, passing the test data as parameters to the test class constructor, and then execute all the tests in the `test` class.

See also

  ▸ The *Creating a data-driven test using JUnit* recipe
  ▸ The *Reading test data from a CSV file using JUnit* recipe

Creating a data-driven test in NUnit

The NUnit framework has been widely used by the Selenium WebDriver community to create test scripts with .NET bindings.

Similar to the JUnit framework, the NUnit framework also supports data-driven testing in the simplest manner. In this recipe, we will create a Selenium WebDriver test using NUnit. We will read the test data from an XML file used in the first recipe.

Getting ready

To begin, follow these steps:

1. Download and install NUnit from `http://www.nunit.org/`

2. Create the test data file in the XML format as follows:

   ```
   <testdata>
   <vars height="160" weight="45" bmi="17.6"
   bmi_category="Underweight" />
   <vars height="168" weight="70" bmi="24.8"
   bmi_category="Normal" />
   <vars height="181" weight="89" bmi="27.2"
   bmi_category="Overweight" />
   <vars height="178" weight="100" bmi="31.6"
   bmi_category="Obesity" />
   </testdata>
   ```

3. Create a new C# class library project and name it `BMICalculator`

4. Add a reference to NUnit, WebDriver, .NET binding, System XML, and `System.Xml.Linq`

How to do it...

Let's create a parameterized test in NUnit. Create a new C# class item with the name `BMICalculatorNUnitTest`, as shown in the following code example, copy the following code to the newly created class by replacing its contents:

```csharp
using System;
using System.Collections.Generic;
using System.Linq;
using System.Text;
using NUnit.Framework;
using System.Collections;
using System.Xml.Linq;
```

```csharp
using OpenQA.Selenium;
using OpenQA.Selenium.Firefox;
using OpenQA.Selenium.Support;
using OpenQA.Selenium.Support.UI;

namespace BMICalculator
{
    [TestFixture]
    public class BMICalculatorNUnitTest
    {
        IWebDriver driver;

        [SetUp]
        public void TestSetup()
        {
            // Create a instance of the Firefox driver
using IWebDriver Interface
            driver = new FirefoxDriver();
        }

        [TestCaseSource("BmiTestData")]
        public void TestBmiCalculator(string height, string
weight, string expectedBmi, string expectedCategory)
        {
            driver.Navigate().GoToUrl("http://cookbook.
seleniumacademy.com/bmicalculator.html");

            IWebElement heightElement =
driver.FindElement(By.Name("heightCMS"));
            heightElement.SendKeys(height);

            IWebElement weightElement =
driver.FindElement(By.Name("weightKg"));
            weightElement.SendKeys(weight);

            IWebElement calculateButton =
driver.FindElement(By.Id("Calculate"));
            calculateButton.Click();

            IWebElement bmiElement =
driver.FindElement(By.Name("bmi"));
            Assert.AreEqual(expectedBmi,
bmiElement.GetAttribute("value"));
```

```csharp
            IWebElement bmiCatElement =
    driver.FindElement(By.Name("bmi_category"));
            Assert.AreEqual(expectedCategory,
    bmiCatElement.GetAttribute("value"));

        }

        [TearDown]
        public void TestCleanUp()
        {
            // Close the browser
            driver.Quit();
        }

        private IEnumerable BmiTestData
        {
            get { return GetBmiTestData(); }
        }
        private IEnumerable GetBmiTestData()
        {
            var doc = XDocument.Load(@"c:\data.xml");
            return
                from vars in doc.Descendants("vars")
                let height = vars.Attribute("height").Value
                let weight = vars.Attribute("weight").Value
                let expectedBmi =
    vars.Attribute("bmi").Value
                let expectedCategory =
    vars.Attribute("bmi_category").Value

                select new object[] { height, weight,
    expectedBmi, expectedCategory };
        }
    }
}
```

How it works...

While creating a data-driven test in NUnit, we use the `TestCaseSource` attribute. We will specify the name of the `IEnumerable` property that will provide test data to this test case with the `TestCaseSource` attribute, as shown in the following code:

```
[TestCaseSource("BmiTestData")]
public void TestBmiCalculator(string height, string weight, string
expected_bmi, string expected_category)
```

When we execute the test, NUnit framework will generate test cases by calling the `BmiTestData` property. This will return an array of arguments as `IEnumerable` by calling the `GetBmiTestData()` method. An array of arguments is created by reading an XML file using a LINQ Query in the `GetBmiTestData()` method. When we open the test in the NUnit GUI, it shows the test cases for all the test data combinations provided in the input XML file, as shown in the following screenshot:

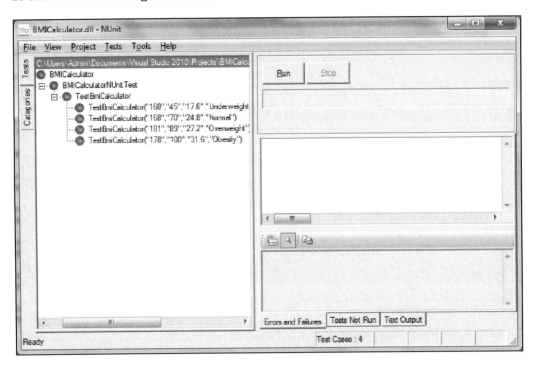

With this, we can get the test data from any source, such as CSV, Excel spreadsheet, or a database. The NUnit GUI will show the results when all the tests are executed, as shown in the following screenshot:

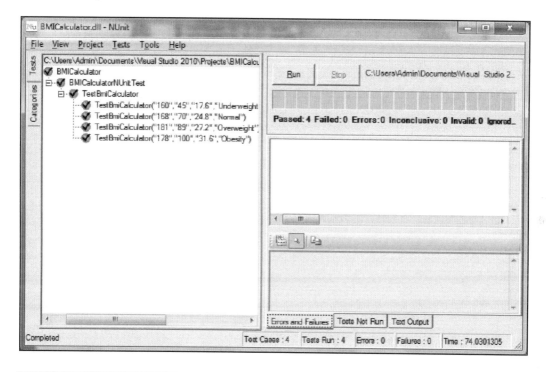

▶ The *Creating a data-driven test in MSTEST* recipe

Creating a data-driven test in MSTEST

To create a data-driven test in MSTEST, the unit testing framework provided by Microsoft Visual Studio is the simplest way to parameterize the test scripts with .NET bindings.

MSTEST has in-built features to support data-driven testing, which can be configured very easily. In this recipe, we will use MSTEST to create a data-driven Selenium test by reading test data from an Excel spreadsheet.

Getting ready

To begin, follow these steps:

▸ Create a new C# test project in Microsoft Visual Studio 2010 and name it BMICalculator

▸ Add a reference to the WebDriver .NET binding

How to do it...

You can parameterize a test in MSTEST by adding the Excel spreadsheet to deployment items of the test project, using the following steps:

1. Click on **Local.testsettings** under **Solution Items**.

2. The **Test Settings** dialog will appear. We need to add the test data file by clicking the **Add File** button in the **Deployment** section.

3. Once you add the file to the **Deployment** section, it will appear in the list.

4. Create a new test class and name it BMICalculatorTests. Copy the following code to this class:

```csharp
using System;
using System.Text;
using System.Collections.Generic;
using System.Linq;
using Microsoft.VisualStudio.TestTools.UnitTesting;
using OpenQA.Selenium;
using OpenQA.Selenium.Firefox;
using OpenQA.Selenium.Support;
using OpenQA.Selenium.Support.UI;
using System.Data;

namespace BMICalculator
{
    [TestClass]
    public class BMICalculatorTests
    {
        IWebDriver driver;

        [TestInitialize]
        public void TestSetup()
        {
```

```
            // Create a instance of the Firefox driver
    using IWebDriver Interface
            driver = new FirefoxDriver();
        }

        private TestContext testContextInstance;

        /// <summary>
        ///Gets or sets the test context which provides
        ///information about and functionality for the
    current test run.
        ///</summary>
        public TestContext TestContext
        {
            get
            {
                return testContextInstance;
            }
            set
            {
                testContextInstance = value;
            }
        }

        [TestMethod]
        [DeploymentItem("Data.xls")]
        [DataSource("System.Data.OleDb",
    "Provider=Microsoft.ACE.OLEDB.12.0;Data Source=Data.xls;Persist
    Security Info=False;Extended
    Properties='Excel 12.0;HDR=Yes'", "Data$",
    DataAccessMethod.Sequential)]
        public void TestBMICalculator()
        {
            driver.Navigate().GoToUrl("http://dl.dropbox.
    com/u/55228056
    /bmicalculator.html");

            IWebElement height =
    driver.FindElement(By.Name("heightCMS"));
            height.SendKeys(TestContext.DataRow["Height"].
    ToString());

            IWebElement weight =
    driver.FindElement(By.Name("weightKg"));
```

```
            weight.SendKeys(TestContext.DataRow["Weight"].
     ToString());

            IWebElement calculateButton =
     driver.FindElement(By.Id("Calculate"));
            calculateButton.Click();

            IWebElement bmi =
     driver.FindElement(By.Name("bmi"));
            Assert.AreEqual(TestContext.DataRow["Bmi"].ToString(),
     bmi.GetAttribute("value"));

            IWebElement bmiCategory =
     driver.FindElement(By.Name("bmi_category"));
            Assert.AreEqual(TestContext.DataRow["Category"].
     ToString(),
     bmiCategory.GetAttribute("value"));
          }

        [TestCleanup]
        public void TestCleanUp()
        {
            // Close the browser
            driver.Quit();
        }

     }
}
```

How it works...

When we add the `DataSource` attribute to a test in MSTEST, it provides data source-specific information for data-driven testing to the framework:

```
[TestMethod]
[DeploymentItem("Data.xls")]
[DataSource("System.Data.OleDb",
"Provider=Microsoft.ACE.OLEDB.12.0;Data Source=Data.xls;Persist
Security Info=False;Extended Properties='Excel 12.0;HDR=Yes'",
"Data$", DataAccessMethod.Sequential)]
public void TestBMICalculator()
```

It reads the test data from the source. In this example, the source is an Excel spreadsheet. The framework internally creates a `DataTable` object to store the values from the source. The `TestContext` test method provides a collection of data rows for parameterization. We can access a field by specifying its name, as follows:

```
IWebElement height =
driver.FindElement(By.Name("heightCMS"));
        height.SendKeys(TestContext.DataRow["Height"].ToString());
```

With the `DataSource` attribute, we can specify the connection string or a configuration file to read data from a variety of sources, including CSV File, Excel spreadsheets, XML files, or databases.

See also

- ▶ The *Creating a data-driven test in NUnit* recipe

Creating a data-driven test in Ruby using Roo

In the previous recipes, we saw parameterization with Java and .NET. Ruby has also been used widely to create Selenium WebDriver tests.

Again, Ruby does not have its own way to parameterize the script. However, we can use the **Roo** (`http://roo.rubyforge.org/`) **gem** in Ruby to read spreadsheets. Roo supports multiple formats, as follows:

- ▶ A locally stored Excel (`.xls`) file
- ▶ A locally stored OpenOffice (`.ods`) file
- ▶ An Excel file (`.xls`) stored in a Confluence wiki page with Confluence Office Connector
- ▶ A Google Docs spreadsheet

Roo is a great alternative to the Ruby Excel COM WIN32 API, as it does not need Excel or OpenOffice installed on the machine. It reads both these files natively.

In this recipe, we will parameterize the Selenium WebDriver test created in Ruby bindings using an Excel spreadsheet as a test data source.

Getting ready

You need to install the Roo gem using the following command:

```
gem install roo
```

This command will download and install all the dependencies required for Roo on your machine.

How to do it...

Let's create a simple Ruby test for parameterization using the following steps. This test will read test data from the Excel spreadsheet used in the *Reading test data from an Excel file using JUnit and Apache POI* recipe earlier. Create a Ruby test by importing the following modules:

```
require 'rubygems'
require 'selenium-webdriver'
require 'roo'
```

Then, follow these steps:

1. Create an instance of WebDriver. We will use the Firefox browser, the following code shows you how:

   ```
   #Create an instance of WebDriver for Firefox
   driver = Selenium::WebDriver.for :firefox
   ```

2. Declare the following variables to print a summary of test combinations executed from the test data source:

   ```
   #Variables for Printing Test Summary
   test_executed = 0
   test_passed = 0
   test_failed = 0
   ```

3. Create an instance of `Excel` class from Roo to read a spreadsheet:

   ```
   #Create an instance of a Excel Spreadsheet
   data = Excel.new("C:\\Data.xls")
   data.default_sheet = data.sheets.first
   ```

4. Add the following code, which will iterate through the spreadsheet, reading each combination and then performing the operations and verifications:

   ```
   #Iterate through the Sheet reading Rows line by line
   data.first_row.upto(data.last_row) do |line|
      if data.cell(line,1) != "Height" #Ignore the first line
   for   Headers
        begin
          test_status = true
          test_executed = test_executed + 1
          puts "Test " + test_executed.to_s()

          driver.get "http://dl.dropbox.com/u/55228056/bmicalculator.
          html"
   ```

```ruby
    height = driver.find_element :name => "heightCMS"
    height.send_keys data.cell(line,1).to_s()

    weight = driver.find_element :name => "weightKg"
    weight.send_keys  data.cell(line,2).to_s()

    calculateButton = driver.find_element :id
=>"Calculate"
    calculateButton.click

    bmi = driver.find_element :name =>"bmi"
    bmi_category = driver.find_element :name
=>"bmi_category"

    if bmi.attribute("value").to_s() ==
data.cell(line,3).to_s()
      puts "Pass, expected value for BMI <" +
data.cell(line,3).
      to_s() + ">, actual <" +
bmi.attribute("value").to_s() + ">"
    else
      puts "Fail, expected value for BMI <" +
data.cell(line,3).
      to_s() + ">, actual <" +
bmi.attribute("value").to_s() + ">"
      test_status=false
    end

    if bmi_category.attribute("value").to_s() == data.
    cell(line,4).to_s()
      puts "Pass, expected value for BMI Category <" +
      data.cell(line,4).to_s() + ">, actual <" +
bmi_category.         attribute("value").to_s() + ">"
    else
      puts "Fail, expected value for BMI Category <" +
      data.cell(line,4).to_s() + ">, actual <" +
bmi_category.         attribute("value").to_s() + ">"
      test_status=false
    end

    if test_status
      test_passed = test_passed + 1
    else
      test_failed = test_failed + 1
```

```
        end
      rescue
        puts "An error occurred: #{$!}"
      end
    end
end
```

5. Finally, we will print a summary of test combinations that were executed and passed, or those that failed the test, using the following code:

```
puts "----------------------------------------------"
puts "Total (" + test_executed.to_s() + ") Tests Executed"
puts "Total (" + test_passed.to_s() + ") Tests Passed"
puts "Total (" + test_failed.to_s() + ") Tests Failed"

driver.quit
```

How it works...

When we execute this test, Roo will read the contents of the Excel spreadsheet into the `data` object, using the following code:

```
#Create an instance of a Excel Spreadsheet
data = Excel.new("C:\\Data.xls")
data.default_sheet = data.sheets.first
```

We can then iterate the `data` object from the first row to the last row using the following code:

```
data.first_row.upto(data.last_row) do |line|
```

This will copy the content from a row in a variable named `line`. The value from a data cell is accessed using the `data.cell()` method by passing the line and position of the cell, using the following code:

```
height = driver.find_element :name => "heightCMS"
height.send_keys data.cell(line,1).to_s()
```

We also added a custom reporting code that will generate a nicely formatted report at the end of the test execution, as shown in the following screenshot:

There's more...

We can also read the Google Docs spreadsheets from Roo. This can be done using the `Google.new()` method by passing the key for the Google Docs spreadsheet, as shown in the following command:

```
data = Google.new("0Al-3LZqhACsidFh1NmdnYktmTkREVEkzb3B0ZnYybHc")
```

If you want to use Google spreadsheets, you must either have set the environment variables to `GOOGLE_MAIL` and `GOOGLE_PASSWORD` or passed the Google-username and password to the `Google#new` method.

Many teams maintain Excel spreadsheets on Confluence Wiki. Using Roo, you can also read a spreadsheet stored on Confluence Wiki. For more information, visit the Roo home page at `http://roo.rubyforge.org/`.

Creating a data-driven test in Python using DDT

Python is also a widely used language for building Selenium WebDriver tests. It offers various ways to parameterize tests.

In this recipe, we will use the **DDT** module along with unittest to create a parameterized test.

Getting ready

You need to install the DDT module by using the following command:

```
pip install ddt
```

This command will download and install all the dependencies required for DDT on your machine.

How to do it...

Let's create a simple Python test for parameterization using the DDT module. Create a new Python file named bmi_calc_ddt.py using the following code:

```python
import unittest
from ddt import ddt, data, unpack
from selenium import webdriver

@ddt
class BmiCalcDDT(unittest.TestCase):
    def setUp(self):
        # create a new Firefox session
        self.driver = webdriver.Firefox()
        self.driver.implicitly_wait(30)
        self.driver.maximize_window()

        # navigate to the BMI Calculator page
        self.driver.get("http://bit.ly/1zdNrFZ")

    # specify test data using @data decorator
    @data(("160", "45", "17.6", "Underweight"),
          ("168", "70", "24.8", "Normal"),
          ("181", "89", "27.2", "Overweight"))
    @unpack
    def test_bmi_calc(self, height, weight, bmi, category):
        driver = self.driver
```

```
        height_field = driver.find_element_by_name("heightCMS")
        height_field.clear()
        height_field.send_keys(height)

        weight_field = driver.find_element_by_name("weightKg")
        weight_field.clear()
        weight_field.send_keys(weight)

        calculate_button = driver.find_element_by_id("Calculate")
        calculate_button.click()

        bmi_label = driver.find_element_by_name("bmi")
        bmi_category_label =
driver.find_element_by_name("bmi_category")

        self.assertEqual(bmi, bmi_label.get_attribute("value"))
        self.assertEqual(category,
bmi_category_label.get_attribute("value"))

    def tearDown(self):
        # close the browser window
        self.driver.quit()

if __name__ == '__main__':
    unittest.main(verbosity=2)
```

How it works...

The DDT module is an extension for the Python unittest library. We can use this module to parameterize unit tests in Python. We need to add a special decorator @ddt to parameterize the test class:

```
@ddt
class BmiCalcDDT(unittest.TestCase):
```

Next, we need to describe the test data above the test method using the @data decorator:

```
    # specify test data using @data decorator
    @data(("160", "45", "17.6", "Underweight"),
          ("168", "70", "24.8", "Normal"),
          ("181", "89", "27.2", "Overweight"))
    @unpack
```

When we execute this test, Python will read the data tuples and pass each row to the test.

8

Using the Page Object Model

In this chapter, we will cover the following topics:

- ▸ Using the PageFactory class for exposing the elements on a page
- ▸ Using the PageFactory class for exposing an operation on a page
- ▸ Using the LoadableComponent class
- ▸ Implementing nested Page Object instances
- ▸ Implementing the Page Object model in .NET
- ▸ Implementing the Page Object model in Python
- ▸ Implementing the Page Object model in Ruby using the page-object gem

Introduction

Developing a maintainable automation code is one of the keys to a successful test-automation project. Test-automation code should to be treated as production code, and similar standards and patterns should be applied while developing this code.

While developing Selenium WebDriver tests, we can use the Page Object model pattern. This pattern helps enhance the tests by making them highly maintainable, reducing the code duplication, building a layer of abstraction, and hiding the inner implementation from tests.

By applying object-oriented development principles, we can develop a class that serves as an interface to a web page in the application, modeling its properties and behavior. This helps in creating a layer of separation between the test code and the code specific to the page by hiding technical implementations such as locators used to identify elements on the page, layout, and so on. The Page Object design pattern provides an interface where a test can operate on that page in a manner similar to the user accessing the page, but by hiding its internals. For example, if we build a Page Object for a login page, then it will provide a method to log in, which will accept the username and password and take the user to the home page of the application. The test need not worry about how input controls are used for the login page, their locator details, and so on. It will instantiate the login page object and call the login method by passing the username and password. Tests should use objects of a page at a high level, where any change in layout or attributes used for the fields in the underlying page should not break the test.

This chapter covers recipes to build tests using the Page Object model and related designs.

Using the PageFactory class for exposing the elements on a page

To implement the Page Object model in tests, we need to create a Page Object class for each page that is being tested. For example, to test the BMI Calculator application, a BMI Calculator page class will be defined, which will expose the internals of the BMI Calculator page to the test, as shown in following diagram. This is done by using the `PageFactory` class of Selenium WebDriver API:

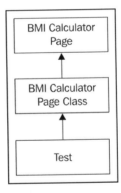

Getting ready

Before exposing the elements of a page, we need to do the following:

- Identify the locators that will be needed to find all the required elements from a page uniquely
- Define the structure of the package and classes for the page

How to do it...

Let's implement a Page Object test for the BMI Calculator page using the `PageFactory` class with the following steps:

1. Define and create a package for all the page objects from the application for logical grouping. For example, `seleniumcookbook.tests.pageobjects` is created to define all the page objects.

2. Create a new Java class file. Give the name of the page we will be testing from the application to this class. For example, we will be creating a page object for the BMI Calculator application, so the class name could be `BmiCalcPage`. This is a single page application. The Java class file will have the following code:

```
package com.secookbook.examples.chapter08.pageobjects;

import org.openqa.selenium.WebDriver;
import org.openqa.selenium.WebElement;
import org.openqa.selenium.support.FindBy;
import org.openqa.selenium.support.PageFactory;

public class BmiCalcPage  {
}
```

3. Define elements from the BMI Calculator page as instance variables in the `BmiCalcPage` class created in step 1. Use the `name` or `id` attributes to name these variables, as follows:

```
private WebElement heightCMS;
private WebElement weightKg;
private WebElement Calculate;
private WebElement bmi;

@FindBy(id = "bmi_category")
private WebElement bmiCategory;

private WebDriver driver;
```

4. Add a constructor to the `BmiCalcPage` class, which will call the `PageFactory.initElements()` method to initialize the elements in the class. In other words, map the elements to the variables in the `BmiCalcPage` class, as follows:

```
public BmiCalcPage(WebDriver driver) {
  this.driver = driver;
  PageFactory.initElements(driver, this);
}
```

5. We will add the accessor methods for Height, Weight, and Calculate button fields so we can set values or perform operation like clicking a button:

```
public void setHeight(String height) {
  heightCMS.sendKeys(height);
}

public void setWeight(String weight) {
  weightKg.sendKeys(weight);
}

public void calculateBmi() {
  Calculate.click();
}
```

6. Also, add the accessor method to read the values from the Bmi and Bmi Category fields, as shown in the following code:

```
public String getBmi() {
  return bmi.getAttribute("value");
}

public String getBmiCategory() {
  return bmiCategory.getAttribute("value");
}
```

7. Finally, create a test that will use the BmiCalcPage class to test the BMI Calculator page, as follows:

```
package com.secookbook.examples.chapter08.tests;

import org.junit.After;
import org.junit.Before;
import org.junit.Test;
import org.openqa.selenium.WebDriver;
import org.openqa.selenium.chrome.ChromeDriver;

import static org.junit.Assert.*;

import com.secookbook.examples.chapter08.pageobjects.BmiCalcPage;

public class BmiCalculatorTests {

  private WebDriver driver;

  @Before
  public void setUp() {
```

```
        driver = new ChromeDriver();
        driver.get("http://cookbook.seleniumacademy.com/bmicalculat
    or.html");
      }

    @Test
    public void testBmiCalculation() {
        // Create an instance of Bmi Calculator Page class
        // and provide the driver
        CopyOfBmiCalcPage bmiCalcPage = new
    CopyOfBmiCalcPage(driver);

        // Set Height
        bmiCalcPage.setHeight("181");

        // Set Weight
        bmiCalcPage.setWeight("80");

        // Click on Calculate button
        bmiCalcPage.calculateBmi();

        // Verify Bmi & Bmi Category values
        assertEquals("24.4", bmiCalcPage.getBmi());
        assertEquals("Normal", bmiCalcPage.getBmiCategory());
      }

    @After
    public void tearDown() {
      driver.quit();
      }
```

How it works...

Using the Page Object model and the PageFactory class, the BMI Calculator page's elements are exposed through the BmiCalcPage class to the test instead of the test directly accessing the internals of the page.

When we initialize the page's object using the PageFactory class in the BmiCalcPage class, the PageFactory class searches for the elements on the page with the name or id attributes matching the name of the WebElement object declared in the BmiCalcPage class, as follows:

```
    public BmiCalcPage(WebDriver driver) {
        PageFactory.initElements(driver, this);
    }
```

The `initElements()` method takes the driver object created in the test and initializes the elements declared in the `BmiCalcPage` class. We can then directly call the methods on these elements, as follows:

```
// Set Height
bmiCalcPage.setHeight("181");

// Set Weight
bmiCalcPage.setWeight("80");

// Click on Calculate button
bmiCalcPage.calculateBmi();
```

The FindBy annotations

Finding elements using the `name` or `id` attributes may not always work and we might need to use advanced locator strategies such as XPath or CSS selectors. Using the `FindBy` annotation, we can locate the elements within the `PageFactory` class, as follows:

```
@FindBy(id = "heightCMS")
public WebElement heightField;
```

We declared a public member for the height element and used the `@FindBy` annotation, specifying the `id` as a locator for finding this element on the page.

The CacheLookUp attribute

One downside to using the `@FindBy` annotation is that every time we call a method on the `WebElement` object, the driver will go and find it on the current page again. This is useful in applications where elements are dynamically loaded, or AJAX-heavy applications.

However, in applications where we know that the element is always going to be there and stay the same without any change, it would be handy if we could cache the element once we find it. In order to do this, we use the `@CacheLookUp` annotation along with the `@FindBy` annotation, as follows:

```
@FindBy(id = "heightCMS")
@CacheLookup
public WebElement heightField;
```

This tells the `PageFactory.initElements()` method to cache the element once it's located. Tests work faster with cached elements when these elements are used repeatedly.

Using the PageFactory class for exposing an operation on a page

In the previous recipe, we created the `BmiCalcPage` class, which provides elements from the BMI Calculator page to the test. Along with elements, we define operations or behaviors on a page. In the BMI Calculator application, we are calculating the BMI by entering height and weight values. We can create an operation named `calculateBmi` and call it directly in a test, instead of calling individual elements and operations.

In this recipe, let's refine the `BmiCalcPage` class. And instead of elements, let's provide the operations that are supported on the page, and some common properties. We will also move the WebDriver instance of the test to the `BmiCalcPage` class to make the test generic.

Getting ready

Identify operations that will be required in a test and can be exposed from a page. This recipe uses the `BmiCalcPage` class created in the previous recipe.

How to do it...

Let's modify the `BmiCalcPage` class created in the previous recipe and refactor it a bit to provide operations and properties to the test through the following steps:

1. Make the page's elements private in the `BmiCalPage` class for better encapsulation. Also, add an instance variable of the `WebDriver` class and a string variable for the URL of the page, as follows:

```
package com.secookbook.examples.chapter08.tests;

import org.openqa.selenium.WebDriver;
import org.openqa.selenium.chrome.ChromeDriver;
import org.openqa.selenium.WebElement;
import org.openqa.selenium.support.PageFactory;

public class BmiCalcPage {

    private WebElement heightCMS;
    private WebElement weightKg;
    private WebElement Calculate;
    private WebElement bmi;
    private WebElement bmi_category;
    private WebDriver driver;
    private String url = "http://dl.dropbox.com/u/55228056/
bmicalculator.html";
}
```

2. Update the `BmiCalcPage` class constructor so that it initializes the WebDriver instance, as follows:

```
public BmiCalcPage() {
    driver = new ChromeDriver();
    PageFactory.initElements(driver, this);
}
```

3. Add the `load()` and `close` methods to the `BmiCalcPage` class, as follows:

```
public void load() {
    this.driver.get(url);
}
public void close() {
    this.driver.close();
}
```

4. Add the `calculateBmi()` method to the `BmiCalcPage` class, as follows:

```
public void calculateBmi(String height, String weight) {
    heightCMS.sendKeys(height);
    weightKg.sendKeys(weight);
    Calculate.click();
}
```

5. Add the `getBmi` and `getBmiCategory()` methods to the `BmiCalcPage` class, as follows:

```
public String getBmi() {
    return bmi.getAttribute("value");
}

public String getBmiCategory() {
    return bmi_category.getAttribute("value");
}
```

6. Finally, create a test that will use the methods defined in the `BmiCalcPage` class to test the BMI Calculator page, as follows:

```
package com.secookbook.examples.chapter08.tests;

import org.junit.Test;

import static org.junit.Assert.*;
import seleniumcookbook.tests.pageobjects.*;

public class BmiCalculatorTests {

@Test
```

```
public void testBmiCalculation()
{
  //Create an instance of Bmi Calculator Page class
  //and provide the driver
  BmiCalcPage bmiCalcPage = new BmiCalcPage();

  //Open the Bmi Calculator Page
  bmiCalcPage.load();

  //Calculate the Bmi by supplying Height and Weight values
  bmiCalcPage.calculateBmi("181", "80");

  //Verify Bmi & Bmi Category values
  assertEquals("24.4", bmiCalcPage.getBmi());
  assertEquals("Normal", bmiCalcPage.getBmiCategory());

  //Close the Bmi Calculator Page
  bmiCalcPage.close();
}
```

How it works...

In this example, the `BmiCalcPage` class defines various methods for loading, closing the page, calculation functionality, and providing access to elements as properties to the test. This simplifies the test development by creating a layer of abstraction, hiding the internals of a page, and exposing only the operations and fields needed for testing from the page.

When any change happens to the structure or behavior of the page, only the `BmiCalcPage` class will be refactored, while the test will remain intact.

In this example, we created the `load()` method, which navigates the application using the URL, as follows:

```
public void load() {
    this.driver.get(url);
}
```

Using this approach, we can also expose the elements as properties, which provide specific attributes, such as the `value` attribute, instead of exposing elements fully. For example, the `getBmi()` method provides only the `value` attribute of the `bmi` label to the test, as follows:

```
public String getBmi() {
    return bmi.getAttribute("value");
}
```

Selenium WebDriver provides a very neat and clean way to implement the Page Object model.

Using the LoadableComponent class

We can implement the objects of the Page Object model using the `LoadableComponent` class of Selenium WebDriver. This helps in building a robust Page Object that provides a standard way to ensure that the page is loaded and that the page load issues are easy to debug.

In this recipe, we will further refactor the `BmiCalcPage` class created in the previous recipes and extend it as a loadable component.

Getting ready

This recipe uses the `BmiCalcPage` class created in the previous recipe.

How to do it...

To implement an object of the Page Object model as the `LoadableComponent` class, we need to extend it from the `LoadableComponent` base class, as shown in the following example:

```
package com.secookbook.examples.chapter08.pageobjects;

import org.openqa.selenium.WebDriver;
import org.openqa.selenium.WebElement;
import org.openqa.selenium.support.PageFactory;
import org.openqa.selenium.support.ui.LoadableComponent;
import static org.junit.Assert.*;

public class BmiCalcPage extends LoadableComponent<BmiCalcPage> {

    private WebElement heightCMS;
    private WebElement weightKg;
    private WebElement calculate;
    private WebElement bmi;
    private WebElement bmiCategory;

    private WebDriver driver;

    private String url =
"http://cookbook.seleniumacademy.com/bmicalculator.html";
    private String title = "BMI Calculator";

    public BmiCalcPage(WebDriver driver) {
        this.driver = driver;
```

```
      PageFactory.initElements(driver, this);
    }

    @Override
    protected void load() {
      this.driver.get(url);
    }

    @Override
    protected void isLoaded() throws Error {
      assertTrue("Bmi Calculator page not loaded",
          driver.getTitle().equals(title));
    }

    public void calculateBmi(String height, String weight) {
      heightCMS.sendKeys(height);
      weightKg.sendKeys(weight);
      calculate.click();
    }

    public String getBmi() {
      return bmi.getAttribute("value");
    }

    public String getBmiCategory() {
      return bmiCategory.getAttribute("value");
    }
  }
}
```

Finally, in the test, change the call of the `bmiCalcPage.load()` method to the `bmiCalcPage.get()` method, as follows:

```
package com.secookbook.examples.chapter08.tests;

import org.junit.After;
import org.junit.Before;
import org.junit.Test;
import org.openqa.selenium.WebDriver;
import org.openqa.selenium.chrome.ChromeDriver;

import static org.junit.Assert.*;

import
com.secookbook.examples.chapter08.pageobjects.BmiCalcPage;
```

```
public class BmiCalculatorTests {

  private WebDriver driver;

  @Before
  public void setUp() {
    driver = new ChromeDriver();
  }

  @Test
  public void testBmiCalculation() {
    // Create an instance of Bmi Calculator Page class
    // and provide the driver
    BmiCalcPage bmiCalcPage = new BmiCalcPage(driver);

    // Open the Bmi Calculator Page
    bmiCalcPage.get();

    // Calculate the Bmi by supplying Height and Weight values
    bmiCalcPage.calculateBmi("181", "80");

    // Verify Bmi & Bmi Category values
    assertEquals("24.4", bmiCalcPage.getBmi());
    assertEquals("Normal", bmiCalcPage.getBmiCategory());
  }

  @After
  public void tearDown() {
    driver.quit();
  }
}
```

How it works...

By extending the object of the Page Object model with the `LoadableComponent` base class, we overrode the `load()` and `isLoaded()` methods to the `BmiCalcPage` class.

The `load()` method will load the URL of the page we encapsulated in the Page Object, and when we create the instance of this Page Object in a test, we call the `get()` method on the `BmiCalcPage` class, which will in turn call the `load()` method, as follows:

```
BmiCalcPage bmiCalcPage = new BmiCalcPage(driver);
bmiCalcPage.get();
```

The `isLoaded()` method will verify that the indented page is loaded by the `load()` method.

Implementing nested Page Object instances

So far, we explored a very simple Page Object implementation for a single page web application. We can use the Page Object model to implement the objects of a page in a complex web application to simplify the testing.

In this recipe, we will create the objects of the Page Object model for the search functionality in an e-commerce application found at `http://demo.magentocommerce.com/`. We can implement a Page Object model even if the specific functionality is not a page of its own.

Each page of the application provides the user with the ability to search for products on the site by entering a query and hitting the search button. When a search query is submitted, the application returns a new page with a list of products matching the search query. Using the approach described in this recipe, we can build a more modular framework as shown in following diagram:

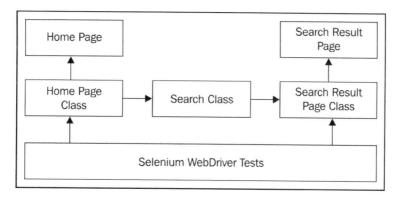

In this recipe, we will create this nested hierarchy, where the `HomePage` class implements the `Search` class, which in turn returns an object of the `SearchResults` class to the test.

Getting ready

Identify the page and logical relationship between pages to build a nested component set.

How to do it...

To implement nested Page Object instances, perform the following steps:

1. Create the `Browser` class, which will provide a static and shared WebDriver instance for all the pages, as follows:

```
package com.secookbook.examples.chapter08.pageobjects;

import org.openqa.selenium.WebDriver;
import org.openqa.selenium.chrome.ChromeDriver;

public class Browser {

  private static WebDriver driver = new ChromeDriver();

  public static WebDriver driver() {
    return driver;
  }

  public static void open(String url) {
    driver.get(url);
  }

  public static void close() {
    driver.quit();
  }
}
```

2. Create the `HomePage` class, which allows the test to navigate to the home page of the application. It also provides access to the `Search` class, which is shared among the various pages of the application, as follows:

```
package com.secookbook.examples.chapter08.pageobjects;

import org.openqa.selenium.WebDriver;
import org.openqa.selenium.support.PageFactory;
import org.openqa.selenium.support.ui.LoadableComponent;

import static org.junit.Assert.*;

public class HomePage extends LoadableComponent<HomePage> {

  private WebDriver driver;
```

```java
static String url = "http://demo.magentocommerce.com/";
private static String title = "Madison Island";

public HomePage(WebDriver driver) {
  this.driver = driver;
  PageFactory.initElements(driver, this);
}

@Override
public void load() {
  Browser.open(url);
}

@Override
public void isLoaded() {
  assertEquals(title, driver.getTitle());
}

public Search Search() {
  Search search = new Search(driver);
  return search;
}
}
```

3. Create the `Search` class. This class provides all the objects of the Page Object model to search for products in the application, as follows:

```java
package com.secookbook.examples.chapter08.pageobjects;

import org.openqa.selenium.WebDriver;
import org.openqa.selenium.WebElement;
import org.openqa.selenium.support.FindBy;
import org.openqa.selenium.support.PageFactory;

public class Search {

  private WebDriver driver;

  private WebElement search;

  @FindBy(css = "button.button")
  private WebElement searchButton;

  public Search(WebDriver driver) {
    this.driver = driver;
```

```
      PageFactory.initElements(driver, this);
   }

   public SearchResults searchInStore(String query) {
      search.sendKeys(query);
      searchButton.click();
      return new SearchResults(driver, query);
   }
}
```

4. Create the `SearchResult` class, which is nested in the `Search` class. The `SearchResult` class represents the results page when the user submits a search query, as discussed previously. The `SearchResult` class also provides access to the `Search` class so that users can search again for a different query. This is done as follows:

```
package com.secookbook.examples.chapter08.pageobjects;

import java.util.ArrayList;
import java.util.List;

import org.openqa.selenium.By;
import org.openqa.selenium.WebDriver;
import org.openqa.selenium.WebElement;
import org.openqa.selenium.support.PageFactory;
import org.openqa.selenium.support.ui.LoadableComponent;

import static org.junit.Assert.*;

public class SearchResults extends LoadableComponent<SearchResul
ts> {

   private WebDriver driver;
   private String query;

   public SearchResults(WebDriver driver, String query) {
      this.driver = driver;
      PageFactory.initElements(driver, this);
   }

   @Override
   public void isLoaded() {
      assertEquals("Search results for: '" + this.query +
"'", driver.getTitle());
   }
```

```java
    public List<String> getProducts() {
      List<String> products = new ArrayList<String>();
      List<WebElement> productList = driver.findElements(
          By.cssSelector("ul.products-grid > li"));

      for (WebElement item : productList)  {
         products.add(item.findElement(By.cssSelector("h2 >
a")).getText());
      }
      return products;
    }

    public Search Search() {
      Search search = new Search(driver);
      return search;
    }

    @Override
    protected void load() {
      // TODO Auto-generated method stub
    }
}
```

5. Finally, create a test which tests the search functionality from the home page of the application, as follows:

```java
package com.secookbook.examples.chapter08.tests;

import org.junit.Test;

import com.secookbook.examples.chapter08.pageobjects.Browser;
import com.secookbook.examples.chapter08.pageobjects.HomePage;
import com.secookbook.examples.chapter08.pageobjects.
SearchResults;

import static org.junit.Assert.*;

public class SearchTest {

  @Test
  public void testProductSearch() {
    try {
      // Create an instance of Home page
      HomePage homePage = new HomePage(Browser.driver());
```

```
        // Navigate to the Home page
        homePage.get();

        // Search for 'phones', the searchInStore method will return
        // SerchResults
        SearchResults searchResult = homePage.Search().
    searchInStore(
            "phones");

        // Verify there are 2 products available with this search
        assertEquals(2, searchResult.getProducts().size());
        assertTrue(searchResult.getProducts().contains(
            "MADISON OVEREAR HEADPHONES"));
      } finally {
        Browser.close();
      }
    }
  }
```

How it works...

The test starts by creating an instance of the HomePage class. As you can see, the application home page provides the user with the ability to search the site. In a similar way, the HomePage class provides the ability to search by using the Search class, as follows:

```
HomePage homePage = new HomePage(Browser.driver());
homePage.get();
SearchResults searchResult = homePage.Search().searchInStore(
    "phones");
```

The searchInStore() method of the Search class takes the query string as arguments and interacts with the search form to send the query. It returns the SearchResults class as a page. The SearchResults class provides a list of products that match the query back to the test using the getProducts() method, as follows:

```
public List<String> getProducts() {
   List<String> products = new ArrayList<String>();
   List<WebElement> productList = driver.findElements(
      By.cssSelector("ul.products-grid > li"));

   for (WebElement item : productList)  {
     products.add(item.findElement(By.cssSelector("h2 >
a")).getText());
   }
   return products;
}
```

The test can verify the number of products as well as the names of the products by checking the return value of the `getProducts()` method, as follows:

```
assertEquals(2, searchResult.getProducts().size());
assertTrue(searchResult.getProducts().contains(
    "MADISON OVEREAR HEADPHONES"));
```

Using the nested objects of the Page Object model, we can build a logical chain of pages within an application and build a robust and maintainable test automation framework.

See also

▸ The *Using the LoadableComponent class* recipe

Implementing the Page Object model in .NET

Similar to Java bindings, Selenium WebDriver provides the `PageFactory` class in .NET bindings to implement the Page Object model.

In this recipe, we will implement the Page Object model for the BMI Calculator page using the `PageFactory` class in C#.

Getting ready

We need to identify the locators that will be needed to locate the elements uniquely.

How to do it...

To implement Page Object model .NET, perform the following steps:

1. Define a class for the Page Object model by creating a new C# class with the name of the page. In this example, we will create the page's object for the BMI Calculator application:

```
using System;
using OpenQA.Selenium;
using OpenQA.Selenium.Chrome;
using OpenQA.Selenium.Support.PageObjects;

namespace PageFactoryTests
{
    public class BmiCalcPage
    {
```

```
        static string Url = " http://cookbook.seleniumacademy.com/
bmicalculator.html";
        private static string Title = "BMI Calculator";

        [FindsBy(How = How.Id, Using = "heightCMS")]
        [CacheLookup]
        private IWebElement HeightField;

        [FindsBy(How = How.Id, Using = "weightKg")]
        private IWebElement WeightField;

        [FindsBy(How = How.Id, Using = "Calculate")]
        private IWebElement CalculateButton;

        [FindsBy(How = How.Name, Using = "bmi")]
        private IWebElement BmiField;

        [FindsBy(How = How.Name, Using = "bmi_category")]
        private IWebElement BmiCategoryField;

        private IWebDriver driver;

        public BmiCalcPage() {
            driver = new ChromeDriver(@"C:\ChromeDriver");
            PageFactory.InitElements(driver, this);
        }

        public void Load()
        {
            driver.Navigate().GoToUrl(Url);
        }

        public void Close()
        {
            driver.Close();
        }

        public bool IsLoaded
        {
            get { return driver.Title.Equals(Title); }
        }
```

```
        public void CalculateBmi(String height, String
weight)
        {
            HeightField.SendKeys(height);
            WeightField.SendKeys(weight);
            CalculateButton.Click();
        }

        public String Bmi
        {
            get { return BmiField.GetAttribute("value"); }
        }

        public String BmiCategory
        {
            get { return BmiCategoryField.GetAttribute("value"); }
        }
    }
}
```

2. Using the `BmiCalcPage` class, let's create a test for the calculation feature, as follows:

```
using NUnit.Framework;

namespace PageFactoryTests
{
    public class BmiCalcTests
    {
        [TestCase]
        public void TestBmiCalculator()
        {
            BmiCalcPage bmiCalcPage = new BmiCalcPage();
            bmiCalcPage.Load();
              Assert.IsTrue(bmiCalcPage.IsLoaded);
            bmiCalcPage.CalculateBmi("181", "80");
            Assert.AreEqual("24.4", bmiCalcPage.Bmi);
            Assert.AreEqual("Normal",
bmiCalcPage.BmiCategory);
            bmiCalcPage.Close();
        }
    }
}
```

How it works...

In this example, the `BmiCalcPage` class provides various operations and properties from the BMI Calculator page to the test. The elements on the page are defined as instances of the `IWebDriver` interface with a `FindsBy` annotation, as follows:

```
[FindsBy(How = How.Id, Using = "heightCMS")]
private IWebElement HeightField;
```

When the page is initialized by the `PageFactory.InitElements()` method, these annotations are used to search the elements on the page.

The `BmiCalcPage` class implements methods to open and close the BMI Calculator page. This will provide a high level of abstraction to the test.

The `BmiCalcPage` class also implements the `IsLoaded` property, which will tell a test if the BMI Calculator page is loaded into the browser. This class also defines properties for the `Bmi` and `BmiCategory` fields, which provide values from these fields to test rather than complete access to the underlying elements, as follows:

```
public bool IsLoaded
{
    get { return driver.Title.Equals(Title); }
}

public String Bmi
{
    get { return BmiField.GetAttribute("value"); }
}

public String BmiCategory
{
    get { return BmiCategoryField.GetAttribute("value"); }
}
```

It also provides a `CalculateBmi()` method, which takes the height and weight as an argument and interacts with underlying elements to perform actions.

Implementing the Page Object model in Python

Implementing the Page Object model in Python is similar to what we have done previously in Java and C#. The Selenium WebDriver Python bindings provide support for objects of the Page Object model.

In this recipe, we will implement the Page Object model using Python bindings.

Getting ready

Before implementing the Page Object model for Python bindings, we must do the following:

- ▸ Identify pages and the elements from the application that will be required in the tests
- ▸ Define locators that will be needed to identify the elements uniquely

How to do it...

To implement the Page Object model in Python, follow these steps:

1. Define a class for the Page Object model by creating a Python script with the name of the page. In this example, we will be creating a Page Object model for the main page of the BMI Calculator application, as follows:

```python
class BmiCalcPage(object):
    def __init__(self, driver):
        self._driver = driver
        self._url = '
http://cookbook.seleniumacademy.com/bmicalculator.html'
        self._title = 'BMI Calculator'

    @property
    def is_loaded(self):
        return self._driver.title == self._title

    @property
    def bmi(self):
        bmi_field = self._driver.find_element_by_id('bmi')
        return bmi_field.get_attribute('value')

    @property
    def bmi_category(self):
```

```
        bmi_category_field =
self._driver.find_element_by_id('bmi_category')
        return bmi_category_field.get_attribute('value')

    def open(self):
        self._driver.get(self._url)

    def calculate(self, height, weight):
        height_field =
self._driver.find_element_by_id('heightCMS')
        weight_field =
self._driver.find_element_by_id('weightKg')
        calc_button =
self._driver.find_element_by_id('Calculate')

        height_field.send_keys(height)
        weight_field.send_keys(weight)
        calc_button.click()
```

2. Using the `BmiCalcPage` object, let's create a test for the calculation feature, as follows:

```
import unittest
from selenium.webdriver.chrome.webdriver import WebDriver
from bmi_calc_page import bmicalcpage

class BmiCalcTest(unittest.TestCase):
    def test_calc(self):
        driver = WebDriver()
        bmi_calc = bmicalcpage(driver)
        bmi_calc.open()
        self.assertEqual(True, bmi_calc.is_loaded)
        bmi_calc.calculate('181','80')
        self.assertEqual('24.4', bmi_calc.bmi)
        self.assertEqual('Normal', bmi_calc.bmi_category)
        driver.close()

if __name__ == '__main__':
    unittest.main()
```

How it works...

Implementing the Page Object model in Python is relatively simple. The Page Object model can be implemented by creating classes, defining methods and properties, and only exposing the functionality from the application page that needed it for testing.

In this example, the `BmiCalcPage` class is defined to represent the BMI Calculator application's main page. This class needs an instance of WebDriver through which it will interact with the main page, as follows:

```
class BmiCalcPage(object):
    def __init__(self, driver):
        self._driver = driver
```

The `bmicalcpage` class implements the `is_loaded` property, which will tell tests if the BMI Calculator page is loaded into the browser. This class also defines properties for the `bmi` and `bmi_category` fields, which provide values from these fields to test, rather than a complete access to the underlying elements:

```
@property
def is_loaded(self):
    return self._driver.title == self._title

@property
def bmi(self):
    bmi_field = self._driver.find_element_by_id('bmi')
    return bmi_field.get_attribute('value')

@property
def bmi_category(self):
    bmi_category_field = self._driver.find_element_by_id('bmi_category')
    return bmi_category_field.get_attribute('value')
```

It provides the `calculate()` method, which takes the height and weight as an argument and interacts with underlying elements to perform actions.

The `BmiCalcPage` class also implements methods to open and close the BMI Calculator page. This will provide a high level of abstraction to the test, hiding the underlying details of page and elements. This makes writing tests, in a kind of domain-specific language, easier and faster.

Implementing the Page Object model in Ruby using the page-object gem

While developing tests in Ruby, we can use the page-object gem to implement the Page Object model within the tests. The page-object gem provides simple features with which to build the objects of a Page Object, along with **Watir WebDriver**.

In this recipe, we will see how to use the page-object gem to implement the Page Object model for the BMI Calculator's main page.

Getting ready

You need to download and install the page-object gem with the help of the following command:

```
gem install page-object
```

How to do it...

To implement the Page Object model in Ruby using the page-object gem, perform the following steps:

1. Define a class for the Page Object model by creating a Ruby script with the name of the page. In this example, we will be creating a Page Object model for the main page of the BMI Calculator application and including the page-object module:

```ruby
require 'page-object'

class BmiCalcPage
    include PageObject

    text_field(:height, :id => 'heightCMS')
    text_field(:weight, :id => 'weightKg')
    button(:calculate, :value => 'Calculate')

    text_field(:bmi, :id => 'bmi')
    text_field(:bmi_category, :id => 'bmi_category')

    def calculate_bmi(height, weight)
        self.height = height
        self.weight = weight
        calculate
    end
```

```
    def open()
        @browser.get '
http://cookbook.seleniumacademy.com/bmicalculator.html'
    end
end
```

2. Using the object of the `BmiCalcPage` class, create a test for the calculation feature, as follows:

```
require 'rubygems'
require 'watir-webdriver'
require 'test/unit'
require_relative 'bmicalcpage.rb'

class BmiCalcTest < Test::Unit::TestCase
    def test_bmi_calculation
        @driver = Selenium::WebDriver.for :chrome
        bmi_calc = BmiCalcPage.new(@driver)
        bmi_calc.open()
        bmi_calc.calculate_bmi('181','80')
        assert_equal '24.4', bmi_calc.bmi
        assert_equal 'Normal', bmi_calc.bmi_category
        @driver.close()
    end
end
```

How it works...

We can use the Page Object model implemented with the page-object gem by creating an instance of the `BmiCalcPage` class and passing the browser as an argument to the constructor. The rest of the magic is performed by the page-object gem.

While defining the elements, we need to specify the type of element and the locator, as follows:

```
text_field(:Height, :id => 'heightCMS')
```

The page-object gem adds a few more methods automatically to these objects at runtime. For example, we created an element for the `Calculate` button in the Page Object model, as follows:

```
button(:Calculate, :value => 'Calculate')
```

The page-object gem creates a method called `calculate`, which will click the `Calculate` button when called from the `calculate_bmi()` method, as follows:

```
def calculate_bmi(height, weight)
    self.height = height
    self.weight = weight
    calculate
end
```

You can find more information about the page-object gem API at `http://rubydoc.info/github/cheezy/page-object/master/PageObject/Accessors`.

9

Extending Selenium

In this chapter, we will cover:

- ▸ Creating an extension class for web tables
- ▸ Creating an extension for the jQueryUI tab widget
- ▸ Implementing an extension for the WebElement object to set the element attribute values
- ▸ Implementing an extension for the WebElement object to highlight elements
- ▸ Creating an object map for Selenium tests
- ▸ Capturing screenshots of elements in Selenium WebDriver
- ▸ Comparing images in Selenium
- ▸ Measuring performance with the Navigation Timing API

Introduction

Selenium WebDriver provides a highly flexible and robust API to extend the features and commands and add customization to build a scalable test automation framework. This chapter covers some of the important recipes to extend Selenium WebDriver for various practical scenarios.

In this chapter, we will write Selenium WebDriver extensions that support web tables, object maps, and image comparison features.

We will also build an extension for **jQuery UI** control. You can use this pattern to implement support for a third-party or the custom controls used in your application by hiding technical details from the tests. This makes test development a lot easier.

Creating an extension class for web tables

Selenium WebDriver provides the `WebElement` interface to work with various types of HTML elements. It also provides helper classes to work with the `Select` element. However, there is no built-in class to support the web tables or the `<table>` elements. In this recipe, we will implement a helper class for web tables. Using this class, we will retrieve properties and perform some basic operations on a web table element.

Getting ready

Create a new Java class `WebTable.java`, which we will use to implement support for the table elements.

How to do it...

Let's implement the web table extension code with `WebTable.java` using the following steps:

1. Add a constructor for the `WebTable` class, and for the setter and getter property methods as well. The `WebTable` constructor will accept the `WebElement` object, as shown in the following code:

```
package com.secookbook.examples.chapter09;

import org.openqa.selenium.NoSuchElementException;
import org.openqa.selenium.WebElement;
import org.openqa.selenium.By;

import java.util.List;

public class WebTable {

  private WebElement _webTable;

  public WebTable(WebElement webTable) {
    set_webTable(webTable);
  }

  public WebElement get_webTable() {
    return _webTable;
  }

  public void set_webTable(WebElement _webTable) {
    this._webTable = _webTable;
  }
}
```

2. Now, add methods to retrieve rows and columns from a table, as shown in following code:

```java
public int getRowCount() {
    List<WebElement> tableRows =
        _webTable.findElements(By.tagName("tr"));
    return tableRows.size();
}


public int getColumnCount() {
    List<WebElement> tableRows =
        _webTable.findElements(By.tagName("tr"));
    WebElement headerRow = tableRows.get(0);

    List<WebElement> tableCols =
        headerRow.findElements(By.tagName("td"));
    return tableCols.size();
}
```

3. Add a method `getCellData()` to retrieve data from a specific cell of the table:

```java
public String getCellData(int rowIdx, int colIdx) {
    List<WebElement> tableRows =
        _webTable.findElements(By.tagName("tr"));
    WebElement currentRow = tableRows.get(rowIdx-1);
    List<WebElement> tableCols =
        currentRow.findElements(By.tagName("td"));
    WebElement cell = tableCols.get(colIdx-1);
    return cell.getText();
}
```

4. Add a method to retrieve the cell editor element; this is useful while working with editable cells:

```java
public WebElement getCellEditor(int rowIdx, int colIdx, int
editorIdx) throws NoSuchElementException {
  try {
    List<WebElement> tableRows =
_webTable.findElements(By.tagName("tr"));
    WebElement currentRow = tableRows.get(rowIdx-1);
    List<WebElement> tableCols =
currentRow.findElements(By.tagName("td"));
    WebElement cell = tableCols.get(colIdx-1);
    WebElement cellEditor =
cell.findElements(By.tagName("input")).get(editorIdx);
    return cellEditor;
  } catch (NoSuchElementException e) {
```

```
        throw new NoSuchElementException("Failed to get cell
    editor");
      }
    }
```

5. Let's create a test on a shopping cart page using a newly created `WebTable` class:

```java
package com.secookbook.examples.chapter09;

import org.openqa.selenium.WebDriver;
import org.openqa.selenium.firefox.FirefoxDriver;
import org.openqa.selenium.WebElement;
import org.openqa.selenium.By;

import static org.junit.Assert.*;

import org.junit.After;
import org.junit.Before;
import org.junit.Test;

public class WebTableTests {
  WebDriver driver;

  @Before
  public void setUp() {
    // Create a new instance of the Firefox driver
    driver = new FirefoxDriver();
    driver.get("http:// cookbook.seleniumacademy.com/Locators.
html");
  }

  @Test
  public void testWebTableTest() {
    // Get the table element as WebTable instance using CSS
Selector
    WebTable table = new WebTable(driver.findElement(By
        .cssSelector("div.cart-info table")));

    // Verify that it has three rows
    assertEquals(3, table.getRowCount());
    // Verify that it has six columns
    assertEquals(5, table.getColumnCount());
    // Verify that specified value exists in second cell of
third row
    assertEquals("iPhone", table.getCellData(3, 1));
```

```
    // Get in cell editor and enter some value
    WebElement cellEdit = table.getCellEditor(3, 3, 0);
    cellEdit.clear();
    cellEdit.sendKeys("2");
}

@After
public void tearDown() {
    // Close the browser
    driver.quit();
}
}
```

How it works...

The `WebTable` class accepts a `WebElement` object and extends it to provide table-specific properties and operations.

To retrieve the number of rows from a table, we locate the `<tr>` elements from the `_webTable` object. We used the `tagName()` method of the `By` class and collected all the `<tr>` elements as a list of `WebElement` objects. Using the `size()` method, we can find out how may rows are available in the table element, as shown in the following code:

```
List<WebElement> tableRows =
_webTable.findElements(By.tagName("tr"));
```

Similarly, we inspected a number of `<td>` elements in the first row of the table (normally the header) to retrieve the number of columns available in the table element, as shown in the following code:

```
List<WebElement> tableRows =
_webTable.findElements(By.tagName("tr"));
    WebElement headerRow = tableRows.get(0);
List<WebElement> tableCols =
headerRow.findElements(By.tagName("td"));
```

To retrieve data from a specific cell, the `getCellData()` function accepts row and column number arguments. First, it gets the `<tr>` element from the list by using the row argument as an index, as shown in the following code:

```
List<WebElement> tableRows =
_webTable.findElements(By.tagName("tr"));
WebElement currentRow = tableRows.get(rowIdx-1);
```

Then, it retrieves the `<td>` elements from `currentRow` using column argument as an index, as shown in following code:

```
List<WebElement> tableCols =
currentRow.findElements(By.tagName("td"));
    WebElement cell = tableCols.get(colIdx-1);
```

To retrieve the text, it calls the `cell` object's `getText()` method, as shown in following code:

```
    return cell.getText();
```

Often we need to test tables with editable cells. These could be dynamic tables based on database values. The `getCellEditor()` method of the `WebTable` object provides access to the first input element of the cell. We can then use this input element and perform actions such as `Click()` or `SendKeys()`. The `getCellEditor()` method uses a similar method to reach the desired cell and then finds the first input element inside a cell, that is, a `<td>` element, using the `ByTagName` locator strategy, as shown in the following code:

```
WebElement cellEditor =
cell.findElements(By.tagName("input")).get(0);
```

Creating an extension for the jQueryUI tab widget

jQuery UI is a jQuery user-interface library. It provides interactions, widgets, effects, and theming to build rich Internet applications. jQuery UI provides a number of UI widgets such as **accordion**, **datepicker**, **slider**, **dialog**, and **tabs**.

These widgets are built using a number of low-level HTML elements, such as DIVs, unordered lists, and input tags. While Selenium can recognize these elements individually, we can build support for Selenium to recognize these controls as native jQuery UI widgets. We can then perform native operations supported by jQuery framework.

In this recipe, we will implement support for the jQuery UI tab widget.

Getting ready

Visit `http://jqueryui.com/demos/tabs/` to understand more about the jQuery UI tabs widget. Explore how they are implemented along with various options, methods, and events related to this widget.

How to do it...

Similar to the `WebTable` extension class we created earlier, we will create a `JQueryUITab` class to represent the tab widget in Selenium by following the ensuing steps:

1. First, create a `JQueryUITab` class with setter and getter properties:

```
package com.secookbook.examples.chapter09;

import org.openqa.selenium.By;
import org.openqa.selenium.JavascriptExecutor;
import org.openqa.selenium.WebElement;
import org.openqa.selenium.internal.WrapsDriver;

import java.util.List;

public class JQueryUITab {

    private WebElement _jQueryUITab;

    public JQueryUITab(WebElement jQueryUITab) {
        set_jQueryUITab(jQueryUITab);
    }

    public WebElement get_jQueryUITab() {
        return _jQueryUITab;
    }

    public void set_jQueryUITab(WebElement _jQueryUITab) {
        this._jQueryUITab = _jQueryUITab;
    }
}
```

2. Add a method to retrieve the count of tabs available on tab widget, as shown in the following code. We can use this to verify that the tab widget is displaying the expected number of tabs:

```
public int getTabCount() {
    List<WebElement> tabs =
    _jQueryUITab.findElements(By.cssSelector(".ui-tabs-nav >
li"));
    return tabs.size();
}
```

3. Add a method to get the name of the selected tab, using the following code:

```
public String getSelectedTab() {
  WebElement tab = _jQueryUITab.findElement(By
       .cssSelector(".ui-tabs-nav > li[class*='ui-tabs-
selected']"));
  return tab.getText();
}
```

4. Add a method to select a tab. We will pass the name of the tab that we want to select to this method by using the following code:

```
public void selectTab(String tabName) {
  int idx = 0;
  boolean found = false;
  List<WebElement> tabs = _jQueryUITab.findElements(By
       .cssSelector(".ui-tabs-nav > li"));

  for (WebElement tab : tabs) {
    if (tabName.equals(tab.getText().toString())) {
      WrapsDriver wrappedElement = (WrapsDriver)
_jQueryUITab;
      JavascriptExecutor driver = (JavascriptExecutor)
wrappedElement
            .getWrappedDriver();
      driver.executeScript(
          "jQuery(arguments[0]).tabs().
tabs('select',arguments[1]);",
          _jQueryUITab, idx);
      found = true;
      break;
    }
    idx++;
  }
  // Throw an exception if specified tab is not found
  if (found == false)
    throw new IllegalArgumentException("Could not find tab
'" + tabName
        + "'");
}
```

5. Let's implement the JQueryUITab class in a sample test, with the following code:

```
package com.secookbook.examples.chapter09;

import org.openqa.selenium.WebDriver;
import org.openqa.selenium.firefox.FirefoxDriver;
```

```java
import org.openqa.selenium.By;
import static org.junit.Assert.*;

import org.junit.After;
import org.junit.Before;
import org.junit.Test;

public class JQueryUITabWidgetTest {

  private WebDriver driver;

  @Before
  public void setUp() {
    driver = new FirefoxDriver();
    driver.get("http://
cookbook.seleniumacademy.com/jQueryUITabDemo.html");
  }

  @Test
  public void testjQueryUITabWidget() {

    JQueryUITab tab = new JQueryUITab(driver.findElement(By
        .cssSelector("div[id=MyTab][class^=ui-tabs]")));

    // Verify Tab Widget has 3 Tabs
    assertEquals(3, tab.getTabCount());

    // Verify Home Tab is selected
    assertEquals("Home", tab.getSelectedTab());

    // Select Options Tab and verify it is selected
    tab.selectTab("Options");
    assertEquals("Options", tab.getSelectedTab());

    // Select Admin Tab and verify it is selected
    tab.selectTab("Admin");
    assertEquals("Admin", tab.getSelectedTab());

    // Select Home Tab
    tab.selectTab("Home");
  }

  @After
  public void tearDown() {
```

```
        // Close the browser
        driver.quit();
    }
}
```

How it works...

The `JQueryUITab` class was ready for use in testing the tab widget. The `JQueryUITab` class accepts a `WebElement` object passed to its constructor. To retrieve the number of tabs in a tab widget, we passed the tab element. Internally, the Tab widget defines an unordered list for tab headers. We located these headers using the `cssSelector()` method of the `By` class in a `WebElement` list using the `findElements()` method. We got the count of the tabs by looking at the list size:

```
List<WebElement> tabs =
_jQueryUITab.findElements(By.cssSelector(".ui-tabs-nav > li"));
    return tabs.size();
```

To retrieve the selected tab name, we used a similar `cssSelector()` method with a filter to locate the `<li>` element whose class was `ui-tabs-selected`. When we select a tab in the tab widget, the jQuery framework adds all these class attributes to the `<li>` element internally, as shown in the following code:

```
WebElement tab = _jQueryUITab.findElement(By.cssSelector
(".ui-tabs-nav > li[class*='ui-tabs-selected']"));
return tab.getText();
```

Finally, to select a tab in the tab widget, we were required to execute the jQuery native API functions. The tab widget has a method to select a tab by its index. However, selecting a tab by its index may not be user-friendly. Therefore, we accept the name of the tab and then find out its index internally, using the following code:

```
int idx=0;
List<WebElement> tabs =
_jQueryUITab.findElements(By.cssSelector(".ui-tabs-nav > li"));
Iterator<WebElement> itr = tabs.iterator();
while(itr.hasNext()) {
    WebElement element = itr.next();
    if(tabName.equals(element.getText().toString()))
        break;
    idx++;
}
```

Then, we call the native jQuery API using `JavaScriptExecutor` and pass the index to the `select` method of the Tab widget, using the following code:

```
WrapsDriver wrappedElement = (WrapsDriver) _jQueryUITab;
JavascriptExecutor driver = (JavascriptExecutor)
wrappedElement.getWrappedDriver();
    driver.executeScript("jQuery(arguments[0]).tabs().tabs('select',ar
guments[1]);",_jQueryUITab,idx);
}
```

There's more...

Using a similar approach, we can also build support for other widgets in jQuery UI or other UI frameworks such as **Yahoo UI**, **Doojo**, and **GWT**. This provides a neat and clean way to work with custom widgets and UI controls.

Implementing an extension for the WebElement object to set the element attribute values

Setting an element's attribute can be useful in various situations where the test needs to manipulate properties of an element. For example, for a masked textbox, the `sendKeys()` method may not work well, and setting the value of the textbox will help to overcome these issues. The `WebElement` interface does not have a direct method that supports setting all types of attributes.

In this recipe, we will create an extension for the `WebElement` and provide a method to set the attribute value of an element at runtime.

Getting ready

Create a new Java class file for the `WebElementExtender.java` class. We will use this class to host all the extension methods for elements.

How to do it...

Add the `setAttribute()` method to the `WebElementExtender` class, as follows:

```
import org.openqa.selenium.JavascriptExecutor;
import org.openqa.selenium.WebElement;
import org.openqa.selenium.internal.WrapsDriver;
```

```
public class WebElementExtender {
    public static void setAttribute(WebElement element, String
    attributeName, String value)
    {
        WrapsDriver wrappedElement = (WrapsDriver) element;

        JavascriptExecutor driver = (JavascriptExecutor)
        wrappedElement.getWrappedDriver();
        driver.executeScript("arguments[0].setAttribute(arguments[1],
        arguments[2])", element, attributeName, value);
    }

}
```

How it works...

In the `setAttribute()` method, we created an object of `JavaScriptExecutor` and retrieved `WrappedDriver` of the `WebElement` object on which we wanted to call the `setAttribute()` method.

Using `JavaScriptExecutor`, we called the JavaScript `setAttribute()` method to set the attribute value of an element. In this example, the contents of an input element are cleared before calling the `SendKeys()` method. This can also be done by calling the `clear()` method of the `WebElement` class:

```
WebElement email = driver.findElement(By.id("email"));
WebElementExtender.setAttribute(userName, "value", "");
userName.sendKeys("test@test.com");
```

See also

▶ The *Implementing an extension for the WebElement object to highlight elements* recipe

Implementing an extension for the WebElement object to highlight elements

During the test execution, there is no way to highlight an element. This will help us to see what is actually going on in the browser. This method will slow down the tests a bit, but sometimes it's a useful way to debug tests.

In this recipe, we will create an extension for `WebElement` and provide the `highlight Elements()` method at runtime.

Getting ready

Create a new Java class file for the `WebElementExtender.java` class, or you can use the class created in the previous recipe.

How to do it...

Add the `highlightElement()` method to the `WebElementExtender` class, as follows:

```java
import org.openqa.selenium.JavascriptExecutor;
import org.openqa.selenium.WebElement;
import org.openqa.selenium.internal.WrapsDriver;

public class WebElementExtender {

    public static void highlightElement(WebElement element) {
        for (int i = 0; i < 5; i++) {
            WrapsDriver wrappedElement = (WrapsDriver) element;
            JavascriptExecutor driver = (JavascriptExecutor)
            wrappedElement.getWrappedDriver();
            driver.executeScript("arguments[0].setAttribute('style',
            arguments[1]);",
                        element, "color: green; border: 2px solid
yellow;");
            driver.executeScript("arguments[0].setAttribute('style',
            arguments[1]);",
                        element, "");
        }
    }
}
```

How it works...

In the `highlightElement()` method, we created an instance of the `JavaScriptExecutor` class and, from the element, got an instance of the `WrappedDriver` class on which we wanted to call the `highlightElement()` method.

Using the `JavaScriptExecutor` class, we called the JavaScript `setAttribute()` method to set the `style` attribute value to green and then back to original. We do this a few times using a loop. During execution, the element is highlighted with a green flash. Here is an example on using the `highlightElement()` method:

```java
WebElement userName = driver.findElement(By.id("username"));
WebElementExtender.highlightElement(userName);
userName.sendKeys("test_user");
```

This comes in very handy while debugging or visualizing the test progress.

See also

▶ The *Implementing an extension for the WebElement object to set the element attribute values* recipe

Creating an object map for Selenium tests

So far, we have seen how the Selenium WebDriver API needs locator information to find the elements on the page. When a large suite of tests is created, a lot of locator information is duplicated in the test code. It becomes difficult to manage locator details when the number of tests increases. If any changes happen in the element locator, we need to find all the tests that use this locator and update these tests. This becomes a maintenance nightmare.

One way to overcome this problem is to use page objects and create a repository of pages as reusable classes.

There is another way to overcome this problem—by using an object map. An object or a UI map is a mechanism that stores all the locators for a test suite in one place for easy modification when identifiers or paths to GUI elements change in the application under test. The test script then uses the object map to locate the elements to be tested.

Object maps help in making test script management much easier. When a locator needs to be edited, there is a central location for easily finding that object, rather than having to search through the test script code. Also, it allows changing the identifier in a single place, rather than having to make the change in multiple places within a test script, or for that matter, in multiple test scripts. The object map files can also be version-controlled.

In this recipe, we will implement the `ObjectMap` class to maintain locator details obtained from the tests.

Getting ready

Set up a new Java project for the `ObjectMap` class. This class will be used by Selenium tests as an extension to read the `ObjectMap` file.

How to do it...

Let's implement an object map to store the locators used in a test with the following steps:

1. We will create a properties file named `objectmap.properties`. We will add the locators in a key/value pair. The part before the equal-to sign (=) will be the key or the logical name of the element, and the part after will be the locator details, in the following format:

```
[logical_name]=[locator_type]>[locator_value]
```

The following code is an example of the object map for the BMI calculator page:

```
height_field=name>heightCMS
weight_field=id>weightKg
calculate_button=id>Calculate
bmi_field=id>bmi
```

2. Implement the `ObjectMap` class to read the property file and provide the locator information to the test:

```java
import java.io.FileInputStream;
import java.io.IOException;
import java.util.Properties;

public class ObjectMap {

    Properties properties;

    public ObjectMap(String mapFile)
    {
        properties = new Properties();
        try {
            FileInputStream in = new FileInputStream(mapFile);
            properties.load(in);
            in.close();
        }catch (IOException e) {
            System.out.println(e.getMessage());
        }

    }

}
```

3. Add a method to the `ObjectMap` class which will read the locator details from the properties file and create and return the locator using the `By` class, as shown in following code:

```java
public By getLocator(String logicalElementName) throws
Exception
{
    //Read value using the logical name as Key
    String locator =
properties.getProperty(logicalElementName);

    //Split the value which contains locator type and locator
value
    String locatorType = locator.split(">")[0];
```

```
      String locatorValue = locator.split(">")[1];


      //Return a instance of By class based on type of locator
      if(locatorType.toLowerCase().equals("id"))
        return By.id(locatorValue);
      else if(locatorType.toLowerCase().equals("name"))
        return By.name(locatorValue);
      else if((locatorType.toLowerCase().equals("classname"))
||
       (locatorType.toLowerCase().equals("class")))
        return By.className(locatorValue);
      else if((locatorType.toLowerCase().equals("tagname")) ||
       (locatorType.toLowerCase().equals("tag")))
        return By.className(locatorValue);
      else if((locatorType.toLowerCase().equals("linktext")) ||
       (locatorType.toLowerCase().equals("link")))
        return By.linkText(locatorValue);
      else if(locatorType.toLowerCase().equals("partiallinktext"))
        return By.partialLinkText(locatorValue);
      else if((locatorType.toLowerCase().equals("cssselector"))
||
       (locatorType.toLowerCase().equals("css")))
        return By.cssSelector(locatorValue);
      else if(locatorType.toLowerCase().equals("xpath"))
        return By.xpath(locatorValue);
      else
      throw new Exception("Locator type '" + locatorType + "'
not   defined!!");
      }
```

4. Finally, create a test that uses the property file to store the locator information, using the following code:

```
package com.secookbook.examples.chapter09;


import org.openqa.selenium.WebDriver;
import org.openqa.selenium.firefox.FirefoxDriver;
import org.openqa.selenium.WebElement;


import org.junit.*;
import static org.junit.Assert.assertEquals;


public class ObjectMapTest {

  private WebDriver driver;
  private ObjectMap map;
```

```java
  @Before
  public void setUp() throws Exception {
    // Create a new instance of the Firefox driver
    driver = new FirefoxDriver();
    driver.get("http:// cookbook.seleniumacademy.com/
bmicalculator.html");
  }


  @Test
  public void testBmiCalculator() {
    // Get the Object Map File
    map = new
ObjectMap("src/test/resources/objectmap/objectmap.propertie
s");

    // Get the Height element
    WebElement height =
driver.findElement(map.getLocator("height_field"));
    ;
    height.sendKeys("181");

    // Get the Weight element
    WebElement weight =
driver.findElement(map.getLocator("weight_field"));
    weight.sendKeys("80");

    // Click on the Calculate button
    WebElement calculateButton = driver.findElement(map
        .getLocator("calculate_button"));
    calculateButton.click();

    // Verify the Bmi
    WebElement bmi =
driver.findElement(map.getLocator("bmi_field"));
    assertEquals("24.4", bmi.getAttribute("value"));
  }

  @After
  public void tearDown() throws Exception {
    // Close the browser
    driver.quit();
  }
}
```

How it works...

First, we created a Java properties file with the key/value pair, storing a logical name for an element and locator value. The properties files are flat text files, and the `java.util.Properties` namespace provides the `Properties` class to access a property file:

```
properties = new Properties();
```

By passing a logical name or key to the `getProperty()` method of the `Properties` class, we can retrieve a value from the pair.

The `getLocator()` method uses the value returned by the `getProperty()` method and returns a matching `By` locator method, along with the value, to the test.

In the test, we created an instance of an object map and then passed the location of the property file, as shown in the following code:

```
map = new
ObjectMap("src/test/resources/objectmap/objectmap.properties");
```

We passed the locator value to the `findElement()` method by passing the logical name or key of the element to the `getLocator()` method of the `ObjectMap` class, as follows:

```
WebElement height =
driver.findElement(map.getLocator("height_field"));
```

We can have a single object map file to store all the locators and can use the same locators in multiple tests.

There's more...

Object maps can also be created in XML files. The following code is an example of an XML-based object map:

```xml
<elements>
  <element name="HeightField" locator_type="name"
locator_value="heightCMS"/>
  <element name="WeightField" locator_type="id"
locator_value="weightKg"/>
  <element name="CalculateButton" locator_type="xpath"
locator_value="//input[@value='Calculate']"/>
  <element name="BmiField" locator_type="id" locator_value="bmi"/>
  <element name="BmiCategoryField" locator_type="css"
locator_value="#bmi_category"/>
</elements>
```

The following code is the C# implementation of the `getLocator()` method:

```csharp
public By GetLocator(string locatorName)
{
  var element = from elements in _root.Elements("element")
          where elements.Attributes("name").First().Value ==
          locatorName
          select elements;
  try
  {
    string locatorType =
element.Attributes("locator_type").First().
    Value.ToString();
    string locatorValue =
element.Attributes("locator_value").First().
    Value.ToString();

    switch (locatorType.ToLower())
    {
      case "id":
        return By.Id(locatorValue);
      case "name":
        return By.Name(locatorValue);
      case "classname":
        return By.ClassName(locatorValue);
      case "linktext":
        return By.LinkText(locatorValue);
      case "partiallinktext":
        return By.PartialLinkText(locatorValue);
      case "css":
        return By.CssSelector(locatorValue);
      case "xpath":
        return By.XPath(locatorValue);
      case "tagname":
        return By.TagName(locatorValue);
      default:
        throw new Exception("Locator Type '" + locatorType + "'
        not supported!!");
    }
  }
  catch (Exception)
  {
    throw new Exception("Failed to generate locator for '" +
    locatorName + "'");
  }
}
```

A similar approach can be taken with other Selenium WebDriver language bindings, such as Java, Python, or Ruby.

Capturing screenshots of elements in the Selenium WebDriver

The `TakesScreenshot` interface captures the screenshot of the entire page, current window, visible portion of the page, or of the complete desktop window in their respective order as supported by the browser. It does not provide a way to capture an image of the specific element.

We can extend the screen capture functionality to capture images of `WebElement` using the Java Image API in addition to the `TakesScreenshot` interface.

In this recipe, we will implement a helper method to capture images of elements.

How to do it...

Let's implement the `captureElementPicture()` method to capture an image of `WebElement`. We will pass a `WebElement` instance to this method; the following code shows an example:

```java
public static File captureElementPicture(WebElement element)
        throws Exception {

    // Get the WrapsDriver of the WebElement
    WrapsDriver wrapsDriver = (WrapsDriver) element;

    // Get the entire Screenshot from the driver of passed
WebElement
    File screen = ((TakesScreenshot)
wrapsDriver.getWrappedDriver())
        .getScreenshotAs(OutputType.FILE);

    // Create an instance of Buffered Image from captured
screenshot
    BufferedImage img = ImageIO.read(screen);

    // Get the Width and Height of the WebElement using getSize()
    int width = element.getSize().getWidth();
    int height = element.getSize().getHeight();

    // Create a rectangle using Width and Height
    Rectangle rect = new Rectangle(width, height);

    // Get the Location of WebElement in a Point.
    // This will provide X & Y co-ordinates of the WebElement
```

```
Point p = element.getLocation();

// Create image by for element using its location and size.
// This will give image data specific to the WebElement
BufferedImage dest = img.getSubimage(p.getX(), p.getY(),
rect.width,
        rect.height);

// Write back the image data for element in File object
ImageIO.write(dest, "png", screen);

// Return the File object containing image data
return screen;
}
```

How it works...

When the `captureElementPicture()` method is called with `WebElement` as an argument, it gets the underlying `driver` instance of the element using the `WrapsDriver` class. Then it captures the screenshot of the page displayed in the driver using the `getScreenShotAs()` method of the `TakesScreenshot` interface using the location and size of the element. We will crop the image of the element from the image of the entire page.

In the following example, the `captureElementPicture()` method is used to capture the image of a `button` element:

```
@Test
public void testElementScreenshot() {
  WebElement searchButton = driver.findElement(By.name("btnK"));
  try {
    FileUtils.copyFile(
        WebElementExtender.captureElementPicture(searchButton),
        new File("target/searchButton.png"));
  } catch (Exception e) {
    e.printStackTrace();
  }
}
```

See also

▶ The *Capturing screenshots with Selenium WebDriver* recipe in *Chapter 4, Working with Selenium API*

Comparing images in Selenium

Many a time, our tests need image-based comparison. For example, verifying whether correct icons are displayed, verifying whether correct images are displayed in web pages, or comparing the baseline screen layout with the actual layout.

Selenium WebDriver does have features to capture screenshots or images from the application under test; however, it does not have the feature to compare the images.

In this recipe, we will create an extension class to compare images and use it in our Selenium tests.

Getting ready

Set up a new Java project for the `CompareUtil` class. This class will be used by Selenium tests as an extension to compare images.

How to do it...

Let's implement the `CompareUtil` class with a method to compare two image files, as shown in the following code:

```
package com.secookbook.examples.chapter09;

import java.awt.Image;
import java.awt.Toolkit;
import java.awt.image.PixelGrabber;

public class CompareUtil {

  public enum Result {
    Matched, SizeMismatch, PixelMismatch
  };

  public static Result CompareImage(String baseFile, String
actualFile) {
    Result compareResult = Result.PixelMismatch;
    Image baseImage = Toolkit.getDefaultToolkit().getImage(baseFile);
    Image actualImage = Toolkit.getDefaultToolkit().
getImage(actualFile);
    try {
      PixelGrabber baseImageGrab = new PixelGrabber(baseImage, 0,
0, -1,
```

```
            -1, false);
        PixelGrabber actualImageGrab = new PixelGrabber(actualImage,
    0, 0,
            -1, -1, false);

        int[] baseImageData = null;
        int[] actualImageData = null;

        if (baseImageGrab.grabPixels()) {
          int width = baseImageGrab.getWidth();
          int height = baseImageGrab.getHeight();
          baseImageData = new int[width * height];
          baseImageData = (int[]) baseImageGrab.getPixels();
        }

        if (actualImageGrab.grabPixels()) {
          int width = actualImageGrab.getWidth();
          int height = actualImageGrab.getHeight();
          actualImageData = new int[width * height];
          actualImageData = (int[]) actualImageGrab.getPixels();
        }

        if ((baseImageGrab.getHeight() !=
    actualImageGrab.getHeight())
            || (baseImageGrab.getWidth() !=
    actualImageGrab.getWidth()))
          compareResult = Result.SizeMismatch;
        else if (java.util.Arrays.equals(baseImageData,
    actualImageData))
          compareResult = Result.Matched;

      } catch (Exception e) {
        e.printStackTrace();
      }
      return compareResult;
    }
}
```

How it works...

The `CompareUtil` class uses the `java.awt.Image` namespace to work with images. The `CompareImage()` method takes the path of the base file and the actual file as an argument. It then retrieves these images to the `Image` class:

```
Image baseImage = Toolkit.getDefaultToolkit().getImage(baseFile);
Image actualImage = Toolkit.getDefaultToolkit().getImage(actualFile);
```

Finally, it uses the `PixelGrabber` class to get the pixels from these images to an array, as shown in the following code:

```
PixelGrabber baseImageGrab = new PixelGrabber(baseImage, 0, 0, -1,
-1, false);
PixelGrabber actualImageGrab = new PixelGrabber(actualImage, 0, 0,
-1, -1, false);

int[] baseImageData = null;
int[] actualImageData = null;

if(baseImageGrab.grabPixels()) {
    int width = baseImageGrab.getWidth();
    int height = baseImageGrab.getHeight();
    baseImageData = new int[width * height];
    baseImageData = (int[])baseImageGrab.getPixels();
}

if(actualImageGrab.grabPixels()) {
    int width = actualImageGrab.getWidth();
    int height = actualImageGrab.getHeight();
    actualImageData = new int[width * height];
    actualImageData = (int[])actualImageGrab.getPixels();
}
```

The images are first tested for size mismatch, and then for pixel mismatch, using the following code:

```
if ((baseImageGrab.getHeight() != actualImageGrab.getHeight()) ||
(baseImageGrab.getWidth() != actualImageGrab.getWidth()))
    compareResult = Result.SizeMismatch;
else if(java.util.Arrays.equals(baseImageData, actualImageData))
    compareResult = Result.Matched;
```

The following code is a sample test, comparing the layout of the application being tested with a base layout captured from an earlier release:

```
package com.secookbook.examples.chapter09;

import org.openqa.selenium.firefox.FirefoxDriver;
import org.openqa.selenium.*;
import org.apache.commons.io.FileUtils;
import org.junit.*;
import static org.junit.Assert.*;
import java.io.File;
```

```java
public class BmiCalculatorTest {

    private WebDriver driver;

    @Before
    public void setUp() throws Exception {
        // Create a new instance of the Firefox driver
        driver = new FirefoxDriver();
    }

    @Test
    public void testBmiCalculatorLayout() throws Exception {

        String scrFile = "c:\\screenshot.png";
        String baseScrFile = "c:\\baseScreenshot.png";

        // Open the BMI Calculator Page and get a Screen Shot of Page into a
        // File
        driver.get("http://dl.dropbox.com/u/55228056/bmicalculator.html");
        File screenshotFile = ((TakesScreenshot) driver)
            .getScreenshotAs(OutputType.FILE);
        FileUtils.copyFile(screenshotFile, new File(scrFile));

        // Verify baseline image with actual image
        assertEquals(CompareUtil.Result.Matched,
            CompareUtil.CompareImage(baseScrFile, scrFile));

    }

    @After
    public void tearDown() throws Exception {
        // Close the browser
        driver.quit();
    }
}
```

There's more...

The following code is the C# implementation of `CompareUtil`. You can use this class for Selenium tests created with .NET bindings:

```csharp
using System;
using System.Collections.Generic;
```

```
using System.Linq;
using System.Text;
using System.Drawing;
using System.Drawing.Imaging;

namespace CompareUtil
{
  public class CompareUtil
  {
    public enum Result { Matched, SizeMismatch, PixelMismatch
};

    public static Result CompareImage(string baseFile,
    string actualFile)
    {
      Result result = Result.Matched;

      Bitmap baseBmp = (Bitmap)Image.FromFile(baseFile);
      Bitmap actBmp = (Bitmap)Image.FromFile(actualFile);

      if (baseBmp.Size != actBmp.Size)
        result = Result.SizeMismatch;
      else
      {
        int height = Math.Min(baseBmp.Height,
actBmp.Height);
        int width = Math.Min(baseBmp.Width, actBmp.Width);

        bool are_identical = true;
        for (int x = 0; x <= width - 1; x++)
        {
          for (int y = 0; y <= height - 1; y++)
          {
            if (baseBmp.GetPixel(x, y).Equals(actBmp.
            GetPixel(x, y)))
            {
            }
            else
            {
              are_identical = false;
            }
          }
        }
        if (are_identical == true)
```

```
        result = Result.Matched;
      else
        result = Result.PixelMismatch;
    }

    return result;
  }
 }
}
```

See also

▶ The *Capturing screenshots with Selenium WebDriver* recipe in *Chapter 4, Working with the Selenium API*

▶ The *Capturing screenshots of elements in the Selenium WebDriver* recipe

Measuring performance with the Navigation Timing API

Measuring and optimizing the client-side performance is essential for a seamless user experience, and this is critical for web 2.0 applications using AJAX.

Capturing vital information, such as the time taken for page load, rendering of the elements, and the JavaScript code execution, helps in identifying the areas where performance is slow, and optimizes the overall client-side performance.

Sometimes, third-party controls, images, and media content also cause degradation in the performance. Using Selenium WebDriver and various other tools together, we can measure the performance and eliminate the weaker content.

Navigation Timing is a W3C Standard JavaScript API to measure performance on the Web. The API provides a simple way to get accurate and detailed timing statistics natively for page navigation and load events. It is available on Internet Explorer 9, Google Chrome, Firefox, and WebKit-based browsers.

The API is accessed via the properties of the timing interface of the `window.performance` object using JavaScript.

Each `performance.timing` attribute shows the time of a navigation event when the page was requested or when the page load event was measured in milliseconds since midnight of January 1, 1970 (UTC). A zero value means that an event did not occur.

The order of the `performance.timing` events is shown in the following diagram from the Navigation Timing draft:

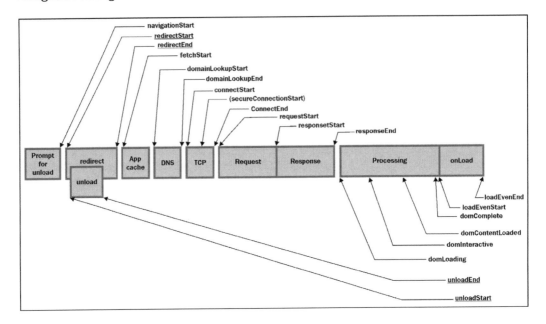

Getting ready

Identify a test where you want to measure the performance as well as decide what performance counters you want to measure.

How to do it...

We need to access the `window.performance` object using `JavascriptExecutor` to collect the timing metric; the following code shows an example for this:

```
// Open the BMI Calculator Mobile Application
driver.get("http://
cookbook.seleniumacademy.com/bmicalculator.html");

JavascriptExecutor js = (JavascriptExecutor) driver;

// Get the Load Event End
long loadEventEnd = (Long) js.executeScript("return
window.performance.timing.loadEventEnd;");

// Get the Navigation Event Start
```

```
long navigationStart = (Long) js.executeScript("return
window.performance.timing.navigationStart;");

// Difference between Load Event End and Navigation Event Start is
// Page Load Time
System.out.println("Page Load Time is " + (loadEventEnd -
navigationStart)/1000 + " seconds.");
```

 Refer to the `NavTimingDemo.java` section in the book's sample code for a complete test.

How it works...

As discussed in the previous code, the `window.performance` object provides us with the performance metric that is available within the Browser Window object. We need to use JavaScript to retrieve this metric, using the following code:

```
JavascriptExecutor js = (JavascriptExecutor) driver;

// Get the Load Event End
long loadEventEnd = (Long) js.executeScript("return
window.performance.timing.loadEventEnd;");
```

Here, we are collecting the `loadEventEnd` time and the `navigationEventStart` time and calculating the difference between them, which will give us the page load time.

10
Testing HTML5
Web Applications

In this chapter, we will cover:

- ▶ Automating the HTML5 video player
- ▶ Automating interaction on the HTML5 canvas element
- ▶ Web storage – testing local storage
- ▶ Web storage – testing session storage
- ▶ Cleaning local and session storage

Introduction

As HTML5 is gaining popularity, major browsers are now equipped to support HTML5, extending the scope of HTML combined with JavaScript and CSS3 into powerful, rich internet applications. There are many applications being developed that use new HTML5 elements such as canvas and video, as well as features such as web storage.

Selenium WebDriver supports testing HTML5 web applications on certain browsers out of the box. However, we can also use JavaScript to test these features, which will work on all the browsers supported by Selenium WebDriver.

In this chapter, we will focus on the most important features of HTML5, and see how to test them using Selenium WebDriver.

Automating the HTML5 video player

HTML5 defines a new element that specifies a standard way to embed a video or movie clip on a web page using the <video> element. Internet Explorer 9+, Firefox, Opera, Chrome, and Safari support the <video> element.

In this recipe, we will explore how we can automate testing of the <video> element. This automated testing provides a JavaScript interface with various methods and properties for automation.

How to do it...

We will create a new test named testHTML5VideoPlayer for testing the <video> element. We will use the JavaScriptExecutor class from Selenium WebDriver to interact with the <video> element. We will control the video from our test code and also verify some properties of the video in the following way:

```java
package com.secookbook.examples.chapter10;

import java.io.File;

import org.openqa.selenium.WebDriver;
import org.openqa.selenium.chrome.ChromeDriver;
import org.openqa.selenium.WebElement;
import org.openqa.selenium.By;
import org.openqa.selenium.JavascriptExecutor;
import org.openqa.selenium.OutputType;
import org.openqa.selenium.TakesScreenshot;
import org.apache.commons.io.FileUtils;
import org.junit.After;
import org.junit.Before;
import org.junit.Test;

import static org.junit.Assert.*;

public class HTML5VideoPlayer {

  private WebDriver driver;

  @Before
  public void setUp() {
    System.setProperty("webdriver.chrome.driver",
        "src/test/resources/drivers/chromedriver.exe");

    driver = new ChromeDriver();
    driver.get("http://cookbook.seleniumacademy.com/html5video.html");
```

```
  }

  @Test
  public void testHTML5VideoPlayer() throws Exception {
    // Get the HTML5 Video Element
    WebElement videoPlayer = driver.findElement(By.id("vplayer"));

    // We will need a JavaScript Executor for interacting with
Video
    // Element's methods and properties for automation
    JavascriptExecutor jsExecutor = (JavascriptExecutor) driver;

    // Get the Source of Video that will be played in Video Player
    String source = (String) jsExecutor.executeScript(
        "return arguments[0].currentSrc;", videoPlayer);
    // Get the Duration of Video
    long duration = (Long) jsExecutor.executeScript(
        "return arguments[0].duration", videoPlayer);

    // Verify Correct Video is loaded and duration
    assertEquals("http://html5demos.com/assets/dizzy.mp4",
source);
    assertEquals(25, duration);

    // Play the Video
    jsExecutor.executeScript("return arguments[0].play()",
videoPlayer);

    Thread.sleep(5000);

    // Pause the video
    jsExecutor.executeScript("arguments[0].pause()", videoPlayer);

    // Take a screenshot for later verification
    File scrFile = ((TakesScreenshot)
driver).getScreenshotAs(OutputType.FILE);
    FileUtils.copyFile(scrFile, new
File("target/screenshots/pause_play.png"));
  }

  @After
  public void tearDown() {
    driver.quit();
  }
}
```

How it works...

Firstly, we locate the `<video>` element so we can call its associated methods in JavaScript as well as in the retrieve/set properties. We can locate the `<video>` element similar to another HTML elements by using the `findElement()` method, as follows:

```
//Get the HTML5 Video Element
WebElement videoPlayer = driver.findElement(By.id("vplayer"));
```

We can verify which video file is being used with video player for playback, and duration of the video, by looking at the `currentSrc` and `duration` properties. We retrieve these properties by accessing the `<video>` element through JavaScript. For this, we created an instance of the `JavaScriptExecutor` class, as follows:

```
JavascriptExecutor jsExecutor = (JavascriptExecutor) driver;
```

Using the `executeScript()` method of the `JavaScriptExecutor` class of Selenium WebDriver, we can execute the JavaScript code within the browser window. We can return a value from the JavaScript code by assigning the value to a variable. However, we need to cast this value appropriately based on the type of value being returned. In this case, the `currentSrc` property will return a URL of the video file as a `String`:

```
String source = (String) jsExecutor.executeScript("return
arguments[0].currentSrc;", videoPlayer);
```

In the preceding example, `arguments[0]` was replaced by the `videoPlayer` WebElement using the `executeScript()` method.

The video playback

As discussed earlier, we can also control the playback of a video using the methods of the `<video>` element such as `play()` and `pause()`. We can call these methods using the `executeScript()` method in the following way:

```
//Play the Video
jsExecutor.executeScript("return arguments[0].play()",
videoPlayer);
```

See also

> ▶ *Executing the JavaScript code* recipe in *Chapter 4, Working with Selenium API*

Automating interaction on the HTML5 canvas element

Web developers can now create cool drawing applications within web browsers using the new HTML5 <canvas> element. This element is used to build drawing and charting applications by using JavaScript. Canvas has several methods for drawing paths, boxes, circles, characters, and adding images.

In this recipe, we will automate a simple drawing application through the Selenium WebDriver action class for mouse movements. We will also implement an image comparison feature to test the drawing on a canvas.

Internet Explorer 9+, Firefox, Opera, Chrome, and Safari support the <canvas> element.

How to do it...

Create a new test named testHTML5CanvasDrawing for testing the <canvas> element. We will draw a shape by using a sequence of mouse movements on the <canvas> element. We will verify the canvas with a previously captured image and check if the shape has been redrawn, as follows:

```
package com.secookbook.examples.chapter10;

import java.io.File;

import org.openqa.selenium.WebDriver;
import org.openqa.selenium.firefox.FirefoxDriver;
import org.openqa.selenium.WebElement;
import org.openqa.selenium.By;
import org.openqa.selenium.interactions.Actions;
import org.openqa.selenium.support.ui.Select;
import org.apache.commons.io.FileUtils;
import org.junit.After;
import org.junit.Before;
import org.junit.Test;

import com.secookbook.examples.chapter09.CompareUtil;
import com.secookbook.examples.chapter09.WebElementExtender;

import static org.junit.Assert.*;

public class HTML5CanvasDrawing {
```

```java
    private WebDriver driver;

    @Before
    public void setUp() {
        driver = new FirefoxDriver();
        driver.get("http://cookbook.seleniumacademy.com/html5canvasdraw.ht
ml");
    }

    @Test
    public void testHTML5CanvasDrawing() throws Exception {
        // Get the HTML5 Canvas Element
        WebElement canvas = driver.findElement(By.id("imageTemp"));

        // Select the Pencil Tool
        Select drawTools = new
Select(driver.findElement(By.id("dtool")));
        drawTools.selectByValue("pencil");

        // Create a Action chain to draw a shape on Canvas
        Actions builder = new Actions(driver);
        builder.clickAndHold(canvas).moveByOffset(10,
50).moveByOffset(50, 10)
            .moveByOffset(-10, -50).moveByOffset(-50, -10).release()
            .perform();

        // Get a screenshot of Canvas element after drawing and
compare it to
        // the base version
        FileUtils.copyFile(WebElementExtender.captureElementPicture(canvas
),
            new File("target/screenshots/drawing.png"));

        assertEquals(CompareUtil.Result.Matched,
CompareUtil.CompareImage(
            "src/test/resources/testdata/base_drawing.png",
"target/screenshots/drawing.png"));
    }

    @After
    public void tearDown() {
        driver.quit();
    }
}
```

How it works...

To draw on the canvas, we will first select a drawing tool by selecting the `pencil` option from the **Drawing Tool** dropdown. Selenium WebDriver provides a `Select` class for working with dropdowns and lists. In the test, the `selectByValue()` method is called to select the `pencil` tool:

```
Select drawTools = new Select(driver.findElement(By.id("dtool")));
drawTools.selectByValue("pencil");
```

We then draw a shape on the canvas using the Selenium WebDriver actions generator. Selenium WebDriver will perform a sequence of mouse movements by calling the `moveByOffset()` method while the mouse button is held down to draw the shape, with the mouse button released at the end:

```
builder.clickAndHold(canvas).moveByOffset(10, 50).
                moveByOffset(50,10).
                moveByOffset(-10,-50).
                moveByOffset(-50,-10).release().perform();
```

The Selenium actions generator mimics the mouse operations exactly like an end user drawing a shape on the canvas.

Finally, we will capture an image of the canvas using the `captureElementBitmap()` method of the `WebElementExtender` class. This image will be compared with a baseline image to verify that the drawing operation works on the canvas as expected, using the Selenium WebDriver.

See also

- ▸ *Executing the JavaScript code* recipe in *Chapter 4, Working with Selenium API*
- ▸ The *Comparing images in Selenium* recipe in *Chapter 9, Extending Selenium*

Web storage – testing local storage

HTML5 introduced a more secure and faster way of storing data locally within the user's browser from the web application. Previously, this was done with cookies. This data is not included with every server request, but used *only* when asked for. It is also possible to store large amounts of data without affecting the website's performance. The data is stored in key/value pairs, and a web application can only access data that is stored by itself.

HTML5 provides a `localStorage` interface through JavaScript that stores the data with no expiration date. The data will not be deleted when the browser is closed, and will be available at all times. You can view this data in Google Chrome by clicking on the **Inspect Element | Resources** tab.

Internet Explorer 8+, Firefox, Opera, Chrome, and Safari support web storage.

In this recipe, we will verify if a web page stores data in local storage as expected.

How to do it...

We will create a test that will verify that the web page has created an entry in local storage and stored a value. We will use the Selenium WebDriver `JavaScriptExecutor` class to access the `localStorage` interface, as follows:

```
package com.secookbook.examples.chapter10;

import org.openqa.selenium.WebDriver;
import org.openqa.selenium.chrome.ChromeDriver;
import org.openqa.selenium.JavascriptExecutor;
import org.junit.After;
import org.junit.Before;
import org.junit.Test;

import static org.junit.Assert.*;

public class HTML5LocalStorage {

  private WebDriver driver;

  @Before
  public void setUp() {
    System.setProperty("webdriver.chrome.driver",
        "src/test/resources/drivers/chromedriver.exe");

    driver = new ChromeDriver();
    driver.get("http://cookbook.seleniumacademy.com/html5storage.html"
);
  }

  @Test
  public void testHTML5LocalStorage() throws Exception {
    JavascriptExecutor jsExecutor = (JavascriptExecutor) driver;

    // Get the current value of localStorage.lastname, this should
be Smith
    String lastName = (String) jsExecutor
        .executeScript("return localStorage.lastname;");
    assertEquals("Smith", lastName);
  }
```

```
@After
public void tearDown() {
    driver.quit();
    }
}
```

How it works...

While executing this test, Selenium WebDriver loads a page that will access the local storage, and creates a new key/value pair as `lastName = Smith`. We can validate this by accessing the `lastName` key from the `localStorage` interface using the `executeScript()` method of the `JavaScriptExecutor` class. This will return the value of the `lastName` key as a `String`:

```
String lastName = (String) jsExecutor.executeScript("return
localStorage.lastname;");
```

There's more...

During testing, there might be a need to directly set the value of the key in local storage. We can assign a new value to an existing key by directly assigning the value in the following way, using JavaScript:

```
//Set the value of localStorage.lastname to Dustin
jsExecutor.executeScript("localStorage.lastname = arguments[0];",
"Dustin");
```

See also

▶   The *Cleaning local and session storage* recipe in this chapter.

Web storage – testing session storage

Similar to local storage, **session storage** stores the data for only one session. The data is deleted when the user closes the browser window. We can access the session storage using the `sessionStorage` interface through JavaScript.

In this recipe, we will verify that a web page stores data in session storage as expected.

How to do it...

Let's create a test case that will load a web page that implements a counter and stores the value of the counter every time a button is clicked in session storage. We will verify that a new counter value is stored in session storage:

```java
package com.secookbook.examples.chapter10;

import org.openqa.selenium.WebDriver;
import org.openqa.selenium.chrome.ChromeDriver;
import org.openqa.selenium.JavascriptExecutor;
import org.openqa.selenium.WebElement;
import org.openqa.selenium.By;
import org.junit.After;
import org.junit.Before;
import org.junit.Test;

import static org.junit.Assert.*;

public class HTML5SessionStorage {

  private WebDriver driver;

  @Before
  public void setUp() {
    System.setProperty("webdriver.chrome.driver",
        "src/test/resources/drivers/chromedriver.exe");

    driver = new ChromeDriver();
    driver.get("http://cookbook.seleniumacademy.com/html5storage.html"
);
  }

  @Test
  public void testHTML5SessionStorage() throws Exception {
    WebElement clickButton = driver.findElement(By.id("click"));
    WebElement clicksField = driver.findElement(By.id("clicks"));

    JavascriptExecutor jsExecutor = (JavascriptExecutor) driver;

    // Get current value of sessionStorage.clickcount, should be
null
    String clickCount = (String) jsExecutor
        .executeScript("return sessionStorage.clickcount;");
```

```
    assertEquals(null, clickCount);
    assertEquals("0", clicksField.getAttribute("value"));

    // Click the Button, this will increase the
sessionStorage.clickcount
    // value by 1
    clickButton.click();

    // Get current value of sessionStorage.clickcount, should be 1
    clickCount = (String) jsExecutor
        .executeScript("return sessionStorage.clickcount;");
    assertEquals("1", clickCount);
    assertEquals("1", clicksField.getAttribute("value"));
  }

  @After
  public void tearDown() {
    driver.quit();
  }
}
```

How it works...

While executing this test, whenever a button is clicked by Selenium WebDriver, a new session storage key is created for the first time in session storage. For subsequent clicks, this value is incremented by the web page.

Similar to local storage, we can validate this by accessing the clickCount key from the sessionStorage interface using the executeScript() method of the JavaScriptExecutor class. This will return the value of the clickCount key as a String:

```
//Click the Button, this will increase the
sessionStorage.clickcount //value by 1
clickButton.click();

//Get current value of sessionStorage.clickcount, should be 1
clickCount = (String) jsExecutor.executeScript("return
  sessionStorage.clickCount;");
```

When the browser is closed and the test has ended, the clickcount key will be removed from session storage.

See also

▶ The *Cleaning local and session storage* recipe in this chapter.

Cleaning local and session storage

When tests are run on HTML5 applications using local or session storage, lots of local and session storage entries will be created. When running tests in a batch on an already used environment, cleaning local and session storage is a good idea before you begin your tests.

In this recipe, we will briefly see how to remove local or session storage items and clean the values.

How to do it...

To remove a specific item from local or session storage, you can use the `removeItem()` method in the following way:

```
// We can use removeItem method to remove a specific Key along
with it's value from local storage
JavascriptExecutor jsExecutor = (JavascriptExecutor) driver;
jsExecutor.executeScript("localStorage.removeItem(lastname);");
```

For session storage, the following code snippet is used:

```
JavascriptExecutor jsExecutor = (JavascriptExecutor) driver;
jsExecutor.executeScript("sessionStorage.removeItem(lastname);");
```

To clear all items, in local or session storage, you can use the `clear()` method in the following way:

```
//To Clear Storage values
JavascriptExecutor jsExecutor = (JavascriptExecutor) driver;
jsExecutor.executeScript("localStorage.clear();");
```

For session storage, the following code snippet is used:

```
//To Clear Storage values
JavascriptExecutor jsExecutor = (JavascriptExecutor) driver;
jsExecutor.executeScript("sessionStorage.clear();");
```

See also

▶ The *Web storage – testing session storage* recipe
▶ The *Web storage – testing local storage* recipe covered earlier in this chapter

11

Behavior-Driven Development

In this chapter, we will cover:

- ▶ Using Cucumber-JVM and Selenium WebDriver in Java for BDD
- ▶ Using SpecFlow.NET and Selenium WebDriver in .NET for BDD
- ▶ Using Capybara, Cucumber, and Selenium WebDriver in Ruby
- ▶ Using Behave and Selenium WebDriver in Python

Introduction

Behavior-driven development (**BDD**) is an agile software development method that enhances the paradigm of **test driven development** (**TDD**) and acceptance tests, and encourages the collaboration between developers, QA, domain experts, and stakeholders. Behavior-driven development was introduced by Dan North in 2003 in his seminal article *Introducing BDD*. The article can be accessed at http://dannorth.net/introducing-bdd/.

Behavior-driven development focuses on obtaining a clear understanding of desired application behavior through discussions with stakeholders using a ubiquitous language as described at http://behaviour-driven.org/.

It extends TDD by writing test cases in a natural language that non-programmers can read. Users describe features and scenarios to test these features in plain text files using the **Gherkin** language in the Given, When, and Then structures. You can find out more about Gherkin language at http://en.wikipedia.org/wiki/Behavior-driven_development and https://github.com/cucumber/cucumber/wiki/Gherkin.

The `Given`, `When`, and `Then` structures in the Gherkin language are described as follows:

- `Given`: This represents the initial context (precondition)
- `When`: This represents the user performing a key action (actor + action)
- `Then`: This ensures some kind of outcome (observable result)

In behavior-driven development, the process starts with users of the system and the development team discussing features, user stories, and scenarios. These are documented in feature or story files using the Gherkin language. Developers then use the red-green-refactor cycle to run these features using the BDD framework, then write step definition files mapping the steps from the scenarios to the automation code and re-running until all the acceptance criteria are met.

 Behavior-driven development is also known as **acceptance test driven development (ATDD)** or **story testing**.

In this chapter, we will explore how to use frameworks like Cucumber-JVM, SpecFlow.NET, and Capybara, Behave with Selenium WebDriver for behavior-driven development.

Using Cucumber-JVM and Selenium WebDriver in Java for BDD

BDD/ATDD is gaining much popularity in agile software development, and Cucumber-JVM is a mainstream tool used to implement this practice in Java. Cucumber-JVM is the Java port of the **Cucumber** framework, widely used in Ruby.

Cucumber-JVM allows developers, QA, and non-technical or business participants to write features and scenarios in a plain text file using Gherkin language. This is done with minimal restrictions about grammar in a typical `Given`, `When`, and `Then` structure.

This feature file is then supported by a step definition file, which implements automated steps to execute the scenarios written in the feature file. Apart from testing APIs with Cucumber-JVM, we can also test UI level tests by combining Selenium WebDriver.

In this recipe, we will use Cucumber-JVM, Maven, and Selenium WebDriver to implement tests for the fund transfer feature of an online banking application.

Getting ready

1. Create a new Maven project named **FundTransfer** in Eclipse.

2. Add the following dependencies to POM.XML:

```xml
<project xmlns="http://maven.apache.org/POM/4.0.0"
xmlns:xsi="http://www.w3.org/2001/XMLSchema-instance"
  xsi:schemaLocation="http://maven.apache.org/POM/4.0.0
http://maven.apache.org/xsd/maven-4.0.0.xsd">
  <modelVersion>4.0.0</modelVersion>
  <groupId>FundTransfer</groupId>
  <artifactId>FundTransfer</artifactId>
  <version>0.0.1-SNAPSHOT</version>
  <dependencies>
    <dependency>
      <groupId>info.cukes</groupId>
      <artifactId>cucumber-java</artifactId>
      <version>1.2.4</version>
      <scope>test</scope>
    </dependency>
    <dependency>
      <groupId>info.cukes</groupId>
      <artifactId>cucumber-junit</artifactId>
      <version>1.2.4</version>
      <scope>test</scope>
    </dependency>
    <dependency>
      <groupId>junit</groupId>
      <artifactId>junit</artifactId>
      <version>4.12</version>
      <scope>test</scope>
    </dependency>
    <dependency>
      <groupId>org.seleniumhq.selenium</groupId>
      <artifactId>selenium-java</artifactId>
      <version>2.47.1</version>
    </dependency>
  </dependencies>
</project>
```

How to do it...

Perform the following steps to create BDD/ATDD tests with Cucumber-JVM:

1. Select the **FundTransfer** project in **Package Explorer** in Eclipse. Select and right-click on **src/test/resources** in **Package Explorer**. Select **New | Package** from the menu to add a new package, as shown in the following screenshot:

2. Enter `fundtransfer.test` in the **Name:** textbox and click on the **Finish** button.

3. Add a new file to this package. Name this file `fundtransfer.feature`, as shown in the following screenshot:

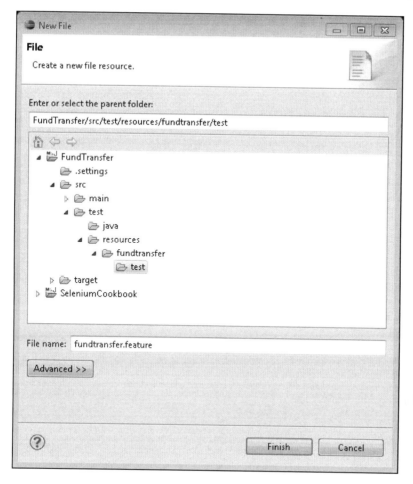

4. Add the Fund Transfer feature and scenarios to this file:

```
Feature: Customer Transfer's Fund
  As a customer,
  I want to transfer funds
  so that I can send money to my friends and family

Scenario: Valid Payee
  Given the user is on Fund Transfer Page
  When he enters "Jim" as payee name
  And he enters "100" as amount
  And he submits request for Fund Transfer
  Then ensure the fund transfer is complete with "$100
transferred successfully to Jim!!" message
```

```
Scenario Outline: Invalid conditions
    Given the user is on Fund Transfer Page
    When he enters "<payee>" as payee name
    And he enters "<amount>" as amount
    And he submits request for Fund Transfer
    Then ensure a transaction failure "<message>" is
displayed

    Examples:
        | payee | amount | message |
        | Unmesh | 100    | Transfer failed!! 'Unmesh' is not
registered in your List of Payees |    | Tim | 100000 |
Transfer failed!! account cannot be overdrawn |
```

5. Select and right-click on **src/test/java** in **Package Explorer**. Select **New | Package** from the menu to add a new package, as shown in the following screenshot:

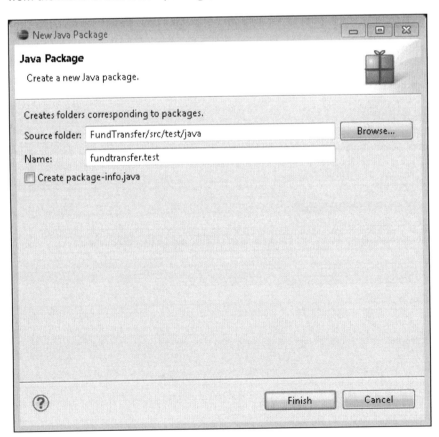

6. Create a class named `FundTransferStepDefs` in the newly created package. Add the following code to this class:

```java
package fundtransfer.test;

import org.openqa.selenium.WebDriver;
import org.openqa.selenium.chrome.ChromeDriver;
import org.openqa.selenium.WebElement;
import org.openqa.selenium.By;

import cucumber.api.java.*;
import cucumber.api.java.en.*;
import static org.junit.Assert.assertEquals;

public class FundTransferStepDefs {
  protected WebDriver driver;

  @Before
  public void setUp() {
    driver = new ChromeDriver();
  }

  @Given("the user is on Fund Transfer Page")
  public void theUserIsOnFundTransferPage() {
    driver.get("http://cookbook.seleniumacademy.com/fundTransfer.html");
  }

  @When("he enters \"([^\"]*)\" as payee name")
  public void heEntersPayeeName(String payeeName) {
    driver.findElement(By.id("payee")).sendKeys(payeeName);
  }

  @And("he enters \"([^\"]*)\" as amount")
  public void heEntersAmount(String amount) {
    driver.findElement(By.id("amount")).sendKeys(amount);
  }

  @And("he submits request for Fund Transfer")
  public void heSubmitsRequestForFundTransfer() {
    driver.findElement(By.id("transfer")).click();
  }
```

```
    @Then("ensure the fund transfer is complete with
\"([^\"]*)\" message")
    public void ensureTheFundTransferIsComplete(String msg) {
      WebElement message =
driver.findElement(By.id("message"));
      assertEquals(message.getText(), msg);
    }


    @Then("^ensure a transaction failure \"([^\"]*)\" is
displayed$")
    public void ensureATransactionFailureMessage(String msg)
{
      WebElement message =
driver.findElement(By.id("message"));
      assertEquals(message.getText(), msg);
    }

    @After
    public void tearDown() {
      driver.close();
    }
}
```

7. Create a support class `RunCukesTest`, which will define the Cucumber-JVM configurations:

```
package fundtransfer.test;

import cucumber.api.CucumberOptions;
import cucumber.api.junit.Cucumber;

import org.junit.runner.RunWith;

@RunWith(Cucumber.class)
@CucumberOptions(plugin = {"pretty",
"html:target/report/report.html",
        "json:target/report/cucu_json_report.json",
        "junit:target/report/cucumber_junit_report.xml"})
public class RunCukesTest {
}
```

8. To run the tests in Maven life cycle, select the **FundTransfer** project in **Package Explorer**. Right-click on the project name and select **Run As | Maven test**. Maven will execute all the tests from the project.

9. At the end of the test, an HTML report will be generated, as shown in the following screenshot. To view this report, open `index.html` in the `target\report` folder:

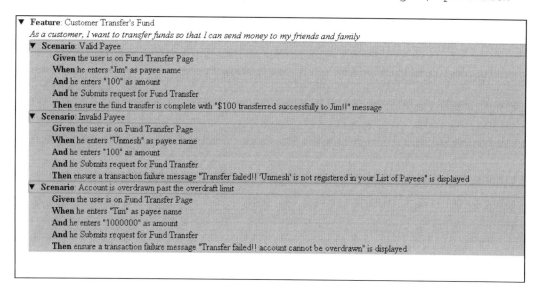

How it works...

Creating tests in Cucumber-JVM involves three major steps: writing a feature file, implementing automated steps using the step definition file, and creating support code as needed.

To write features, Cucumber-JVM uses the Gherkin syntax. The feature file describes the feature and then the scenarios to test the feature:

```
Feature: Customer Transfer's Fund
        As a customer,
        I want to transfer funds
        so that I can send money to my friends and family
```

You can write as many scenarios as needed to test the feature in the feature file. The scenario section contains the name and steps to execute the defined scenario, along with test data required to execute that scenario using the application:

```
Scenario: Valid Payee
        Given the user is on Fund Transfer Page
        When he enters "Jim" as payee name
        And he enters "100" as amount
        And he Submits request for Fund Transfer
        Then ensure the fund transfer is complete with "$100
        transferred successfully to Jim!!" message
```

Team members use these feature files and scenarios to build and validate the system. Frameworks like Cucumber provide an ability to automatically validate the features by allowing us to implement automated steps. For this we need to create the step definition file that maps the steps from the feature file to the automation code. Step definition files implement a method for steps using special annotations. For example, in the following code, the `@When` annotation is used to map the step `"When he enters "Jim" as payee name"` from the feature file in the step definition file. When this step is to be executed by the framework, the `heEntersPayeeName()` method will be called by passing the data extracted using regular expressions from the step:

```
@When("he enters \"([^\"]*)\" as payee name")
public void heEntersPayeeName(String payeeName) {
    driver.findElement(By.id("payee")).sendKeys(payeeName);
}
```

In this method, the WebDriver code is written to locate the `payee name` textbox and enter the name value using the `sendKeys()` method.

The step definition file acts like a template for all the steps from the feature file, while scenarios can use a mix and match of the steps based on the test conditions.

A helper class `RunCukesTest` is defined to provide Cucumber-JVM configurations, such as how to run the features and steps with JUnit, report format, and location, shown as follows:

```
@RunWith(Cucumber.class)
@CucumberOptions(plugin = {"pretty",
"html:target/report/report.html",
    "json:target/report/cucu_json_report.json",
    "junit:target/report/cucumber_junit_report.xml"})
public class RunCukesTest {
}
```

There's more...

In this example, step definition methods are calling Selenium WebDriver methods directly. However, a layer of abstraction can be created using the `Page` object where a separate class is defined with the definition of all the elements from `FundTransferPage`:

```
import org.openqa.selenium.WebDriver;
import org.openqa.selenium.WebElement;
import org.openqa.selenium.support.CacheLookup;
import org.openqa.selenium.support.FindBy;
import org.openqa.selenium.support.PageFactory;

public class FundTransferPage {
```

```
@FindBy(id = "payee")
@CacheLookup
public WebElement payeeField;

@FindBy(id = "amount")
public WebElement amountField;

@FindBy(id = "transfer")
public WebElement transferButton;

@FindBy(id = "message")
public WebElement messageLabel;

public FundTransferPage(WebDriver driver)
{
  if(!"Online Fund Transfers".equals(driver.getTitle()))
    throw new IllegalStateException("This is not Fund
            Transfer Page");
  PageFactory.initElements(driver, this);
}
}
```

See also

▶ The *Configuring Selenium WebDriver test development environment for Java with Eclipse and Maven* recipe in *Chapter 1, Getting Started*

▶ The *Using the PageFactory class for exposing the elements on a page* recipe in *Chapter 8, Using the Page Object Model*

Using SpecFlow.NET and Selenium WebDriver in .NET for BDD

We saw how to use Selenium WebDriver with Cucumber-JVM for BDD/ATDD. Now let's try using a similar combination in .NET using SpecFlow.NET. We can implement BDD in .NET using the SpecFlow.NET and Selenium WebDriver .NET bindings.

SpecFlow.NET is inspired by Cucumber and uses the same Gherkin language to write specs. In this recipe, we will implement tests for the Fund Transfer feature using SpecFlow.NET. We will also use the Page objects for FundTransferPage in this recipe.

Getting ready

This recipe is created with SpecFlow.NET Version 1.9.0 and Microsoft Visual Studio Professional 2013; follow these steps:

▸ Download and install SpecFlow from Visual Studio Gallery from `http://visualstudiogallery.msdn.microsoft.com/9915524d-7fb0-43c3-bb3c-a8a14fbd40ee`.

▸ Download and install NUnit Test Adapter from `http://visualstudiogallery.msdn.microsoft.com/9915524d-7fb0-43c3-bb3c-a8a14fbd40ee`.

This will install the project template and other support files for SpecFlow.NET in Visual Studio 20132.

How to do it...

Let's test the fund transfer feature using SpecFlow.NET by performing the following steps:

1. Launch Microsoft Visual Studio.

2. In Visual Studio, create a new project by going to **File | New | Project**. Select **Visual C# Class Library Project**. Name the project `FundTransfer.specs`, as shown in the following screenshot:

3. Next, add SpecFlow.NET, WebDriver, and NUnit using NuGet. Right-click on the
   `FundTransfer.specs` solution in **Solution Explorer** and select **Manage NuGet
   Packages...**, as shown in the following screenshot:

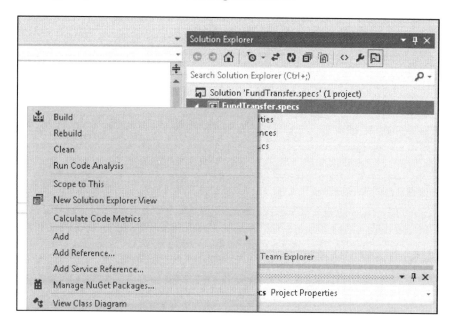

4. On the **FundTransfer.specs - Manage NuGet Packages** dialog box, select **Online** and
   search for the **SpecFlow** packages. The search will result in the following suggestions:

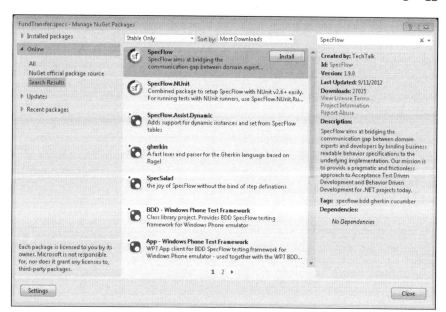

5. Select **SpecFlow.NUnit** from the list and click on the **Install** button. NuGet will download and install **SpecFlow.NUnit** and any other package dependencies to the solution. This will take a while.

6. Next, search for the **WebDriver** package on the **FundTransfer.specs - Manage NuGet Packages** dialog box.

7. Select **Selenium WebDriver** and **Selenium WebDriver Support Classes** from the list and click on the **Install** button.

8. Close the **FundTransfer.specs - Manage NuGet Packages** dialog box.

Creating a spec file

The steps to create a spec file are as follows:

1. Right-click on the FundTransfer.specs solution in **Solution Explorer**. Select **Add | New Item**.

2. On the **Add New Item – FundTransfer.specs** dialog box, select **SpecFlow Feature File** and enter FundTransfer.feature in the **Name:** textbox. Click on the **Add** button, as shown in the following screenshot:

3. In the **Editor** window you will see the FundTransfer.feature tab.

4. By default, `SpecFlow` will add a dummy feature in the feature file. Replace the content of this file with the following feature and scenarios:

```
Feature: Customer Transfer's Fund
        As a customer,
        I want to transfer funds
        so that I can send money to my friends and family


Scenario: Valid Payee
        Given the user is on Fund Transfer Page
        When he enters "Jim" as payee name
        And he enters "100" as amount
        And he Submits request for Fund Transfer
        Then ensure the fund transfer is complete with "$100
        transferred successfully to Jim!!" message


Scenario: Invalid Payee
        Given the user is on Fund Transfer Page
        When he enters "Jack" as payee name
        And he enters "100" as amount
        And he Submits request for Fund Transfer
        Then ensure a transaction failure message "Transfer
        failed!! 'Jack' is not registered in your List of
Payees" is displayed


Scenario: Account is overdrawn past the overdraft limit
        Given the user is on Fund Transfer Page
        When he enters "Tim" as payee name
        And he enters "1000000" as amount
        And he Submits request for Fund Transfer
        Then ensure a transaction failure message "Transfer
        failed!! account cannot be overdrawn" is displayed
```

Creating a step definition file

The steps to create a step definition file are as follows:

1. To add a step definition file, right-click on the `FundTransfer.sepcs` solution in **Solution Explorer**. Select **Add | New Item**.

2. On the **Add New Item - FundTransfer.specs** dialog box, select **SpecFlow Step Definition File** and enter `FundTransferStepDefs.cs` in the **Name:** textbox.

3. Click on the **Add** button. A new C# class will be added with dummy steps. Replace the content of this file with the following code:

```
using System;
using System.Collections.Generic;
using System.Linq;
using System.Text;
using TechTalk.SpecFlow;
using NUnit.Framework;
using OpenQA.Selenium;

namespace FundTransfer.specs
{
    [Binding]
    public class FundTransferStepDefs
    {
        FundsTransferPage _ftPage = new
        FundsTransferPage(Environment.Driver);

        [Given(@"the user is on Fund Transfer Page")]
        public void GivenUserIsOnFundTransferPage()
        {
            Environment.Driver.Navigate().GoToUrl("http://
            cookbook.seleniumacademy.com/fundTransfer.html");
        }

        [When(@"he enters ""(.*)"" as payee name")]
        public void WhenUserEneteredIntoThePayeeNameField(string
        payeeName)
        {
            _ftPage.payeeNameField.SendKeys(payeeName);
        }

        [When(@"he enters ""(.*)"" as amount")]
        public void WhenUserEneteredIntoTheAmountField(string
        amount)
        {
            _ftPage.amountField.SendKeys(amount);
        }

        [When(@"he enters ""(.*)"" as amount above his
limit")]
        public void WhenUserEneteredIntoTheAmountFieldAboveLimit
        (string amount)
        {
```

```
        _ftPage.amountField.SendKeys(amount);
    }

    [When(@"he Submits request for Fund Transfer")]
    public void WhenUserPressTransferButton()
    {
        _ftPage.transferButton.Click();
    }

    [Then(@"ensure the fund transfer is complete with
""(.*)""
    message")]
    public void ThenFundTransferIsComplete(string
message)
    {
        Assert.AreEqual(message,
_ftPage.messageLabel.Text);
    }

    [Then(@"ensure a transaction failure message
""(.*)"" is displayed")]
    public void ThenFundTransferIsFailed(string
message)
    {
        Assert.AreEqual(message, _ftPage.messageLabel.Text);
    }
  }

}
```

Defining a Page object and a helper class

The steps to define a Page object and a helper class are as follows:

1. Define a Page object for the Fund Transfer Page by adding a new C# class file. Name this class FundTransferPage. Copy the following code to this class:

```
using System;
using System.Collections.Generic;
using System.Linq;
using System.Text;
using OpenQA.Selenium;
using OpenQA.Selenium.Support.PageObjects;

namespace FundTransfer.specs
{
```

```
class FundTransferPage
{
    public FundTransferPage(IWebDriver driver)
    {
        PageFactory.InitElements(driver, this);
    }

    [FindsBy(How = How.Id, Using = "payee")]
    public IWebElement payeeNameField { get; set; }

    [FindsBy(How = How.Id, Using = "amount")]
    public IWebElement amountField { get; set; }

    [FindsBy(How = How.Id, Using = "transfer")]
    public IWebElement transferButton { get; set; }

    [FindsBy(How = How.Id, Using = "message")]
    public IWebElement messageLabel { get; set; }
}
}
```

2. We need a helper class that will provide a WebDriver instance and perform clean up activity at the end. Name this class `Environment` and copy the following code to this class:

```
using System;
using System.Collections.Generic;
using System.Linq;
using System.Text;
using OpenQA.Selenium;
using OpenQA.Selenium.Chrome;
using TechTalk.SpecFlow;

namespace FundTransfer.specs
{
    [Binding]
    public class Environment
    {
        private static ChromeDriver driver;

        public static IWebDriver Driver
        {
            get { return driver ?? (driver = new
            ChromeDriver(@"C:\ChromeDriver")); }
        }
```

```
    [AfterTestRun]
    public static void AfterTestRun()
    {
        Driver.Close();
        Driver.Quit();
        driver = null;
    }
    }
}
```

3. Build the solution.

Running the tests

The steps to run the tests are as follows:

1. Open the **Test Explorer** window by clicking the **Test Explorer** option on **Test | Windows** on **Main Menu**.

2. It will display the three scenarios listed in the feature file, as shown in the following screenshot:

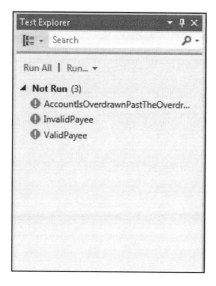

3. Click on **Run All** to test the feature, as shown in the following screenshot:

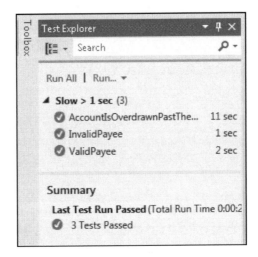

How it works...

SpecFlow.NET first needs the feature files for the features we will be testing. SpecFlow.NET supports the Gherkin language for writing features.

In the step definition file, we must create a method for each step written in a feature file using the `Given`, `When`, and `Then` attributes. These methods can also take the parameter values specified in the steps using the arguments. Following is an example of entering the name of the payee:

```
[When(@"he enters ""(.*)"" as payee name")]
public void WhenUserEneteredIntoThePayeeNameField(string
payeeName)
{
    _ftPage.payeeNameField.SendKeys(payeeName);
}
```

In this example, we are automating the `"When he enters "Jim" as payee name"` step. We used the `When` attribute and created a method: `WhenUserEneteredIntoThePayeeNameField`. This method will need the value of the payee name embedded in the step, which is extracted using the regular expression by the SpecFlow.NET. Inside the method, we are using an instance of the `FundTransferPage` class and calling its `payeeNameField` member's `SendKeys()` method, passing the name of the payee extracted from the step. Using the `Page` object helps in abstracting locator and page details from the step definition files, making it more manageable and easy to maintain.

SpecFlow.NET automatically generates the NUnit test code when the project is built. Using the Visual Studio Test Explorer and NUnit Test Adaptor for Visual Studio, these tests are executed and the features are validated.

See also

▶ The *Configuring Selenium WebDriver test development environment for Java with Eclipse and Maven* in *Chapter 1, Getting Started*

Using Capybara, Cucumber, and Selenium WebDriver in Ruby

Capybara is an acceptance test framework for web applications in Ruby. It integrates with Ruby-based BDD frameworks such as Cucumber and **RSpec**, along with Selenium WebDriver, for web testing capabilities. Capybara is widely used in testing Rails applications.

In this recipe, we will see how to use Capybara, Cucumber, and Selenium to test the BMI Calculator application.

Getting ready

1. You need to install Capybara Gem by using the following command:

   ```
   gem install capybara
   ```

2. Additionally, you also need to install Cucumber and RSpec Gem on a fresh Ruby installation, as follows:

   ```
   gem install cucumber
   ```

   ```
   gem install rspec
   ```

How to do it...

In Capybara, we need to create a features file for the stories under test. These stories are written in the Gherkin language with the `Given`, `When`, and `Then` structures in the Cucumber format. Perform the following steps to create a feature and step definition file with Capybara:

1. Create a plain text file named `BmiCalculate.feature`, as follows:

   ```
   Feature: BMI Calculator has a Calculate Function

   Scenario: Calculate BMI
     Given I am on BMI Calculator
     When I fill in the following:
   ```

```
| heightCMS | 181 |
| weightKg | 80 |
When I press "Calculate"
Then I should see following:
| bmi | 24.4 |
| bmi_category | Normal |
```

2. Next, we need to create a step file for the feature file created earlier. This file maps each step from the feature file to a Capybara function to work on UI. Create a Ruby file with the following code and name it `BmiCalculate.rb`:

```ruby
Given /^I am on BMI Calculator$/ do
    visit "http:// cookbook.seleniumacademy.com/bmicalculator.
html"
end

When /^I fill in the following:$/ do |table|
    table.rows_hash.each {|field, value| fill_in field,
        :with => value }
end

When /^I press "([^"]*)"$/ do |button|
    click_button(button)
end

Then /^I should see following:$/ do |table|
    table.rows_hash.each {|field, value| find_field(field).
        value.should == value }
end
```

3. Finally, we need to create a configuration file that provides required support to run the features with Cucumber. Create a new file with the following code and name it `env.rb`:

```ruby
require 'capybara'
require 'capybara/cucumber'
require 'selenium/webdriver'

Capybara.default_driver = :selenium
Capybara.register_driver :selenium do |app|
    Capybara::Selenium::Driver.new(app, :browser => :firefox)
end
```

How it works...

We need to copy all of these files together in a directory named `features`, and use the cucumber command, as follows:

```
cucumber
```

Since we are using Cucumber along with Capybara, it first needs feature files written in plain English. In the following example, we have a step which will populate the `height` and `weight` fields in the BMI Calculator application:

```
When I fill in the following:
  | heightCMS | 181 |
  | weightKg  | 80  |
```

The steps from a feature file are then mapped to Capybara commands using a step file written in Ruby. In the following example, the previously mentioned table format is mapped to the Capybara command, `fill_in`:

```
When /^I fill in the following:$/ do |table|
  table.rows_hash.each {|field, value| fill_in field, :with =>
value }
end
```

To run these features with Cucumber, we need a configuration file that will tell Capybara to use Selenium as a driver:

```
require 'capybara'
require 'capybara/cucumber'
require 'selenium/webdriver'

Capybara.default_driver = :selenium
Capybara.register_driver :selenium do |app|
  Capybara::Selenium::Driver.new(app, :browser => :firefox)
end
```

When Cucumber runs the features, a default report is generated in the following format:

```
c:\>cucumber
*** WARNING: You must use ANSICON 1.31 or higher (http://adoxa.110mb.com/ansicon
) to get coloured output on Windows
Feature: BMI Calculator has a Calculate Function

  Scenario: Calculate BMI             # features\bmicalculate.feature:3
    Given I am on BMI Calculator      # eatures/bmicalculate_steps.rb:1
    When I fill in the following:     # eatures/bmicalculate_steps.rb:5
      | heightCMS | 181 |
      | weightKg  | 80  |
    When I press "Calculate"          # eatures/bmicalculate_steps.rb:9
    Then I should see following:      # eatures/bmicalculate_steps.rb:13
      | bmi          | 24.4   |
      | bmi_category | Normal |

1 scenario (1 passed)
4 steps (4 passed)
0m22.547s

c:\>_
```

See also

▶ The *Using Cucumber-JVM and Selenium WebDriver in Java for BDD* recipe

▶ The *Using SpecFlow.NET and Selenium WebDriver in .NET for BDD* recipe

▶ The *Using Capybara, Cucumber, and Selenium WebDriver in Ruby* recipe

Using Behave and Selenium WebDriver in Python

Behave is a BDD framework available in Python. It provides a very similar approach to Cucumber.

In this recipe, we will see how to use Behave and Selenium WebDriver to test a fund transfer application.

Getting ready

You need to install Behave using the following command:

```
pip install behave
```

How to do it...

In Behave, we need to create a features file for the stories under test. These stories are written in the Gherkin language with the Given, When, and Then structures in the Cucumber format. Perform the following steps to create a feature and step definition file with Behave:

1. Create a folder named fundtransfer and then create two subfolders, features and steps, in the fundtransfer folder.

2. In the feature folder, create a plain text file named fundtransfer.feature, as follows:

```
Feature: Customer Transfer's Fund
        As a customer,
        I want to transfer funds
        so that I can send money to my friends and family


Scenario: Valid Payee
        Given the user is on Fund Transfer Page
        When he enters Jim as payee name
        And he enters 100 as amount
        And he Submits request for Fund Transfer
        Then ensure the fund transfer is complete with $100
transferred successfully to Jim!! message


Scenario: Invalid Payee
        Given the user is on Fund Transfer Page
        When he enters Unmesh as payee name
        And he enters 100 as amount
        And he Submits request for Fund Transfer
        Then ensure a transaction failure message Transfer
failed!! 'Unmesh' is not registered in your List of Payees
is displayed


Scenario: Account is overdrawn past the overdraft limit
        Given the user is on Fund Transfer Page
        When he enters Tim as payee name
        And he enters 1000000 as amount
        And he Submits request for Fund Transfer
        Then ensure a transaction failure message Transfer
failed!! account cannot be overdrawn is displayed
```

3. Next, we need to create a step definition file for the feature file created earlier. This file maps each step from the feature file to Python method, which then calls the Selenium WebDriver API. Create a new Python script file in the `steps` folder with the following code, and name it `fundtransfer_steps.py`:

```python
from behave import given, when, then



@given('the user is on Fund Transfer Page')
def step_user_is_on_fund_transfer_page(context):
    context.driver.get("http://
cookbook.seleniumacademy.com/fundTransfer.html")

@when('he enters {name} as payee name')
def step_he_enters_payee_name(context, name):
    context.driver.find_element_by_id("payee").send_keys(name)

@when('he enters {amount} as amount')
def step_he_enters_amount(context, amount):
    context.driver.find_element_by_id("amount").send_keys(amoun
t)

@when('he Submits request for Fund Transfer')
def step_he_enters_amount(context):
    context.driver.find_element_by_id("transfer").click()

@then('ensure the fund transfer is complete with {text}
message')
def step_ensure_fund_transfer_is_complete(context, text):
    assert context.driver.find_element_by_id("message").text ==
text

@then('ensure a transaction failure message {text} is
displayed')
def step_ensure_fund_transfer_is_complete(context, text):
    assert
context.driver.find_element_by_id("message").text == text
```

4. Finally, we need to create a configuration file that provides required support to run the features with `Behave`. Create a new file with the following code in the `fundtransfer` folder and name it `environment.py`:

```python
from selenium import webdriver

def before_all(context):
    context.driver = webdriver.Chrome()
```

```
def after_all(context):
    context.driver.quit()
```

5. We need to copy all of these files together in the directory named `fundtransfer` and use the Behave command, as follows:

behave

How it works...

Similar to Cucumber, for Behave we need to write feature files in the Gherkin language. The feature files are then linked to step definitions using the step definition file.

To run these features with Behave, we need a configuration file that provides access to the Selenium WebDriver instance:

```
from selenium import webdriver

def before_all(context):
    context.driver = webdriver.Chrome()

def after_all(context):
    context.driver.quit()
```

When Behave runs the features, a default report is generated in the following format:

See also

- ▶ The *Using Cucumber-JVM and Selenium WebDriver in Java for BDD* recipe
- ▶ The *Using SpecFlow.NET and Selenium WebDriver in .NET for BDD* recipe
- ▶ The *Using Capybara, Cucumber, and Selenium WedDriver in Ruby* recipe

12
Integration with Other Tools

In this chapter, we will cover:

- ▶ Configuring Jenkins for continuous integration
- ▶ Using Jenkins and Maven for Selenium WebDriver test execution in continuous integration
- ▶ Using Ant for Selenium WebDriver test execution
- ▶ Using Jenkins and Ant for Selenium WebDriver test execution in continuous integration
- ▶ Automating a non-web UI in Selenium WebDriver with AutoIt
- ▶ Automating a non-web UI in Selenium WebDriver with Sikuli

Introduction

Selenium WebDriver has been widely used with a combination of various other tools to build test automation frameworks.

The initial sections of this chapter explore Selenium WebDriver's integration with development and build tools such **Maven**, **Ant**, and **Jenkins CI server**. These tools provide an easy way to develop test automation frameworks and extend the capabilities of Selenium WebDriver API to build a continuous testing approach. The following recipes will explain how to set up and configure these tools with Selenium.

Lastly, we will explore how to automate non-web GUIs using tools such as **AutoIt and Sikuli** with Selenium WebDriver. Both the tools are famous in the free and open-source software world for automating user tasks and providing their own approaches to automating the GUI.

Configuring Jenkins for continuous integration

Jenkins is a popular continuous integration server in the Java development community. It is derived from the Hudson CI server. It supports SCM tools including **CVS**, **Subversion**, **Git**, **Mercurial**, **Perforce**, and **ClearCase**, and can execute Apache Maven and Apache Ant-based projects, as well as arbitrary shell scripts and Windows batch commands.

Jenkins can be deployed to set up an automated testing environment where you can run Selenium WebDriver tests unattended based on a defined schedule, or every time changes are submitted in SCM.

In this recipe, we will set up Jenkins Server to run Maven and Ant projects. Later recipes describe how Ant and Maven is used to run Selenium WebDriver tests with Jenkins.

Getting ready

Download and install the Jenkins CI server from `http://jenkins-ci.org/`. For this recipe, the Jenkins Windows installer is used to set up Jenkins on a Windows 7 machine.

How to do it...

Before using Jenkins, we need to set up the following options in the Jenkins configuration:

1. Navigate to **Jenkins Dashboard** (`http://localhost:8080` by default) in the browser window.
2. On **Jenkins Dashboard**, click on the **Manage Jenkins** link.
3. On the **Manage Jenkins** page, click on the **Configure System** link.

Adding JDK

The following are the steps for adding the JDK:

1. On the **Configure System** page, locate the **JDK** section.
2. Click on the **Add JDK** button in the **JDK** section.
3. Specify JDK8 in the **Name** field and unselect the **Install automatically** checkbox.

4. In the **JAVA_HOME** textbox, enter the path of the JDK folder from your system. In the following screenshot, `C:\Program Files\Java\jdk1.8.0_25` has been specified:

Adding Ant

1. On the **Configure System** page, locate the **Ant** section.

2. Click on the **Add Ant** button in the **Ant** section.

3. Specify `Ant` in the **Name** field and unselect the **Install automatically** checkbox.

4. In the **ANT_HOME** textbox, enter the path of the Ant folder from your system. In the following screenshot, `C:\Program Files\WinAnt` has been specified for the WinAnt version:

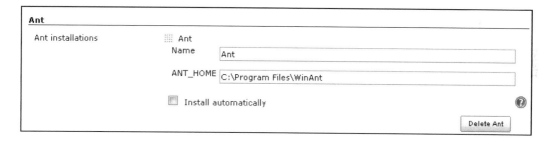

Adding Maven

Follow the given steps to add Maven:

1. On the **Configure System** page, locate the **Maven** section.

2. Click on the **Add Maven** button in the **Maven** section.

3. Specify `Maven` in the **Name** field and unselect the **Install automatically** checkbox.

4. In the **MAVEN_HOME** textbox, enter the path of the Maven folder from your system. In the following screenshot, **MAVEN_HOME** contains `C:\apache-maven`:

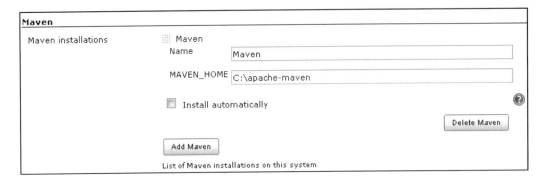

5. Click on the **Save** button to save the configuration.

There's more...

Jenkins also runs a Selenium standalone server that can be used as a remote web driver. Using Jenkins master/slave architecture, we can build a distributed build and test environment for large-scale test automation projects.

See also

▶ The *Using Jenkins and Maven for Selenium WebDriver test execution in continuous integration* recipe

▶ The *Using Jenkins and Ant for Selenium WebDriver test execution in continuous integration* recipe

Using Jenkins and Maven for Selenium WebDriver test execution in continuous integration

Jenkins supports Maven for building and testing a project in continuous integration. In this recipe, we will set up Jenkins to run tests from a Maven project.

Getting ready

Running tests with Jenkins and Maven needs both the tools installed on the machine. In this recipe, the `SeleniumCookbook` project is used from the earlier *Configuring Eclipse and Maven for Selenium WebDriver test development* recipe.

This recipe refers to Subversion as the **Source Code Management** (**SCM**) tool for the `SeleniumCookbook` project.

You can use various SCM tools along with Jenkins. If Jenkins does not support the SCM tool that you are using, please check the Jenkins plugin directory for specific SCM tool plugins.

How to do it...

1. Navigate to the **Jenkins Dashboard** (`http://localhost:8080` by default) in the browser window.

2. On **Jenkins Dashboard**, click on the **New Job** link to create a CI job.

3. Enter `Selenium Cookbook` in the **Job name** textbox.

4. Select the **Build a maven2/3 project** radio button, as shown in the following screenshot:

Job name `Selenium Cookbook`

○ **Build a free-style software project**
  This is the central feature of Jenkins. Jenkins will build your project, combining any SCM with any build than software build.

◉ **Build a maven2/3 project**
  Build a maven2 project. Jenkins takes advantage of your POM files and drastically reduces the configur

○ **Build multi-configuration project**
  Suitable for projects that need a large number of different configurations, such as testing on multiple en

○ **Monitor an external job**
  This type of job allows you to record the execution of a process run outside Jenkins, even on a remote dashboard of your existing automation system. See the documentation for more details.

○ **Copy existing Job**
  Copy from

OK

5. Click on **OK**.

6. A new job will be created with the specified name.

7. On the job configuration page, go to the **Source Code Management** section and select the **Subversion** radio button.

8. Enter the URL of your test code in the **Repository URL** textbox, as shown in the following screenshot. Optionally, Jenkins will ask for the Subversion login details. Provide user credentials as configured on your SVN server:

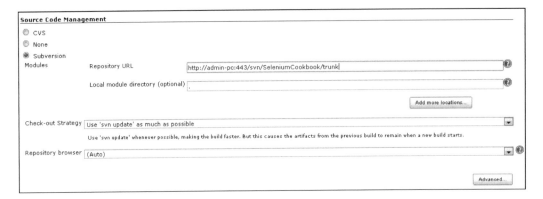

9. Go to the **Build** section. In the **Root POM** textbox, enter pom.xml, and in the **Goals and options** textbox, enter clean test, as shown in the following screenshot:

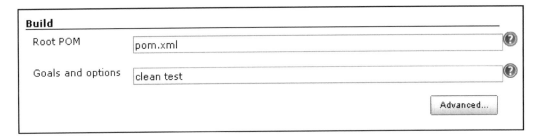

10. On the **Selenium Cookbook** project page, click on the **Build Now** link. Go back to **Jenkins Dashboard**.

11. Maven builds the project and executes tests from the project. Once the build process has been completed, click on the **Selenium Cookbook** project from the list, as shown in the following screenshot:

The **Selenium Cookbook** project page displays the build history and links to the results, as shown in the following screenshot:

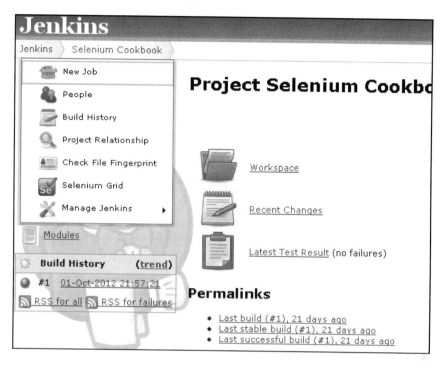

12. Click on the **Latest Test Result** link to view the test results, as shown in the following screenshot:

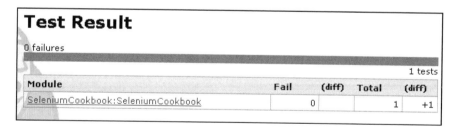

Scheduling build for an automatic execution

1. Go to the **Selenium Cookbook** project configuration in Jenkins.

2. In the **Build Triggers** section, select the **Build periodically** checkbox.

3. Enter 0 22 * * * in the **Schedule** textbox, as shown in the following screenshot. This will trigger the build process every day at 10 p.m. and the test will run unattended:

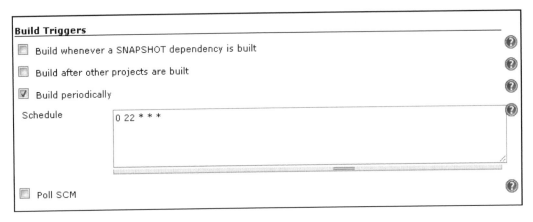

4. Click on the **Save** button to save the configurations.

How it works...

Using the **Build a Maven2/3 Project** option, Jenkins supports building and testing Maven projects.

Jenkins supports various SCM tools such as CVS and Subversion. To get the source code from SCM, specify the repository location and check out the strategy. Since Maven is used in this example, specify the path of root POM and Maven Goal.

While building the project, Jenkins gets the latest source from SCM to the Jenkins project workspace. It will then call Maven with specified goals. When the build process is complete, Jenkins gets the test results from Maven and displays these results on the project page.

Scheduling builds

One of the important features of Jenkins is that it automatically triggers the build, based on defined criteria. Jenkins provides multiple ways to trigger the build process under the Build Trigger configuration. Build Trigger can be set at a specific time. In the previous example, it was set to trigger the process every day at 10 p.m. This provides the ability to nightly run tests unattended, so that you can see the results the next morning.

Test results

Jenkins provides the ability to display test results by reading the results files generated by unit test frameworks. It also archives these results, which can be used to generate various metrics over time.

▶ The *Configuring Jenkins for continuous integration* recipe

Using Ant for Selenium WebDriver test execution

Apache Ant is a popular build management tool available for Java developers. It is similar to Apache Maven, but does not support project management and dependency management features like Maven. It's a pure build tool.

Ant is another choice to run Selenium WebDriver tests from the command line or through continuous integration tools such as Jenkins.

In this recipe, we will add Ant support to the `SeleniumCookbook` project created in the *Configuring Eclipse and Maven for Selenium WebDriver test development* recipe.

Getting ready

You can download and install **WinAnt** on Windows. WinAnt comes with an installer that can configure Ant through the installer. The WinAnt installer is available at `http://code.google.com/p/winant/`.

You can also download and configure Ant from `http://ant.apache.org/bindownload.cgi` for other OS platforms. This recipe uses WinAnt on the Windows OS.

How to do it...

Let's set up the `SeleniumCookbook` project for Ant with the following steps:

1. Create a `lib` folder and copy the JAR files for the dependencies used for this project, that is, Selenium WebDriver and JUnit.

2. Create the `build.xml` file in the project folder with the following XML:

```xml
<?xml version="1.0" encoding="UTF-8"?>
<project name="test" default="exec" basedir=".">

    <property name="src" value="./src" />
    <property name="lib" value="./lib" />
    <property name="bin" value="./bin" />
    <property name="report" value="./report" />
    <path id="test.classpath">
        <pathelement location="${bin}" />
```

```
        <fileset dir="${lib}">
            <include name="**/*.jar" />
        </fileset>
    </path>

    <target name="init">
        <delete dir="${bin}" />
        <mkdir dir="${bin}" />
    </target>

    <target name="compile" depends="init">
        <javac source="1.6" srcdir="${src}" fork="true"
            destdir="${bin}" >
            <classpath>
                    <pathelement path="${bin}">
                    </pathelement>
                <fileset dir="${lib}">
                    <include name="**/*.jar" />
                </fileset>
            </classpath>
        </javac>
    </target>

    <target name="exec" depends="compile">
        <delete dir="${report}" />
        <mkdir dir="${report}" />
            <mkdir dir="${report}/xml" />
        <junit printsummary="yes" haltonfailure="no">
            <classpath>
                <pathelement location="${bin}" />
                <fileset dir="${lib}">
                    <include name="**/*.jar" />
                </fileset>
            </classpath>

            <test name="seleniumcookbook.
                examples.test.GoogleSearchTest"
                haltonfailure="no" todir="${report}/xml"
                outfile="TEST-result">
```

```
                    <formatter type="xml" />
                </test>
            </junit>
            <junitreport todir="${report}">
                <fileset dir="${report}/xml">
                    <include name="TEST*.xml" />
                </fileset>
                <report format="frames"
                        todir="${report}/html" />
            </junitreport>
        </target>
    </project>
```

3. Navigate to the project directory through the command line and type the
following command:

   `ant`

   This will trigger the build process. You will see the test running. At the end, Ant will
   create a `report` folder in the project folder. Navigate to the `html` subfolder in the
   `report` folder and open the `index.html` file to view the results.

How it works...

Ant needs a `build.xml` file with all the configurations and steps that are needed to build
the project. We can add steps for report generation, sending e-mail notification, and so on to
`build.xml`. Ant provides a very dynamic framework to define steps in the build process.

Ant also needs the necessary library/JAR files that are needed to build the project to be
copied in the `lib` folder.

Ant scans for all the tests in the project and executes these tests in a way similar to Maven.

See also

▶ The *Using Jenkins and Ant for Selenium WebDriver test execution in continuous
integration* recipe

Using Jenkins and Ant for Selenium WebDriver test execution in continuous integration

Ant can also be configured to run tests in continuous integration with Jenkins. In this recipe, we will set up Jenkins to run tests with Ant.

Getting ready

Running tests with Jenkins and Ant needs both the tools installed on the machine. Refer to the *Using Ant for Selenium WebDriver test execution* and *Configuring Jenkins for continuous integration* recipes to install and configure Ant and Jenkins respectively.

How to do it...

Let's configure Jenkins and Ant to run tests in CI:

1. Navigate to **Jenkins Dashboard** (`http://localhost:8080` by default) in the browser window.

2. On **Jenkins Dashboard,** click on the **New Job** link to create a CI job.

3. Enter `Selenium Cookbook` in the **Job name:** textbox.

4. Select the **Build a free-style software project** radio button, as shown in the following screenshot:

Job name | Selenium Cookbook

⦿ **Build a free-style software project**
This is the central feature of Jenkins. Jenkins will build your project, combining any SCM with any bui than software build.

⦾ **Build a maven2/3 project**
Build a maven2 project. Jenkins takes advantage of your POM files and drastically reduces the config

⦾ **Build multi-configuration project**
Suitable for projects that need a large number of different configurations, such as testing on multiple

⦾ **Monitor an external job**
This type of job allows you to record the execution of a process run outside Jenkins, even on a remot dashboard of your existing automation system. See the documentation for more details.

⦾ **Copy existing Job**
Copy from

OK

5. Click on **OK**.

6. A new job will be created with the **Selenium Cookbook** name.

7. On the job configuration page, go to the **Source Code Management** section and select the **Subversion** radio button.

8. Enter the URL of your test code in the **Repository URL** textbox, as shown in the following screenshot. Optionally, Jenkins will ask for Subversion login details. Provide user credentials as configured on your SVN server:

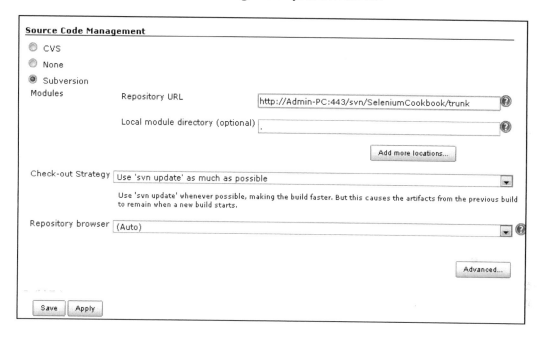

9. Go to the **Build** section. Click on the **Add build step** button once again and select the **Invoke Ant** option from the drop-down list.

10. The **Ant version** textbox will display **Default**, as shown in the following screenshot:

11. Go to the **Post-build Actions** section.

12. Click on the **Add post-build action** button and select **Publish JUnit test result report** from the drop-down list.

13. In the **Test report XMLs** textbox, enter `**/report/*.xml`, as shown in the following screenshot:

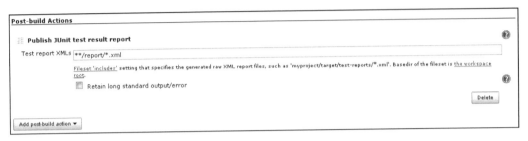

14. Click on the **Save** button to save the configuration.

15. Go back to the **Jenkins Dashboard** page.

16. Click on the **Schedule a Build** button to trigger the build. Ant will execute the test. Once the build process is complete, click on the **Selenium Cookbook** project from the list, as shown in the following screenshot:

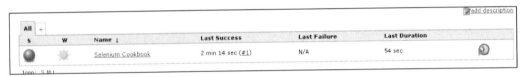

The project page displays the build history and links to the results, as shown in the following screenshot:

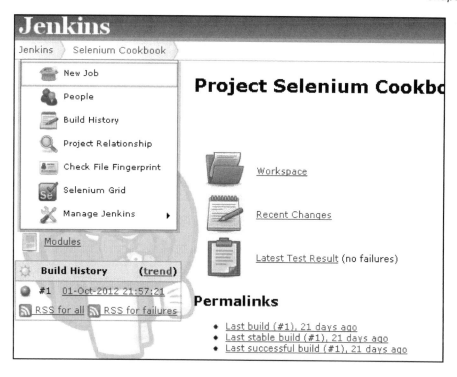

17. Click on the **Latest Test Result** link to view the test results, as shown in the following screenshot:

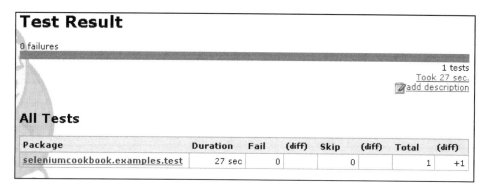

Test Result

0 failures

1 tests
Took 27 sec.
add description

All Tests

Package	Duration	Fail	(diff)	Skip	(diff)	Total	(diff)
seleniumcookbook.examples.test	27 sec	0		0		1	+1

Scheduling the build for an automatic execution

1. Go to the `Selenium Cookbook` project configuration in Jenkins.

2. In the **Build Triggers** section, select the **Build periodically** checkbox.

3. Enter `0 22 * * *` in the **Schedule** textbox, as shown in the following screenshot. This will trigger the build process every day at 10 p.m:

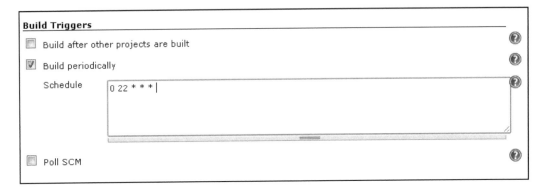

4. Click on the **Save** button to save the configurations.

See also

▸ The *Using Ant for Selenium WebDriver test execution* recipe

▸ The *Configuring Jenkins for continuous integration* recipe

Automating a non-web UI in Selenium WebDriver with AutoIt

Selenium WebDriver is a pure browser automation API and works with HTML/web elements. It does not support the native UI built with C++, .NET, Java, or any other desktop technologies. It also does not support Flex, Flash, or Silverlight native controls out of the box.

While testing applications that interact with the native UI, it becomes difficult to automate the functionality involved. For example, the web application provides a file upload feature that invokes the native OS UI for selecting a file.

We can use tools such as AutoIt to handle the native UI. AutoIt is a freeware BASIC-like scripting language designed to automate the Windows GUI and general scripting. Using AutoIt, we can simulate a combination of keystrokes, mouse movement, and window/control manipulation in order to automate. It is a very small, self-contained utility. It runs on all versions of Windows operating system. AutoIt scripts can be compiled as self-contained executables.

AutoIt has certain limitations in terms of OS support as it is not supported on Linux and Mac OSX, and it will not work with RemoteWebDriver.

In this recipe, we will explore the integration of AutoIt with Selenium WebDriver to test the file upload functionality on a sample page.

Getting ready

Download and install AutoIt tools from `http://www.autoitscript.com/site/autoit/downloads/`.

How to do it...

To implement the file upload functionality, there are a number of libraries or plugins available that provide a number of additional features for uploading files. We will use the jQuery File Upload plugin. It offers multiple ways in which users can upload files on the server. Users can either drag-and-drop a file on the browser or can click on the **Add Files** button, which opens the native **Open** dialog box, as shown in the following screenshot:

We will automate a test where the user to upload a file by clicking on the **Add Files** button. This invokes the **Open** dialog box, as shown in the preceding screenshot. We will create an AutoIt script to automate interactions on this dialog box.

Creating the AutoIt script

Let's create an AutoIt script that works with the **Open** dialog box.

1. Launch **SciTE Script Editor** from **Start | AutoIt**.

2. Create a new script by selecting **File | New** from the **SciTE Script Editor** main menu.

3. Name and save this file as **OpenDialogHandler.au3** (AutoIt scripts have .au3 extension) and copy the following code to the script, then save the script:

```
WinWaitActive("Open","","20")
If WinExists("Open") Then
    ControlSetText("Open","","Edit1",$CmdLine[1])
    ControlClick("Open","","&Open")
EndIf
```

4. Launch the `Compile Script to .exe` utility from **Start | AutoIt**. Using the `Compile Script to .exe` utility, we will convert the AutoIt script into an executable file.

5. On the **Aut2Exe v3 - AutoIt Script to EXE Converter** window, enter the path of the AutoIt script in the **Source (AutoIt .au3 file)** textbox, and the path of the executable in the **Destination (.exe/.a3x file)** textbox, and click on the **Convert** button, as shown in the following screenshot:

Using OpenDialogHandler in Selenium WebDriver script

1. Now create a test that allows us to click on the **Add Files** button and then call `OpenDialogHandler.exe` and validate that the specified file is uploaded on the page.

2. Create a new test class named `FileUpload` and copy the following code in it:

```java
import org.openqa.selenium.WebDriver;
import org.openqa.selenium.chrome.ChromeDriver;
import org.openqa.selenium.By;
import org.openqa.selenium.support.ui.ExpectedCondition;
import org.openqa.selenium.support.ui.WebDriverWait;

import org.junit.*;
import static org.junit.Assert.*;

public class FileUpload {
    protected WebDriver driver;

    @Before
    public void setUp() {
        driver = new ChromeDriver();
        driver.get("http://blueimp.github.com/jQuery-
            File-Upload/");
    }

    @Test
    public void testFileUpload() throws
        InterruptedException {
        try {

            // Click on Add Files button
            driver.findElement(By.className("fileinput-
                button")).click();

            // Call the OpenDialogHandler, specify the
            // path of the file to be uploaded
            Runtime.getRuntime().exec(new String[]
                {"C:\\Utils\\OpenDialogHandler.exe",
                "\"C:\\Users\\Admin\\Desktop\\
                Picture1.png\""});

            //Wait until file is uploaded
            boolean result = (new WebDriverWait
                (driver, 30)).until(new
                ExpectedCondition<Boolean>() {
```

```
            public Boolean apply(WebDriver d) {
                return d.findElement(By.xpath
                ("//table[@role='presentation']"))
                .findElements(By.tagName
                ("tr")).size() > 0;
        }});

        assertTrue(result);

    } catch (Exception e) {
        e.printStackTrace();
    }
}

@After
public void tearDown() {
    driver.close();
}
}
```

How it works...

AutoIt provides an API to automate a native Windows UI control. In this example, we used the `WinWaitActive()` function, which waits for a window. It takes the title of the expected window, text of the window, and timeout as parameters. We supplied the title as `Open` and the timeout of `20` seconds. The text of the windows is passed as blank, as the title is enough to identify the window:

```
WinWaitActive("Open","","20")
```

Once the open window is activated, the `ControlSetText()` function is called to enter the text in the **File name:** textbox:

```
ControlSetText("Open","","Edit1",$CmdLine[1])
```

This function takes the title of the window, text of the window, control ID, and text that needs to be entered in the textbox. Similar to locators in Selenium, AutoIt identifies controls using control IDs. You can find control IDs using the AutoIt V3 Window Info tool installed with AutoIt. You can spy on a window or control using this tool and find out various properties. In this example, the `ControlSetText()` function takes the last parameter as `$CmdLine[1]`. Instead of hardcoding the path of the filename that we want to upload, we will pass the filename to AutoIt script using command line arguments; `$CmdLine[1]` will hold this value.

To click on the **Open** button, the `ControlClick()` function is called. This function takes the title of the window, text of the windows, and control ID as parameters:

```
ControlClick("Open","","&Open")
```

You can find more about AutoIt API in AutoIt help documentation.

Using the **Aut2Exe v3 - AutoIt Script to EXE Converter** utility, AutoIt script is compiled as an executable, that is, `OpenDialogHandler.exe`.

The Selenium WebDriver test calls this executable file using the `exec()` method of the `RunTime` class, which allows the Java code to interact with the environment in which the code is running. The complete path of `OpenDialogHandler`, as well as the path of the file to be uploaded, is passed through the `exec()` method. Please note that `OpenDialogHandler` needs quotes for arguments:

```
Runtime.getRuntime().exec(new String[]
    {"C:\\Utils\\OpenDialogHandler.exe",
    "\"C:\\Users\\Admin\\Desktop\\Picture1.png\""});
```

There's more...

You can use AutoIt scripts with other Selenium WebDriver bindings such as .NET, Ruby, or Python, as long as these languages allow you to call external processes.

AutoIt also comes with a lightweight AutoItX COM library that can be used with languages that support **Component Object Model** (**COM**). Using the COM API will save you from writing the AutoIt script and compiling it into an executable.

You will come across web applications using HTTP authentication, which requires users to authenticate before displaying the application. An HTTP authentication dialog is displayed, as shown in the following screenshot:

This dialog box is displayed using the native UI. In addition, the layout and controls on this dialog box may change for different browsers. In the following example, AutoItX API is called directly in the Ruby script to automate the HTTP authentication dialog box displayed in Google Chrome:

```ruby
require 'rubygems'
require 'selenium-webdriver'
require 'test/unit'
require 'win32ole'

class HttpAuthTest < Test::Unit::TestCase
    def setup
        @driver = Selenium::WebDriver.for :chrome
        @driver.get 'http://www.httpwatch.com/
            httpgallery/authentication'
        @verification_errors = []
    end

    def test_http_auth_window
        #Create instance of AutoItX3 control.
        #This will provide access to AutoItX COM API
        au3 = WIN32OLE.new("AutoItX3.Control")

        #Get the Display Image button and
        #click on it to invoke the Http Authentication dialog
        display_image_button = @driver.find_element :id =>
            "displayImage"
        display_image_button.click

        #Wait for couple of seconds for Http Authentication
        #dialog to appear
        sleep(2)

        #Check if Http Authentication dialog exists and
        #enter login details using send method
        result = au3.WinExists("HTTP Authentication -
            Google Chrome")
        if result then
            au3.WinActivate("HTTP Authentication -
                Google Chrome","")
            au3.Send("httpwatch{TAB}")
            au3.Send("jsdhfkhkhfd{Enter}")
        end
        assert_equal 1, result
    end
```

```
    def teardown
        @driver.quit
        assert_equal [], @verification_errors
    end
end
```

In the previous example, Ruby's `win32ole` module was used to create an instance of AutoItX COM interface:

```
au3 = WIN32OLE.new("AutoItX3.Control")
```

Using this interface, the AutoIt methods are called to interact with non-web UIs.

See also

▶ The *Automating a non-web UI in Selenium WebDriver with Sikuli* recipe

Automating a non-web UI in Selenium WebDriver with Sikuli

Sikuli is another tool that can be used along with Selenium WebDriver to automate a non-web UI. It uses visual identification technology to automate and test graphical user interfaces (GUIs). The Sikuli script automates anything you see as a user on the screen rather than an API.

Sikuli is supported on Windows, Linux, and Mac OSX operating systems. Similar to Selenium IDE, Sikuli provides an IDE for script development and API that can be used within Java.

Sikuli works well for non-web UI. However, it also has certain limitations, as it is not supported by RemoteWebDriver. The Sikuli script might fail if it does not find a captured image due to overlapping windows at runtime.

In this recipe, we will explore the integration of the Sikuli API with Selenium WebDriver to test a non-web UI.

Getting ready

Download and install Sikuli from `http://sikuli.org/`.

How to do it...

We will use the HTTP authentication example from the previous recipe to automate the steps with Sikuli, as follows:

1. Before we automate the steps on the **Authentication Required** dialog box, we need to capture images of the **User Name:** and **Password:** textboxes, and the **Log In** button:

2. Capture the screenshot of the **Authentication Required** dialog box and extract images, as follows, for each control:

Control	Screenshot
User Name: textbox	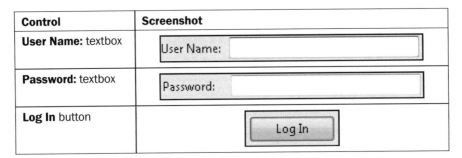
Password: textbox	
Log In button	

3. Save these extracted images separately in **PNG (Portable Network Graphics)** format in a folder that can be accessed from tests easily.

4. Add the `Sikuli-script.jar` file to the test project. You can get this file from the Sikuli installation folder.

5. Create a new test, name it `HttpAuthTest`, and copy the following code to this test:

```
import org.openqa.selenium.WebDriver;
import org.openqa.selenium.chrome.ChromeDriver;
```

```
import org.openqa.selenium.By;

import org.sikuli.script.FindFailed;
import org.sikuli.script.Screen;

import org.junit.*;
import static org.junit.Assert.fail;

public class HttpAuthTest {
    private WebDriver driver;
    private StringBuffer verificationErrors = new
        StringBuffer();

    @Before
    public void setUp() {
        driver = new ChromeDriver();
        driver.get("http://www.httpwatch.com/
            httpgallery/authentication/");
    }

    @Test
    public void testHttpAuth() throws
        InterruptedException {
        driver.findElement(By.id
        ("displayImage")).click();

        //Get the system screen.
        Screen s = new Screen();

        try {

            //Sikuli type command will use the image file
            //of the control
            //and text that needs to be entered in to the
            //control
            s.type("C:\\UserName.png", "httpwatch");
            s.type("C:\\Password.png","dhjhfj");

            //Sikuli click command will use the image
            //file of the control
            s.click("C:\\Login.png");

        } catch (FindFailed e) {
            //Sikuli raises FindFailed exception it fails
```

```
                    //to locate the image on to the screen
                    e.printStackTrace();
            }
    }

    @After
    public void tearDown() {
        driver.close();
        String verificationErrorString =
            verificationErrors.toString();
        if (!"".equals(verificationErrorString)) {
            fail(verificationErrorString);
        }
    }
}
```

How it works...

As Sikuli uses visual identification technology to identify and interact with windows and controls, it requires images of the controls to perform the action. During the execution, it locates the regions captured in the image on the screen and performs the specified action:

```
s.type("C:\\UserName.png", "httpwatch");
```

In this example, it searches the screen for a region that matches the image captured in UserName.png, and performs the type () command. Sikuli replays these commands as if a real user is working on the screen.

Sikuli may fail to interact with the application if the region captured in the image is not displayed on the screen or is overlapped with other windows.

There's more...

By using Sikuli, you can automate RIA technologies such as Flash and Silverlight, along with the Selenium WebDriver.

See also

> ▶ The *Automating a non-web UI in Selenium WebDriver with AutoIt* recipe

13

Cross-Browser Testing

In this chapter, we will cover:

- ▸ Setting up Selenium Grid Server for parallel execution
- ▸ Adding nodes to Selenium Grid for cross-browser testing
- ▸ Creating and executing the Selenium script in parallel with TestNG
- ▸ Creating and executing the Selenium script in parallel with Python
- ▸ Using Cloud tools for cross-browser testing
- ▸ Running tests in headless mode with PhantomJS

Introduction

Organizations are adopting virtualization and cloud-based technologies to reduce costs and increase efficiency. Virtualization and cloud-based infrastructure can also be used to scale the test automation by reducing investment in physical hardware needed to set up the test environment. Using these technologies, web applications can be tested on a variety of browser and operating system combinations. Selenium WebDriver has unmatched support for testing applications in virtual environment, executing tests in parallel, reducing costs, and increasing speed and coverage. This chapter will cover recipes to configure and execute Selenium WebDriver tests for parallel or distributed execution.

Running tests in parallel requires two things: an infrastructure to distribute the tests, and a framework that will run these tests in parallel in the given infrastructure. In this chapter, we will first create a distributed infrastructure, and then create some tests that will be executed in this distributed test environment.

Selenium Grid transparently distributes our tests across multiple physical or virtual machines so that we can run them in parallel, cutting down the time required to run tests. This dramatically speeds up testing, giving us quick and accurate feedback.

With Selenium Grid, we can leverage our existing computing infrastructure. It allows us to easily run multiple tests in parallel, on multiple nodes or clients, in a heterogeneous environment where we can have a mixture of OS and browser support. Here is an example of the Selenium Grid architecture with the capabilities to run tests on Linux, Windows, Mac, iOS, and Android platforms:

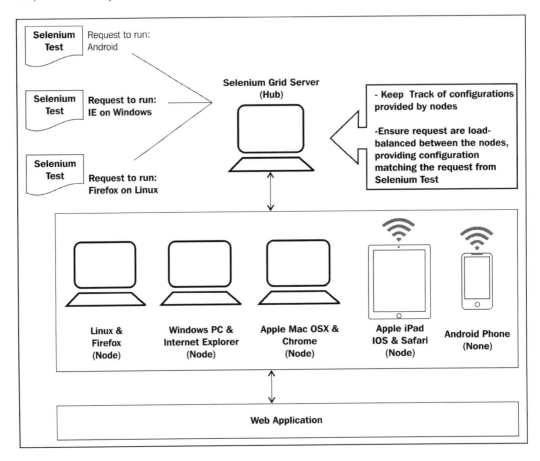

Selenium Grid allows us to run multiple instances of WebDriver or Selenium Remote Control in parallel. It makes all these nodes appear as a single instance, so tests do not have to worry about the actual infrastructure. Selenium Grid cuts down on the time required to run Selenium tests to a fraction of the time that a single instance of Selenium would take to run, and it is very easy to set up and use.

The Selenium Server standalone package includes the Hub, WebDriver, and Selenium RC that are needed to run the Grid.

Testing the framework for parallel execution

In this chapter, we need a testing framework that supports parallel runs of our tests. We will use **TestNG** (`http://testng.org/`) to run parallel tests with Selenium WebDriver Java bindings. TestNG has a threading model to support running multiple instances of the same test using an XML-based configuration. TestNG is pretty similar to JUnit.

We will also use a raw method to run tests in parallel for Python bindings using the `subprocess` module. However, you can also use `nose` for parallel execution in Python.

To run tests in parallel with .NET bindings, you can use **PUnit** or **MSTEST**, and for Ruby, you can use **DeepTest**.

Setting up Selenium Grid Server for parallel execution

To run Selenium WebDriver tests in parallel, we need to set up the Selenium Grid Server as a **Hub**. The Selenium Server hub will provide the available configurations or capabilities to the Selenium WebDriver tests. The slave machines, also called **node**, connect to the hub for parallel execution. Selenium WebDriver tests use the JSON wire protocol to talk to the Hub to execute Selenium commands.

The Hub acts like the central point that will receive the entire test request and distribute it to the right nodes.

In this recipe, we will set up a Selenium Grid Server and then add nodes with different OS and browser combinations. We will then use this setup to run tests in parallel using TestNG.

Getting ready

Download the latest Selenium Server standalone JAR file from `http://docs.seleniumhq.org/download/`. For this recipe, the selenium-server-standalone-2.47.1 version is used.

How to do it...

Setting up a Hub is a fairly simple job. Launch the Selenium Server using the following command:

```
java -jar selenium-server-standalone-2.46.0.jar -port 4444 -role hub
-nodeTimeout 600
```

This command will start the Selenium Server in Hub role with the following output on the command prompt:

How it works...

When we launch the Selenium Standalone Server in Hub role, it starts listening to nodes and Selenium tests on port 4444. If you browse to `http://localhost:4444/grid/console` on the Hub machine, it will display the following information in the browser:

There's more...

To run tests with Selenium Grid, Selenium WebDriver tests need to use the instance of the `RemoteWebDriver` and `DesiredCapabilities` classes to define which browser, version, and platform tests will be executed. Based on preferences set in the `DesiredCapabilities` instance, the Hub will point the test to a node that matches these preferences. In this example, Hub will point the test to a node running on the Windows operating system and Firefox browser with the specified version:

```
DesiredCapabilities cap = new DesiredCapabilities();
    cap.setBrowserName("firefox");
    cap.setPlatform(org.openqa.selenium.Platform.WINDOWS);
```

These preferences are set using the `setBrowserName()`, `setVersion()`, and `setPlatform()` methods of the `DesiredCapabillities` class.

An instance of the `DesiredCapabilities` class is passed to `RemoteWebDriver`:

```
driver = new RemoteWebDriver(new
URL("http://192.168.1.100:4444/wd/hub"),cap);
```

In this example, the test is connecting to the Hub running on `http://192.168.1.100:4444/wd/hub` with the instance of `DesiredCapabilities` named `cap`.

Adding nodes to Selenium Grid for cross-browser testing

In this recipe, we will add nodes to the Selenium Hub that we set up in the previous recipe. We will use multiple OS platforms and browser combinations for cross-browser testing

How to do it...

We will add nodes with the following OS and browser configurations to the Hub:

Adding an IE node

Let's begin with a node which provides Internet Explorer capabilities to run on Windows. Open a new command prompt or terminal window and navigate to the location where Selenium server jar is located. To launch and add a node to the Grid, type the following command:

```
java -Dwebdriver.ie.driver="C:\SeDrivers\IEDriverServer.exe" -jar
selenium-server-standalone-2.46.0.jar -role webdriver -browser
"browserName=internet
explorer,version=10,maxinstance=1,platform=WINDOWS" -hubHost
192.168.1.103 -port 5555
```

To add a node to the Grid, we need to use the `-role` argument and pass `webdriver` as the value. We also need to pass the browser configuration for the node. This is passed through the browser argument. In this example, we passed `browserName` as `internet explorer`, the version as `10`, `maxinstance` as `1`, and `platform` as `WINDOWS`. The `maxinstance` value tells the Grid how many concurrent instances of the browser will be supported by the node.

To connect the node to the hub or Grid server, we need to specify the `-hubHost` argument with the hostname or IP address of the Grid server. Lastly, we need to specify the port on which the node will be running.

When we run the preceding command, and after the node is launched, the following configuration will appear in the Grid console:

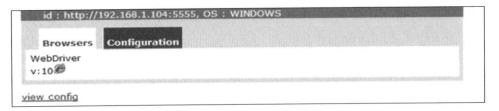

Alternatively, a node can be added by creating a configuration file in the JSON format and then using the following command:

```
{
    "class": "org.openqa.grid.common.RegistrationRequest",
    "capabilities": [
      {
      "seleniumProtocol": "WebDriver",
      "browserName": "internet explorer",
      "version": "10",
      "maxInstances": 1,
      "platform" : "WINDOWS"
      }
    ],
    "configuration": {
      "port": 5555,
      "register": true,
      "host": "192.168.1.103",
      "proxy": "org.openqa.grid.selenium.proxy.
      DefaultRemoteProxy",
      "maxSession": 2,
      "hubHost": "192.168.1.100",
      "role": "webdriver",
      "registerCycle": 5000,
      "hub": "http://192.168.1.100:4444/grid/register",
      "hubPort": 4444,
      "remoteHost": "http://192.168.1.102:5555"
    }
}
```

We can now pass the `selenium-node-win-ie10.cfg.json` configuration file through command-line arguments, as shown in the following command:

```
java -Dwebdriver.ie.driver="C:\SeDrivers\IEDriverServer.exe"-jar
selenium-server-standalone-2.46.0.jar -role webdriver -nodeConfig
selenium-node-win-ie10.cfg.json
```

Adding a Firefox node

To add a Firefox node, open a new command prompt or terminal window and navigate to the location where the Selenium server JAR file is located. To launch and add a node to the Grid, type the following command:

```
java -jar selenium-server-standalone-2.47.1.jar -role webdriver -
browser
"browserName=firefox,version=38.0.5,maxinstance=2,platform=WINDOWS" -
hubHost localhost -port 6666
```

In this example, we set `maxinstance` to 2. This tells the Grid that this node will support two instances of Firefox. Once the node is started, the following configuration will appear in the Grid console:

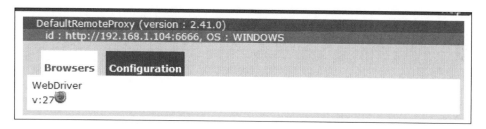

Adding a Chrome node

To add a Chrome node, open a new command prompt or terminal window and navigate to the location where the Selenium server jar is located. To launch and add a node to the grid, type the following command:

```
java -Dwebdriver.chrome.driver="C:\SeDrivers\chromedriver.exe" -jar
selenium-server-standalone-2.47.1.jar -role webdriver -browser
"browserName=chrome,version=35,maxinstance=2,platform=WINDOWS" -
hubHost localhost -port 7777
```

Once the node is started, the following configuration will appear in the Grid console:

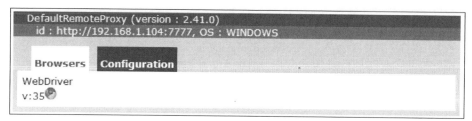

Mac OS X with Safari

We added IE, Firefox, and Chrome instances on a Windows machine. Let's add a Safari node from a Mac OS. Open a new terminal window and navigate to the location where Selenium server jar is located. To launch and add a node to the Grid, type the following command:

```
java -jar selenium-server-standalone-2.47.1.jar -role webdriver -
browser "browserName=safari,version=7,maxinstance=1,platform=MAC" -
hubHost 192.168.1.104 -port 8888
```

Once the node is started, the following configuration will appear in the Grid console:

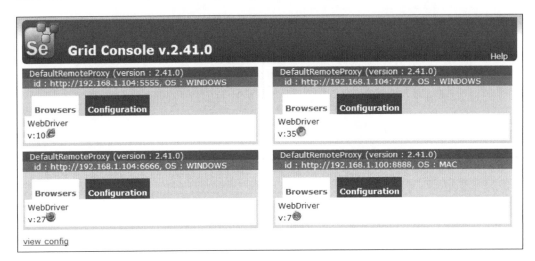

Creating and executing the Selenium script in parallel with TestNG

Now that we have our Selenium Grid Hub and nodes ready and configured from previous recipes, it's time to run tests in parallel with this distributed environment.

To run tests in parallel, we need a test framework that supports distributing tests on these nodes. We will use TestNG to run tests in parallel for Selenium tests developed with Java bindings.

TestNG (http://testng.org) is another popular unit testing frameworks used by the Java community after JUnit. TestNG allows us to create tests that can be executed in parallel. We can set up a group of tests or test suites and have parameters configured to run these tests in parallel. It uses a multithreading model to run tests in parallel.

TestNG requires that we have an XML configuration file with details of configurations that are needed to run the tests in parallel. Before starting the run, TestNG reads this configuration file to set up the test.

In this recipe, we use TestNG to create tests that are parameterized for parallel runs. This recipe is divided in two parts: in the first part, we will create a configuration file based on the Hub and the nodes that we have configured so far; and then in the second part, we will be creating a test case using TestNG annotations and parameterization features.

Getting ready

Make sure you have TestNG installed on the machine from where the tests will be launched. You can download TestNG from `http://testng.org/doc/index.html`.

How to do it...

Let's create and execute a test in parallel with the following steps:

1. Before we create a test for parallel execution, we need to first create a configuration file, which TestNG will need to run the tests in parallel. We will provide four parameters for the tests, platform, browser, version, and URL.

    Create a new `conf.xml` file in your projects source directory and add the following code to this file:

    ```xml
    <!DOCTYPE suite SYSTEM http://testng.org/testng-1.0.dtd>
    <suite name="Parallel Tests" verbose="1" thread-count="3"
    parallel="tests">
    </suite>
    ```

2. Add the `<test>` node for a test that will be executed on the Windows and Internet Explorer combination in the `conf.xml` file, as follows:

    ```xml
    <tests>
      <test name="Windows+IE10 Test">
        <parameters>
          <parameter name="platform" value="Windows" />
          <parameter name="browser" value="Internet Explorer"
    />
          <parameter name="version" value="10" />
          <parameter name="url" value="http://bit.ly/1zdNrFZ"
    />
        </parameters>
        <classes>
          <class name="SeGridTest" />
        </classes>
      </test>
    </tests>
    ```

3. Add the following combinations to `conf.xml`. It should have the following entries:

```xml
<suite name="Parallel Tests" verbose="1" thread-count="3"
  parallel="tests">
  <tests>
    <test name="Windows+IE10 Test">
      <parameters>
        <parameter name="platform" value="Windows" />
        <parameter name="browser" value="Internet Explorer"
/>
        <parameter name="version" value="10" />
        <parameter name="url" value="http://bit.ly/1zdNrFZ"
/>
      </parameters>
      <classes>
        <class name="SeGridTest" />
      </classes>
    </test>
    <test name="Windows+Firefox Test">
      <parameters>
        <parameter name="platform" value="Mac" />
        <parameter name="browser" value="Firefox" />
        <parameter name="version" value="38.0.5" />
        <parameter name="url" value="http://bit.ly/1zdNrFZ" />
      </parameters>
      <classes>
        <class name="SeGridTest" />
      </classes>
    </test>
    <test name="Mac+Safari Test">
      <parameters>
        <parameter name="platform" value="Mac" />
        <parameter name="browser" value="Safari" />
        <parameter name="version" value="8.0.2" />
        <parameter name="url" value="http://bit.ly/1zdNrFZ" />
      </parameters>
      <classes>
        <class name="SeGridTest" />
      </classes>
    </test>
  </tests>
</suite>
```

4. Now, we need to create a test using TestNG. We will create a parameterized test using TestNG's parameterization features. We will create a test for the BMI calculator application. We will use both the normal web and mobile web version of this application. Create a new test with the name `SeGridTest` and copy the following code:

```java
package com.secookbook.examples.chapter13;

import org.openqa.selenium.WebDriver;
import org.openqa.selenium.WebElement;
import org.openqa.selenium.By;

import org.openqa.selenium.remote.DesiredCapabilities;
import org.openqa.selenium.remote.RemoteWebDriver;

import static org.testng.Assert.*;
import org.testng.annotations.AfterTest;
import org.testng.annotations.Parameters;
import org.testng.annotations.Test;
import org.testng.annotations.BeforeTest;

import java.net.MalformedURLException;
import java.net.URL;

public class SeGridTest {

  WebDriver driver = null;

  @Parameters({ "platform", "browser", "version", "url" })
  @BeforeTest(alwaysRun = true)
  public void setup(String platform, String browser, String
version,
      String url) throws MalformedURLException {
    DesiredCapabilities caps = new DesiredCapabilities();

    // Platforms
    if (platform.equalsIgnoreCase("Windows")) {
      caps.setPlatform(org.openqa.selenium.Platform.WINDOWS);
    }

    if (platform.equalsIgnoreCase("MAC")) {
      caps.setPlatform(org.openqa.selenium.Platform.MAC);
    }
```

```
    // Browsers
    if (browser.equalsIgnoreCase("Internet Explorer")) {
      caps = DesiredCapabilities.internetExplorer();
    }

    if (browser.equalsIgnoreCase("Firefox")) {
      caps = DesiredCapabilities.firefox();
    }

    if (browser.equalsIgnoreCase("Chrome")) {
      caps = DesiredCapabilities.chrome();
    }

    if (browser.equalsIgnoreCase("Safari")) {
      caps = DesiredCapabilities.safari();
    }

    // Version
    caps.setVersion(version);

    driver = new RemoteWebDriver(new
URL("http://localhost:4444/wd/hub"),
        caps);

    // Open the BMI Calculator Application
    driver.get(url);

  }

  @Test(description = "Test Bmi Calculator")
  public void testBmiCalculator() throws
InterruptedException {

    WebElement height =
driver.findElement(By.name("heightCMS"));
    height.sendKeys("181");

    WebElement weight =
driver.findElement(By.name("weightKg"));
    weight.sendKeys("80");

    WebElement calculateButton =
driver.findElement(By.id("Calculate"));
    calculateButton.click();
```

```
WebElement bmi = driver.findElement(By.name("bmi"));
assertEquals(bmi.getAttribute("value"), "24.4");

WebElement bmiCategory =
driver.findElement(By.name("bmi_category"));
assertEquals(bmiCategory.getAttribute("value"), "Normal");

}

@AfterTest
public void afterTest() {
    driver.quit();
}
```

How it works...

First, we created a test configuration file listing the combination of tests that we want to run in parallel. Each instance of a test is listed in the `<test>` tag:

```
<tests>
  <test name="Windows+IE10 Test">
    <parameters>
      <parameter name="platform" value="Windows" />
      <parameter name="browser" value="Internet Explorer" />
      <parameter name="version" value="10" />
      <parameter name="url" value="http://bit.ly/1zdNrFZ" />
    </parameters>
    <classes>
      <class name="SeGridTest" />
    </classes>
  </test>
</tests>
```

In the `<parameters>` section, we provided the platform, browser, and the browser version. Next, we added URL as we want to run this test both for normal and mobile web versions of the application. Next, we need to specify the name of the test class in the `<class>` node. If you are storing the test class in a package, then specify the complete path. For example, if we keep `SeGridTest` in the package `com.bmicalcapp.test`, then the following will be the value that we will pass:

```
<classes>
    <class name="com.bmicalcapp.test.SeGridTest" />
</classes>
```

Next, we created a parameterized test in TestNG. We added a `setup()` method, which accepts arguments to set the options for the `DesiredCapabilities` class to run tests for each combination specified in the configuration file:

```java
@Parameters({ "platform", "browser", "version", "url" })
  @BeforeTest(alwaysRun = true)
    public void setup(String platform, String browser, String version,
        String url) throws MalformedURLException {
    DesiredCapabilities caps = new DesiredCapabilities();

    // Platforms
    if (platform.equalsIgnoreCase("Windows")) {
      caps.setPlatform(org.openqa.selenium.Platform.WINDOWS);
    }

    if (platform.equalsIgnoreCase("MAC")) {
      caps.setPlatform(org.openqa.selenium.Platform.MAC);
    }

    // Browsers
    if (browser.equalsIgnoreCase("Internet Explorer")) {
      caps = DesiredCapabilities.internetExplorer();
    }

    if (browser.equalsIgnoreCase("Firefox")) {
      caps = DesiredCapabilities.firefox();
    }

    if (browser.equalsIgnoreCase("Chrome")) {
      caps = DesiredCapabilities.chrome();
    }

    if (browser.equalsIgnoreCase("Safari")) {
      caps = DesiredCapabilities.safari();
    }

    // Version
    caps.setVersion(version);

    driver = new RemoteWebDriver(new URL("http://localhost:4444/wd/
hub"),
        caps);
```

```
   // Open the BMI Calculator Application
   driver.get(url);
}
```

When we execute the tests, we need to tell TestNG to use the `conf.xml` file for test configurations. TestNG will read this file and create a pool of threads (for this example, it will create three threads) for each combination calling the test class. It will then create and assign an instance of test class to each thread by passing the parameters from the configuration file to the `setup()` method. TestNG will run the test concurrently for each combination, monitoring and reporting the test status and the final results. The following is the report it generates after running the test for combinations specified in the configuration file:

Creating and executing the Selenium script in parallel with Python

In this recipe, we will create and execute tests in parallel with Python bindings using the `subprocess` module. We will use the Hub and nodes configured in earlier recipes to run these tests.

How to do it...

We will create two test scripts to test the application with Firefox and Internet Explorer using the following steps. You can also create a single test and parameterize it similar to what we did for TestNG:

1. For the first Python test, which will test the application functionality using the Firefox browser, name this test as `test_on_firefox.py` and copy the following code:

    ```python
    import unittest

    from selenium import webdriver
    from selenium.webdriver.common.desired_capabilities import
    DesiredCapabilities
    from selenium.webdriver.support.ui import WebDriverWait


    class OnFirefox(unittest.TestCase):
        def setUp(self):
            self.driver = webdriver.Remote(
                command_executor='http://localhost:4444/wd/hub',

    desired_capabilities=DesiredCapabilities.FIREFOX)

        def test_gogle_search_ie(self):
    ```

```
        driver = self.driver
        driver.get("http://www.google.com")

        inputElement = driver.find_element_by_name("q")
        inputElement.send_keys("Cheese!")
        inputElement.submit()

        WebDriverWait(driver, 20).until(lambda driver:
driver.title.lower().startswith("cheese!"))
        self.assertEqual("cheese! - Google Search",
driver.title)

    def tearDown(self):
        self.driver.quit()

if __name__ == "__main__":
    unittest.main(verbosity=2)
```

2. For the second Python test, which will test the application functionality using the Internet Explorer browser, name this test as `test_on_ie.py` and copy the following code:

```
import unittest

from selenium import webdriver
from selenium.webdriver.common.desired_capabilities import
DesiredCapabilities
from selenium.webdriver.support.ui import WebDriverWait

class OnFirefox(unittest.TestCase):
    def setUp(self):
        self.driver = webdriver.Remote(

command_executor='http://localhost:4444/wd/hub',
            desired_capabilities=DesiredCapabilities.
INTERNETEXPLORER)

    def test_google_search_ff(self):
        driver = self.driver
        driver.get("http://www.google.com")

        inputElement = driver.find_element_by_name("q")
        inputElement.send_keys("Cheese!")
        inputElement.submit()
```

```
        WebDriverWait(driver, 20).until(lambda driver:
driver.title.lower().startswith("cheese!"))
        self.assertEqual("cheese! - Google Search",
driver.title)

    def tearDown(self):
        self.driver.quit()

if __name__ == "__main__":
    unittest.main(verbosity=2)
```

3. Finally, we need to create a Python script, which will use the `subprocess` module to run these tests concurrently on different nodes. Name this script as `runner.py` and copy the following code:

```
import glob

from subprocess import Popen

tests = glob.glob('test*.py')
processes = [Popen('python %s' % test, shell=True) for test
in tests]

for process in processes:
    process.wait()
```

How it works...

We need to place all three scripts in the same directory. When we execute `runner.py`, it collects all the tests with names starting with `test` using the `glob` function. Then we append each test using the `Popen` function from the `subprocess` module. The `Popen()` function calls each test using Python as a `subprocess` of the main process and waits for the script to complete.

There's more...

We can also use the `nose` module for Python to run the tests in parallel. First, we need to install the `nose` unit testing framework using the following command:

```
pip nose
```

After the `nose` module is installed, you need to open the folder where all the tests are stored and use the following command:

```
nosetests --processes=2
```

This will call the `nosetests` scripts, which will locate all the files with a test prefix in the current directory and start running tests concurrently. In this example we are running two tests, so we need to specify the value for processes argumented as 2. The `nose` module internally uses a multiprocessing module for concurrent execution.

See also

> ► The *Creating and executing the Selenium script in parallel with TestNG* recipe

Using Cloud tools for cross-browser testing running tests in the Cloud

We set up a local Grid in previous recipes to run the tests for cross-browser testing. This requires setting up physical or virtual machines with different browsers and operating systems. There are costs and efforts needed get the required hardware, software, and support to run the test lab. You also need to put in effort to keep this infrastructure updated with the latest versions and patches, and so on. Not everybody can afford these costs and effort.

Instead of investing and setting up a cross-browser test lab, you can easily outsource a virtual test lab to a third-party cloud provider. The **Sauce Labs** and **BrowserStack** are leading cloud-based cross-browser testing cloud providers. Both of these have support for over 400 different browser and operating system configurations including mobile and tablet devices, and support running Selenium WebDriver tests in their cloud.

In this section, we will set up and run a test in the Sauce Labs cloud. The steps are similar if you want to run tests with BrowserStack.

Getting ready

Let's set up and run a test with Sauce Labs. You need a free Sauce Labs account to begin with. Register for a free account on Sauce Labs at `https://saucelabs.com/` and get the user name and access key. Sauce Labs provides all the needed hardware and software infrastructure to run your tests in the cloud.

You can get the access key from Sauce Labs dashboard after the login:

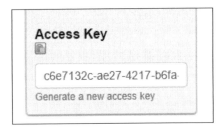

How to do it...

Let's modify the test we created earlier to run with grid, and add steps to run this test on Sauce Labs cloud. We need to add the Sauce username and access key to the test and change the Grid address to Sauce's Gird address, passing the username and access key, as shown in the following code example:

```java
package com.secookbook.examples.chapter13;

import static org.junit.Assert.*;
import static org.testng.Assert.assertEquals;

import java.net.URL;
import java.text.MessageFormat;

import org.junit.After;
import org.junit.Before;
import org.junit.Test;
import org.openqa.selenium.By;
import org.openqa.selenium.WebDriver;
import org.openqa.selenium.WebElement;
import org.openqa.selenium.remote.DesiredCapabilities;
import org.openqa.selenium.remote.RemoteWebDriver;

public class SauceTest {

  WebDriver driver;

  @Before
  public void setUp() throws Exception {
    String SAUCE_USER = "<your username>";
    String SAUCE_KEY = "<your key>";

    DesiredCapabilities caps = new DesiredCapabilities();
    caps.setCapability("platform", "OS X 10.9");
    caps.setCapability("browserName", "Safari");
    caps.setCapability("name", "BMI Calculator Test");
    driver = new RemoteWebDriver(new
URL(MessageFormat.format("http://{0}:{1}@ondemand.saucelabs.com:80
/wd/hub'", SAUCE_USER, SAUCE_KEY)), caps);
    driver.get("http://bit.ly/1zdNrFZ");

  }
```

```
@After
public void tearDown() throws Exception {
  driver.quit();
}

@Test
public void testBmiCalc() {
  WebElement height = driver.findElement(By.name("heightCMS"));
  height.sendKeys("181");

  WebElement weight = driver.findElement(By.name("weightKg"));
  weight.sendKeys("80");

  WebElement calculateButton =
driver.findElement(By.id("Calculate"));
  calculateButton.click();

  WebElement bmi = driver.findElement(By.name("bmi"));
  assertEquals(bmi.getAttribute("value"), "24.4");

  WebElement bmiCategory =
driver.findElement(By.name("bmi_category"));
  assertEquals(bmiCategory.getAttribute("value"), "Normal");
  }

}
```

You can get a list of platforms supported on Sauce Labs
at `https://saucelabs.com/platforms`.

While running the test, it will connect to Sauce Lab's hub and request the desired operating
system and bowser configuration. Sauce assigns a virtual machine for our test to run on
a given configuration. We can monitor this run on the Sauce dashboard, as shown in the
following screenshot:

We can further drill down into the Sauce session and see exactly what happened during the run. It provide details of the Selenium commands, screenshots, logs, and video of the execution on multiple tabs, as shown in the following screenshot:

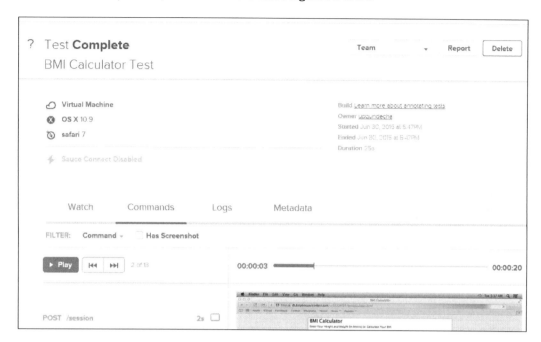

 You can also test applications securely hosted on internal servers by using the **Sauce Connect** utility. Sauce Connect creates a secure tunnel between your machine and the Sauce cloud.

Running tests in headless mode with PhantomJS

PhantomJS is a headless Webkit-based browser. We can use PhantomJS in conjunction with Selenium WebDriver to run basic functional tests.

In this recipe, we will set up and use PhantomJS to run a simple test.

Getting ready

You will need PhantomJS binary for this example. You can download the appropriate binary from http://phantomjs.org/.

In this example, the Windows version of PhantomJS is used.

You will also need to add a dependency in the maven `pom.xml` file, as follows:

```
<dependency>
    <groupId>com.github.detro</groupId>
    <artifactId>phantomjsdriver</artifactId>
    <version>1.2.0</version>
    <scope>test</scope>
</dependency>
```

How to do it...

Let's create a new test `PhantomjsTest` that uses PhantomJS to run a test in headless mode, as shown in the following code example:

```java
package com.secookbook.examples.chapter13;

import static org.junit.Assert.*;
import static org.testng.Assert.assertEquals;

import org.junit.After;
import org.junit.Before;
import org.junit.Test;
import org.openqa.selenium.By;
import org.openqa.selenium.WebDriver;
import org.openqa.selenium.WebElement;
import org.openqa.selenium.phantomjs.PhantomJSDriver;
import org.openqa.selenium.phantomjs.PhantomJSDriverService;
import org.openqa.selenium.remote.DesiredCapabilities;

public class PhantomjsTest {

    WebDriver driver;

    @Before
    public void setUp() throws Exception {
        DesiredCapabilities caps =
DesiredCapabilities.phantomjs();
        caps.setJavascriptEnabled(true);
        caps.setCapability(
                PhantomJSDriverService.PHANTOMJS_EXECUTABLE_PATH_
PROPERTY,
                "./src/test/resources/drivers/phantomjs.exe");
        driver = new PhantomJSDriver(caps);
        driver.get("http://bit.ly/1zdNrFZ");
    }
```

```
    @After
    public void tearDown() throws Exception {
        driver.quit();
    }


    @Test
    public void testBmiCalc() {
        WebElement height =
driver.findElement(By.name("heightCMS"));
        height.sendKeys("181");

        WebElement weight = driver.findElement(By.name("weightKg"));
        weight.sendKeys("80");

        WebElement calculateButton = driver.findElement(By.
id("Calculate"));
        calculateButton.click();

        WebElement bmi = driver.findElement(By.name("bmi"));
        assertEquals(bmi.getAttribute("value"), "24.4");

        WebElement bmiCategory =
driver.findElement(By.name("bmiCategory"));
        assertEquals(bmi_category.getAttribute("value"),
"Normal");
    }
}
```

How it works...

When tests are run with PhantomJS, you will not see graphical browser opening and actions being performed. You will see the execution log on the console, that looks as shown in the following screenshot:

```
Jun 30, 2015 6:11:38 PM org.openqa.selenium.phantomjs.PhantomJSDriverService <init>
INFO: executable: C:\workspace\SeleniumCookbook\.\src\test\resources\drivers\phantomjs.exe
Jun 30, 2015 6:11:38 PM org.openqa.selenium.phantomjs.PhantomJSDriverService <init>
INFO: port: 45866
Jun 30, 2015 6:11:38 PM org.openqa.selenium.phantomjs.PhantomJSDriverService <init>
INFO: arguments: [--webdriver=45866, --webdriver-logfile=C:\workspace\SeleniumCookbook\phantomjsdriver.log]
Jun 30, 2015 6:11:38 PM org.openqa.selenium.phantomjs.PhantomJSDriverService <init>
INFO: environment: {}
[INFO  - 2015-06-30T12:41:52.470Z] GhostDriver - Main - running on port 45866
[INFO  - 2015-06-30T12:41:53.814Z] Session [62e2cd30-1f25-11e5-a947-3d50e305fa96] - page.settings - {"XSSAuditingEnabled":false,"javascriptCanCloseWindows"
[INFO  - 2015-06-30T12:41:53.814Z] Session [62e2cd30-1f25-11e5-a947-3d50e305fa96] - page.customHeaders:  - {}
[INFO  - 2015-06-30T12:41:53.815Z] Session [62e2cd30-1f25-11e5-a947-3d50e305fa96] - Session.negotiatedCapabilities - {"browserName":"phantomjs","version":"
[INFO  - 2015-06-30T12:41:53.816Z] SessionManagerReqHand - _postNewSessionCommand - New Session Created: 62e2cd30-1f25-11e5-a947-3d50e305fa96
[INFO  - 2015-06-30T12:41:59.258Z] ShutdownReqHand - _handle - About to shutdown
```

Using PhantomJS requires a new instance of the `PhantomJSDriver` class, as shown in the following code snippet:

```
driver = new PhantomJSDriver(caps);
```

We need to pass the path of PhantomJS executable using `DesiredCapabilities` through following way:

```
DesiredCapabilities caps = DesiredCapabilities.phantomjs();
caps.setJavascriptEnabled(true);
caps.setCapability(
    PhantomJSDriverServ-
ice.PHANTOMJS_EXECUTABLE_PATH_PROPERTY,
    "./src/test/resources/drivers/phantomjs.exe");
```

There's more...

We can also run PhantomJS as a Selenium node and connect to the Hub using PhantomJS binary, using following command line:

```
phantomjs --webdriver=9090 --webdriver-selenium-grid-
hub=http://localhost:4444
```

This will register a new node to Selenium Grid. You can run tests with the following capabilities using `RemoteWebDriver`:

```
DesiredCapabilities caps = DesiredCapabilities.phantomjs();
caps.setJavascriptEnabled(true);
driver = new RemoteWebDriver(new
URL("http://localhost:4444/wd/hub"), caps);
```

14

Testing Applications on Mobile Browsers

In this chapter, we will cover:

- ▶ Setting up Appium to test mobile applications
- ▶ Testing mobile web applications on iOS using Appium
- ▶ Testing mobile web applications on Android using Appium

Introduction

With ever-increasing number of mobile users, the adoption of smartphones and tablet computers has increased significantly. Mobile apps have penetrated the consumer and enterprise markets, replacing desktops and laptops with smart devices. Small businesses and large scale enterprises has great potential to use the mobile platform as a channel to connect with users. Testing mobile apps have become crucial for the various mobile platforms available in the market. In this chapter, we will learn more about how to test mobile apps using Selenium WebDriver, more specifically, with **Appium**.

Appium is an open source mobile automation framework used to test mobile apps on **iOS** and **Android** platforms using the JSON wire protocol with Selenium WebDriver. Appium replaces the **iPhoneDriver** and **AndroidDriver** APIs in Selenium 2 that were used to test mobile web applications

Appium enables the use and extension of the existing Selenium WebDriver framework to build mobile tests. As it uses Selenium WebDriver to drive the tests, we can use any language to create tests for which a Selenium client library exists. Appium supports the testing of native, hybrid, and mobile web apps. In this chapter, we will see how to use Appium to test mobile web applications.

We will test a mobile web application developed using jQuery mobile on Android and iOS.

Setting up Appium for testing mobile applications

Before we start testing mobile apps with Appium, we need to download and install Appium. We will use the GUI version of Appium. If you wish to run tests for iOS on iPhone or iPad, you need to install and set up Appium on a Mac OS X machine. To test Android applications, you can set up the test environment on a Windows or Linux machine. Setting up Appium is fairly easy with the new Appium App for Mac OS X.

 In addition to the GUI version, you can also install the Appium server, which runs with Node.js.

How to do it...

You can download the latest Appium binaries from `http://appium.io/`. Click on the **Download Appium** button on the front page. It will download the version based on your choice of operating system:

In the following examples, we will be using Appium on Mac OS X:

1. You can install Appium on a Mac by launching the installer and copying Appium to the applications folder.

   When you launch Appium from the applications for the first time, it will ask for an authorization to run the iOS simulators.

> By default, Appium starts at `http://127.0.0.1:4723` or localhost. This is the URL to which your test should direct the test commands. We will be testing a mobile version of the sample application that we used in the book on the iPhone Safari browser.

2. On the **Appium** main window, click on the **Apple** icon to open **iOS Settings**, as shown in the following screenshot:

3. On the **iOS Settings** dialog, select the **Force Device** checkbox and specify (**iPhone 4s**) in the iOS section. Also, select the **Use Mobile Safari** checkbox, as shown in the following screenshot:

4. Click on the Launch button in the Appium window to start the Appium server.

Testing mobile web applications on iOS using Appium

Appium drives automation using a native automation framework and provides an API based on Selenium's WebDriver JSON wire protocol. To automate an iOS application, it uses the UI Automation feature offered as part of **Apple Instruments**.

Appium works as an HTTP server and receives the commands from test scripts over the JSON wire protocol. Appium sends these commands to Apple Instruments so that these can be executed on the app that is launched in a simulator or real device. While doing so, Appium translates the JSON commands into UI Automation JavaScript commands that are understood by the Instruments. The Instruments take care of launching and closing the app in the simulator or device. This process is shown in the following diagram:

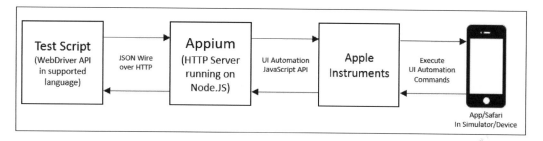

When a command is executed against the app on the simulator or device, the target app sends the response back to the Instruments, which then send it back to Appium in the JavaScript response format. Appium translates the UI Automation JavaScript responses into Selenium WebDriver JSON wire protocol responses and sends them back to the test script.

Getting ready

Before we start writing tests with Appium, we need to add the Appium client library to the project. This example uses Maven for dependency management, so we will add the following dependency for the Appium Java Client library to the POM.xml file:

```
<dependency>
    <groupId>io.appium</groupId>
    <artifactId>java-client</artifactId>
    <version>3.1.0</version>
    <scope>test</scope>
</dependency>
```

How to do it...

Now we have Appium running, so let's create a test that will check the BMI Calculator application on the iPhone Safari browser. Create a new test MobileBmiCalculator with the following code:

```
package com.secookbook.examples.chapter14.ios;

import java.net.URL;
```

```
import io.appium.java_client.ios.IOSDriver;

import org.openqa.selenium.WebDriver;
import org.openqa.selenium.WebElement;
import org.openqa.selenium.By;
import org.openqa.selenium.remote.DesiredCapabilities;
import org.junit.*;

import static org.junit.Assert.*;

public class MobileBmiCalculatorTest {

    private WebDriver driver;

    @Before
    public void setUp() throws Exception {
        // Set the desired capabilities for iOS- iPhone 6
        DesiredCapabilities caps = new DesiredCapabilities();
        caps.setCapability("platformName", "iOS");
        caps.setCapability("platformVersion", "8.4");
        caps.setCapability("deviceName", "iPhone 6");
        caps.setCapability("browserName", "safari");

        // Create an instance of IOSDriver for testing on iOS platform
        // connect to the local Appium server running on a different
machine
        // We will use WebElement type for testing the Web application
        driver = new IOSDriver<WebElement>(new URL(
            "http://192.168.0.101:4723/wd/hub"), caps);

        // Open the BMI Calculator Mobile Application
        driver.get("http://cookbook.seleniumacademy.com/mobilebmicalculato
r.html");
    }

    @Test
    public void testMobileBmiCalculator() throws Exception {
        // Get the height field and set the value
        WebElement height = driver.findElement(By.name("heightCMS"));
        height.sendKeys("181");

        // Get the weight field and set the value
        WebElement weight = driver.findElement(By.name("weightKg"));
        weight.sendKeys("80");
```

```java
    // Click on Calculate button
    WebElement calculateButton =
driver.findElement(By.id("Calculate"));
    calculateButton.click();

    // Check the Bmi Result
    WebElement bmi = driver.findElement(By.name("bmi"));
    assertEquals("24.4", bmi.getAttribute("value"));

    // Check the Category Result
    WebElement bmi_category =
driver.findElement(By.name("bmi_category"));
    assertEquals("Normal", bmi_category.getAttribute("value"));
  }

  @After
  public void tearDown() throws Exception {
    // Close the browser
    driver.quit();
  }
}
```

How it works...

The Appium Java Client library provides the `IOSDriver` class that supports executed tests on the iOS platform to run the tests with Appium. However, for Appium to use the desired platform, we need to pass a set of desired capabilities, as shown in the following code:

```java
DesiredCapabilities caps = new DesiredCapabilities();
caps.setCapability("platformName", "iOS");
caps.setCapability("platformVersion", "8.4");
caps.setCapability("deviceName", "iPhone 6");
caps.setCapability("browserName", "safari");
```

The `platformName` capability is used by Appium to decide on which platform the test script should get executed. In this example, we used the iPhone 6 Simulator. To run tests on an iPad, we can specify the iPad Simulator.

When running tests on a real device, we need to specify the value of `iPhone` or `iPad` for the device capability. Appium will pick the device that is connected to the Mac via USB.

The last desired capability that we used is `browserName`, which is used by Appium to launch the Safari browser.

Finally, we need to connect to Appium server using `IOSDriver` and program the desired capabilities that we need. This is done by creating an instance of `IOSDriver`, as shown in the following code:

```
driver = new IOSDriver<WebElement>(new URL(
    "http://192.168.0.101:4723/wd/hub"), caps);
```

The rest of the test uses Selenium API to interact with the mobile web version of the application. Run the test as normal. You will see that Appium will establish a session with the test's script and launch the iPhone Simulator with the Safari app. Appium will execute all the test steps by running commands on the Safari app in the simulator window.

Testing mobile web applications on Android using Appium

Appium drives the automation of Android applications using a UI Automator bundled with Andorid SDK. The process is pretty much the same as testing on iOS.

Appium works as an HTTP server and receives the commands from test scripts over the JSON wire protocol. Appium sends these commands to the UI Automator so that these can be executed on the app launched in an emulator or real device. While doing so, Appium translates the JSON commands into UI Automator Java commands that are understood by Android SDK. This process is shown in the following diagram:

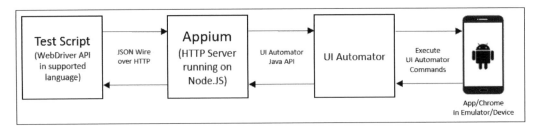

When a command is executed on the app in the emulator or device, the target app sends the response back to the UI Automator, which is sent back to the Appium. It translates the UI Automator responses into Selenium WebDriver JSON wire protocol responses, and sends them back to the test script.

Getting Ready

Testing apps on Android is similar to testing on iOS. For Android, we will use a real device instead of an emulator (a simulator is called an emulator in the Android community). We will use the same application to test in Chrome for Android.

For this example, I am using the Samsung Galaxy S4 Android handset. We need to install the Google Chrome browser on the device. You can get Google Chrome at Google's Play store if case it is not pre-installed on your device. Next, we need to connect the device to the machine on which Appium server is running.

Let's run the following command to get a list of emulator or devices connected to the machine:

`./adb devices`

The **Android Debug Bridge** (**ADB**) is a command line tool available in the Android SDK that lets you communicate with an emulator instance or an actual Android device connected to your computer.

The `./adb devices` command will display a list of all the Android devices that are connected to the host. In this example, we connected to a real device, which is listed as seen in the following screenshot:

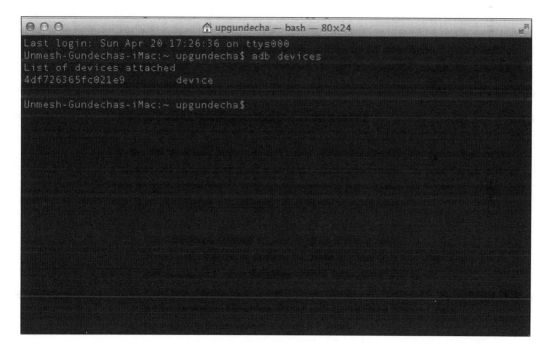

How to do it...

Let's change the test that we created for iOS and modify it for Android. We will change the desired capabilities, as shown in the following code example, to run a test on Android:

```java
package com.secookbook.examples.chapter14.android;

import java.net.URL;

import io.appium.java_client.android.AndroidDriver;
import org.openqa.selenium.WebDriver;
import org.openqa.selenium.WebElement;
import org.openqa.selenium.By;
import org.openqa.selenium.remote.DesiredCapabilities;
import org.junit.*;

import static org.junit.Assert.*;

public class MobileBmiCalculatorTest {

    private WebDriver driver;

    @Before
    public void setUp() throws Exception {
        // Set the desired capabilities for Android Device
        DesiredCapabilities caps = DesiredCapabilities.android();
        caps.setCapability("deviceOrientation", "portrait");
        caps.setCapability("platformVersion", "4.4");
        caps.setCapability("platformName", "Android");
        caps.setCapability("browserName", "Chrome");

        // Create an instance of AndroidDriver for testing on Android
platform
        // connect to the local Appium server running on a different
machine
        // We will use WebElement type for testing the Web application
        driver = new AndroidDriver<WebElement>(new URL(
            "http://192.168.0.101:4723/wd/hub"), caps);

        // Open the BMI Calculator Mobile Application
        driver.get("http://cookbook.seleniumacademy.com/
mobilebmicalculator.html");
    }
```

```java
@Test
public void testMobileBmiCalculator() throws Exception {
    // Get the height field and set the value
    WebElement height = driver.findElement(By.name("heightCMS"));
    height.sendKeys("181");

    // Get the weight field and set the value
    WebElement weight = driver.findElement(By.name("weightKg"));
    weight.sendKeys("80");

    // Click on Calculate button
    WebElement calculateButton =
driver.findElement(By.id("Calculate"));
    calculateButton.click();

    // Check the Bmi Result
    WebElement bmi = driver.findElement(By.name("bmi"));
    assertEquals("24.4", bmi.getAttribute("value"));

    // Check the Category Result
    WebElement bmi_category =
driver.findElement(By.name("bmi_category"));
    assertEquals("Normal", bmi_category.getAttribute("value"));
}

@After
public void tearDown() throws Exception {
    // Close the browser
    driver.quit();
}
}
```

How it works...

In the preceding example, we assigned the `platformName` capability value to Android, which will be used by Appium to run tests on Android.

As we want to run the tests in Chrome for Android, we have mentioned `Chrome` in the `browser` capability section of the code. The other important change we made was using the `AndroidDriver` class from the Appium Java client libraries.

Appium will use the first device from the list of devices that adb returns, as shown in the following screenshot. It will use the desired capabilities that we mentioned and will launch the Chrome browser on the device and start executing the test script commands, as shown in the following screenshot:

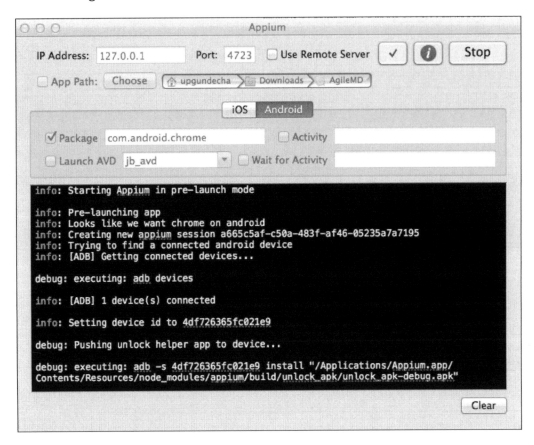

The following screenshot shows the test running on a real device:

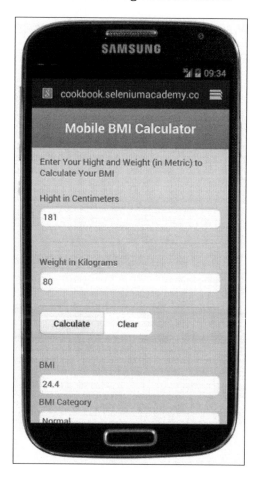

Index

Symbols

.NET
Page Object model, implementing
in 199-202
Selenium WebDriver, using in 261-264
SpecFlow.NET, using in 261-264

A

absolute path
elements, finding with 53, 59
**Acceptance Test Driven Development
(ATDD) 252**
advanced CSS selectors
used, for finding elements 65
Advanced User Interactions API
about 96
using, for keyboard events 96-98
using, for mouse events 96-98
alert
about 128
explicit wait condition, creating for 130
ancestors 51
Android Debug Bridge (ADB) 337
AndroidDriver 329
Android platform 329
Ant
about 279, 287
for Selenium WebDriver test
execution 12-15
URL 287
using, for Selenium WebDriver test
execution 287-289
using for Selenium WebDriver
test, in 290-293

Apache POI
test data, reading from Excel file 161-164
Appium
about 329
setting up, for testing mobile
applications 330-332
URL 330
used, for testing mobile web applications
on Android 336-341
used, for testing mobile web applications
on iOS 332-336
Apple Instruments 332
atomic values 51
attribute
checking, of element 76, 77
elements, finding with 54
matching, value used 55
attributes name selector
elements, finding with 61
attributes selector
elements, finding with 60
attributes values
elements, finding with 53
partial match, performing on 54, 62
AutoIt
about 280
non-web UI in Selenium WebDriver,
automating with 294, 295
URL 295
working 298
AutoIt script
creating 296
using 299-301
automatic execution
build, scheduling for 285, 294

B

Behave
about 274
using, in Python 274-277
Behavior-driven Development (BDD)
about 251
Cucumber-JVM, using in Java 252-260
references 251
Selenium WebDriver, using in .NET 261-264
SpecFlow.NET, using in .NET 261-264
BMI calculator application 149
Browser Developer tools 40
browser navigation
working with 110, 111
BrowserStack 322
browser tools
used, for inspecting elements 34, 35
used, for inspecting page structure 34, 35
browser window
maximizing 107
build
scheduling 286
scheduling, for automatic
execution 285, 294
button element
click, performing on 73
buttons
automating 72-74

C

CacheLookUp attribute 186
Capybara
about 271
using, in Ruby 271-274
Cascading Style Sheets (CSS) 33, 76
checkboxes
automating 89, 90
child elements
finding 65
children 51
child window
handling 141-143
identifying 141-143
ChromeDriver
about 27, 29
reference 27-29

setting up, for Google Chrome 27-29
Chrome node
adding to Selenium Grid, for cross-browser
testing 311
Class attribute
elements, finding by 44
Class selector
elements, finding with 59
ClearCase 280
click
performing, on button element 73
Cloud tools
using, for cross browser testing 322-324
Component Object Model (COM) 299
conditions
reference link 119
confirm box
handling 131-133
content
pop-up window, identifying by 146-148
Content Delivery Network (CDN) 69
contextMenu plug-in
reference link 101
context menus
working with 101-103
continuous integration
Jenkins, configuring for 280
cross browser testing
Cloud tools, using for 322-324
CSS selectors
reference link 58
used, for finding elements 58, 59
working 62
CSS values
checking, of element 76, 77
CSV file
test data, reading from 158-161
Cucumber
about 252
using, in Ruby 271-274
Cucumber-JVM
about 252
using in Java, for BDD 252-260
custom-expected conditions
test, synchronizing with 121, 122
custom wait, examples
waiting, for DOM events 123

waiting, for element's attribute value
    update 122
waiting, for element's visibility 122
CVS 280

D

data-driven-approach
  workflow 150
data-driven test, creating
  in MSTEST 169-172
  in NUnit 165, 168
  in Python 178, 179
  in Ruby 173-177
  JUnit used 151-155
  TestNG used 155-158
data-driven testing approach
  about 149
  benefits 150
DDT module
  about 178
  data-driven test, creating in
      Python 178, 179
DeepTest 307
descendants 51
Document Object Model (DOM) 34
DOM Level 3 XPath
  URL 49
Doojo 219
double-click
  performing, on element 98-100
drag-and-drop operations
  performing 100, 101
dropdowns
  automating 77-79
  selected options, checking in 83-85

E

Eclipse 1
e-commerce application
  reference link 193
element
  attribute, checking of 76, 77
  CSS values, checking of 76, 77
  double-click, performing on 98-100
  finding, findElement method used 41-43

presence, checking 94, 95
state, checking 95, 96
text, checking of 74, 75
elements
  finding, advanced CSS selectors used 65
  finding, attributes name selector used 61
  finding, attributes selector used 60
  finding, attributes used 54
  finding, attributes values used 53
  finding, by Class attribute 44
  finding, by ID attribute 43, 44
  finding, by Name attribute 44
  finding, by tag name 48, 49
  finding, Class selector used 59
  finding, CSS selectors used 58, 59
  finding, exact text value used 63
  finding, findElements method used 46, 47
  finding, ID selector used 60
  finding, predicates used 53
  finding, UI state pseudo-classes used 66
  finding, user action pseudo-classes used 66
  finding, with absolute path 53, 59
  finding, with relative path 53, 59
  finding, XPath used 49, 51
  inspecting, browser tools used 34, 35
  inspecting, with Google Chrome 38, 39
  inspecting, with Microsoft Internet
      Explorer 39, 40
  inspecting, with Mozilla Firefox 35-37
  locating, text used 63
  locating, with XPath axes 56-58
  locating, XPath text function used 63
elements, exposing of page
  PageFactory class used 182-186
exact text value
  used, for finding elements 63
Excel file
  test data, reading from 161-164
ExpectedConditions class
  predefined conditions 119
explicit wait condition
  creating, for alert 130
  test, synchronizing with 119, 120
extension
  creating, for jQueryUI tab widget 214-218
extension class
  creating, for web tables 210-214

extension, for WebElement object
  implementing, for highlighting
      elements 220, 221
  implementing, for setting element
      attribute values 219, 220

F

FindBy annotations 186
findElement method
  used, for finding element 41-43
findElements method
  used, for finding elements 46, 47
Firebug add-in, in Firefox
  URL 35
Firefox node
  adding to Selenium Grid, for cross-browser
      testing 311
FluentWait class
  test, synchronizing with 123, 124
forms
  submitting 72
frames
  handling 134-137
  identifying 134-137
  working with 137, 138
framework
  testing, for parallel execution 307

G

Gherkin
  about 251
  URL 251
Git 280
Google Chrome
  about 38
  elements, inspecting with 38, 39
  pages, inspecting with 38, 39
GWT 219

H

headless mode
  tests, running in 326, 327
helper class
  defining 267, 268

HTML5 canvas elements
  interaction, automating on 243-245
HTML5 video player
  automating 240-242
HTML table 90
Hub 307
Hyper Text Markup Language (HTML) 33

I

ID attribute
  elements, finding by 43, 44
ID selector
  elements, finding with 60
IE node
  adding to Selenium Grid, for cross-browser
      testing 309, 310
IFRAME
  working with 139-141
images
  comparing, in Selenium 230-233
implicit wait
  test, synchronizing with 117-119
index
  option, deselecting by 80
  option, selecting by 80
IntelliJ IDEA 2
interaction
  automating, on HTML5 canvas
      elements 243-245
Internet Explorer Driver Server
  download link 22
  reference link 26
  setting up 22-26
iOS platform 329
iPhoneDriver 329
isElementPresent() method
  implementing 94, 95

J

Java
  Cucumber-JVM, using in 252-260
JavaScript alert box
  handling 128-130
JavaScript code
  executing 103-105

Jenkins
about 12, 280
configuring, for continuous integration 280
using for Selenium WebDriver test execution,
in continuous integration 282-285
using for Selenium WebDriver test, in
continuous integration 290-293

Jenkins CI server
about 279
URL 280

Jenkins configuration
Ant, adding 281
JDK, adding 280
Maven, adding 281, 282

jQuery selectors
URL 68
using 67, 68

jQuery UI 214

jQuery UI control 209

jQueryUI tab widget
extension, creating for 214-218
URL 214

JUnit
about 150, 151
test data, reading from CSV file 158-161
test data, reading from Excel file 161-164
used, for creating data-driven test 151-155

K

keyboard events
Advanced User Interactions API,
using for 96-98

Keys
reference link 73

L

links, finding
about 47
by partial text 48
by text 47

lists
automating 77-79
selected options, checking in 83-85

LoadableComponent class
using 190-192

local storage
cleaning 250
testing 245-247

M

Mac OS X, with Safari
adding to Selenium Grid, for cross-browser
testing 312

Maven
about 279
URL 2
using for Selenium WebDriver test execution,
in continuous integration 282-285

Maven Central
URL 11

Mercurial 280

methods, WebDriver.Navigation interface
back() 110
forward() 110
refresh() 110
to(java.net.URL url) 110
to(String url) 110

methods, WebDriver.Options interface
addCookie(Cookie cookie) 108
deleteAllCookies() 108
deleteCookie(Cookie cookie) 108
deleteCookieNamed(String name) 108
getCookieNamed(String name) 108
getCookies() 108

methods, WebElement interface
isDisplayed() 95
isEnabled() 95
isSelected() 95

Microsoft Edge 30

Microsoft Internet Explorer
elements, inspecting with 39, 40
pages, inspecting with 39, 40

Microsoft Visual Studio
configuring, for Selenium WebDriver test
development 15-18

Microsoft WebDriver
setting up, for Microsoft Edge 30-32

Microsoft WebDriver Server
references 30
working 32

mobile web applications, on Android
testing, with Appium 336-341
mobile web applications, on iOS
testing, with Appium 332-336
mouse events
Advanced User Interactions API,
using for 96-98
Mozilla Firefox
about 35
used, for inspecting elements 35-37
used, for inspecting pages 35-37
MSTEST
about 307
data-driven test, creating in 169-172
multi-select dropdown
selected options, checking in 85, 86

N

Name attribute
elements, finding by 44
Navigation Timing API
about 235
performance, measuring with 235-237
nested Page Object instances
implementing 193-199
NetBeans 2
NoAlertPresentException 130
nodes
about 51
adding to Selenium Grid, for cross-browser
testing 309
selecting, from tree 52
non-web UI in Selenium WebDriver
automating, with AutoIt 294, 295
automating, with Sikuli 301-304
NoSuchElementFoundException 46
NoSuchWindowException 143
NuGet
download link 15
NuGet Package Manager
about 18
URL 15
NUnit
about 150
data-driven test, creating in 165-168
URL 165

NUnit Test Adapter
URL, for downloading 262

O

object map
creating, for Selenium tests 222-226
creating, in XML files 226, 227
OpenCSV
URL 158
OpenDialogHandler
using, in Selenium WebDriver script 297
operations, exposing on page
PageFactory class used 187-189
option
checking, in Select element 81, 82
deselecting, by index 80
deselecting, by value 80
deselecting, by visible text 79
selecting, by index 80
selecting, by value 80
selecting, by visible text 79

P

PageFactory class
used, for exposing elements
from page 182-186
used, for exposing operation
on page 187-189
Page object
defining 267-269
page-object gem
Page Object model, implementing
in Ruby 206, 207
page-object gem API
URL 208
Page Object model, implementing
in .NET 199-202
in Python 203-205
in Ruby 206, 207
pages
inspecting, with Google Chrome 38, 39
inspecting, with Microsoft Internet
Explorer 39, 40
inspecting, with Mozilla Firefox 35-37
page structure
inspecting, browser tools used 34, 35

parallel execution
  framework, testing for 307
  Selenium Grid Server, setting up for 307, 308
parents 51
partial match
  performing, on attribute values 54, 62
partial text
  links, finding by 48
Perforce 280
performance
  measuring, with Navigation
    Timing API 235-237
PhantomJS
  about 325
  tests, running in headless mode 326, 327
  URL 325
PNG (Portable Network Graphics) 106, 302
pop-up window
  handling 146-148
  identifying, by content 146-148
predicates
  elements, finding with 53
prompt alert box
  handling 131-133
PUnit 307
PyPI (Python Package Index) 22
Python
  about 178
  Behave, using in 274-277
  data-driven test, creating in 178, 179
  installing 19
  Page Object model, implementing
    in 203-205
  Selenium script, creating with 319-322
  Selenium script, executing with 319-322
  Selenium WebDriver, using in 274-277

R

radio buttons
  automating 86, 87
radio groups
  automating 86, 87
  working with 88
relative path
  elements, finding with 53, 59

RemoteWebDriver
  screenshots, capturing with 107
Roo
  data-driven test, creating in Ruby 173-177
  URL 173
RSpec 271
Ruby
  Capybara, using in 271-274
  Cucumber, using in 271-274
  data-driven test, creating in 173-177
  installing 19
  Page Object model, implementing
    in 206, 207
  Selenium WebDriver, using in 271-274

S

Sauce Connect utility 325
Sauce Labs
  about 322
  URL 322
screenshots
  capturing, with RemoteWebDriver/Selenium
    Grid 107
  capturing, with Selenium WebDriver 105, 106
screenshots, of elements
  capturing, in Selenium WebDriver 228, 229
selected options, checking
  in dropdowns 83-85
  in lists 83-85
  in multi-select dropdown 85, 86
Select element
  options, checking in 81, 82
selectors 58
Selenium
  images, comparing in 230-233
Selenium Grid
  about 305, 306
  screenshots, capturing with 107
Selenium Grid Server
  setting up, for parallel execution 307, 308
Selenium script
  creating, with Python 319-322
  creating, with TestNG 312-319
  executing, with Python 319-322
  executing, with TestNG 312-319

Selenium Server standalone JAR file
  URL, for downloading 307
Selenium tests
  object map, creating for 222-226
Selenium WebDriver
  about 1
  configuring, for Python and Ruby 19
  installing, with Python 19, 20
  installing, with Ruby 21, 22
  screenshots, capturing with 105, 106
  screenshots of elements,
        capturing in 228, 229
  using in .NET, for BDD 261-264
  using, in Python 274-277
  using, in Ruby 271-274
Selenium WebDriver script
  OpenDialogHandler, using in 297
Selenium WebDriver test development
  Microsoft Visual Studio,
        configuring for 15-18
Selenium WebDriver test development
  environment
  configuring, for Java with Eclipse and
        Maven 2-11
Selenium WebDriver test execution
  Ant using for 12-14
  Ant, using for 287-289
Selenium WebDriver test execution,
  in continuous integration
  Jenkins, using for 282-285
  Maven, using for 282-285
session cookies
  handling 108, 109
session storage
  cleaning 250
  testing 247-249
several paths
  selecting 56, 61
sibling elements
  finding 66
siblings 51
Sikuli
  about 280, 301
  non-web UI in Selenium WebDriver,
        automating with 301-304
  URL 301

Source Code Management (SCM) 283
spec file
  creating 264
SpecFlow, from Visual Studio Gallery
  URL, for downloading 262
SpecFlow.NET
  using in .NET, for BDD 261-264
step definition file
  creating 265
Story Testing 252
Subversion 280

T

tag name
  elements, finding by 48, 49
test data, reading
  from CSV file 158-161
  from Excel file 161-164
Test Driven Development (TDD) 251
TestNG
  about 7, 150, 155, 312
  Selenium script, creating with 312-319
  Selenium script, executing with 312-319
  URL 7
  used, for creating data-driven test 155-158
test results
  displaying 286
tests, running
  about 269, 270
  in headless mode 326, 327
test, synchronizing
  with custom-expected conditions 121, 122
  with explicit wait 119, 120
  with FluentWait class 123, 124
  with implicit wait 117, 118
text
  checking, of element 74, 75
  clearing, from text-area element 72
  clearing, from textbox 72
  entering, in text-area element 72
  entering, in textbox 72
  links, finding by 47
  used, for locating elements 63
text area
  automating 72-74

text-area element
text, clearing from 72
text, entering in 72
textbox
automating 72-74
text, clearing from 72
text, entering in 72
title
window, identifying by 144, 145

U

UI state pseudo-classes
used, for finding elements 66
Uniform Resource Locator (URL) 33
unknown nodes
selecting 56
user action pseudo-classes
used, for finding elements 66

V

value
option, deselecting by 80
option, selecting by 80
used, for matching attribute 55
video playback 242
visible text
option, deselecting by 79
option, selecting by 79

W

Watir WebDriver 206
WebDriver events
afterChangeValueOf 112
afterClickOn 112
afterFindBy 112
afterNavigateBack 112
afterNavigateForward 112
afterNavigateTo 112
afterScript 113
beforeChangeValueOf 112
beforeClickOn 112
beforeFindBy 112
beforeNavigateBack 112
beforeNavigateForward 112

beforeNavigateTo 112
beforeScript 113
onException 113
working with 112-115
WebDriver.Navigation interface
methods 110
WebDriver.Options interface
methods 108
WebElement interface
about 72
methods 95
web tables
extension class, creating for 210-214
WebTables
working with 90-92
widgets, jQueryUI
accordion 214
datepicker 214
dialog 214
slider 214
tabs 214
WinAnt 287
window
handling 144, 145
identifying, by title 144, 145

X

XML files
object maps, creating in 226, 227
XPath
about 49, 58, 87
elements, finding with attributes 54
elements, finding with attributes values 53
exact text value, used for finding elements 63
used, for finding elements 49-51
XPath axes
elements, locating with 56-58
XPath text function
used, for locating elements 63

Y

Yahoo UI 219

Thank you for buying
Selenium Testing Tools Cookbook
Second Edition

About Packt Publishing

Packt, pronounced 'packed', published its first book, *Mastering phpMyAdmin for Effective MySQL Management*, in April 2004, and subsequently continued to specialize in publishing highly focused books on specific technologies and solutions.

Our books and publications share the experiences of your fellow IT professionals in adapting and customizing today's systems, applications, and frameworks. Our solution-based books give you the knowledge and power to customize the software and technologies you're using to get the job done. Packt books are more specific and less general than the IT books you have seen in the past. Our unique business model allows us to bring you more focused information, giving you more of what you need to know, and less of what you don't.

Packt is a modern yet unique publishing company that focuses on producing quality, cutting-edge books for communities of developers, administrators, and newbies alike. For more information, please visit our website at www.packtpub.com.

About Packt Open Source

In 2010, Packt launched two new brands, Packt Open Source and Packt Enterprise, in order to continue its focus on specialization. This book is part of the Packt open source brand, home to books published on software built around open source licenses, and offering information to anybody from advanced developers to budding web designers. The Open Source brand also runs Packt's open source Royalty Scheme, by which Packt gives a royalty to each open source project about whose software a book is sold.

Writing for Packt

We welcome all inquiries from people who are interested in authoring. Book proposals should be sent to author@packtpub.com. If your book idea is still at an early stage and you would like to discuss it first before writing a formal book proposal, then please contact us; one of our commissioning editors will get in touch with you.

We're not just looking for published authors; if you have strong technical skills but no writing experience, our experienced editors can help you develop a writing career, or simply get some additional reward for your expertise.

Learning Selenium Testing Tools with Python

ISBN: 978-1-78398-350-6 Paperback: 216 pages

A practical guide on automated web testing with Selenium using Python

1. Write and automate tests for your applications with Selenium.

2. Explore the Selenium WebDriver API for easy implementations of small to complex operations on browsers and web applications.

3. Packed with easy and practical examples that get you started with Selenium WebDriver.

Learning Selenium Testing Tools

Third Edition

ISBN: 978-1-78439-649-7 Paperback: 318 pages

Leverage the power of Selenium to build your own real-time test cases from scratch

1. Automate tests to ensure error free, quality software.

2. A comprehensive guide with real-world examples and screenshots to automate browser testing using Selenium.

Please check **www.PacktPub.com** for information on our titles

Selenium WebDriver Practical Guide

ISBN: 978-1-78216-885-0   Paperback: 264 pages

Interactively automate web applications using Selenium WebDriver

1. Covers basic to advanced concepts of WebDriver.

2. Learn how to design a more effective automation framework.

3. Explores all of the APIs within WebDriver.

4. Acquire an in-depth understanding of each concept through practical code examples.

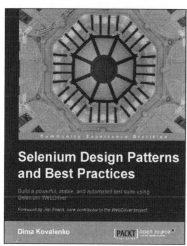

Selenium Design Patterns and Best Practices

ISBN: 978-1-78398-270-7   Paperback: 270 pages

Build a powerful, stable, and automated test suite using Selenium WebDriver

1. Keep up with the changing pace of your web application by creating an agile test suite.

2. Save time and money by making your Selenium tests 99% reliable.

3. Improve the stability of your test suite and your programing skills by following a step-by-step continuous improvement tutorial.

22396989R00207

Printed in Great Britain
by Amazon